HNC HND BUSINESS

Core Unit 5:

Quantitative Techniques for Business

Course Book

BPP

PUBLISHING

EDEXCEL HNC & HND BUSINESS

First edition August 2000
ISBN 0 7517 7035 3

British Library Cataloguing-in Publication Data
A catalogue record for this book is available from the British Library

Printed in Great Britain by Ashford Colour Press, Gosport, Hants

Published by
BPP Publishing Limited
Aldine House, Aldine Place
London W12 8AW

www.bpp.com

CONTENTS

INTRODUCTION

The HNC and HND qualifications in Business are very demanding. The suggested content, set out by Edexcel in guidelines for each unit, includes topics which are normally covered at degree level. Students therefore need books which get straight to the core of these topics, and which build upon the student's existing knowledge and experience. BPP's series of Course Books have been designed to meet that need.

This book has been written specifically for Unit 5: *Quantitative Techniques for Business*. It covers the Edexcel guidelines and suggested content in full, and includes the following features.

- The Edexcel guidelines

- A study guide explaining the key features of the book and how to get the most from your studies

- A glossary and index

Each chapter contains:

- An introduction and study objectives

- Summary diagrams and signposts, to guide you through the chapter

- Numerous activities, definitions and examples

- A chapter roundup, a quick quiz, answers to activities and an assignment (with answer guidelines at the end of the book.)

BPP Publishing are the leading providers of targeted texts for professional qualifications. Our customers need to study effectively. They cannot afford to waste time. They expect clear, concise and highly-focused study material. This series of Course Books for HNC and HND Business has been designed and produced to fulfil those needs.

BPP Publishing
August 2000

Other titles in this series:

Core Unit 1	Marketing
Core Unit 2	Managing Financial Resources
Core Unit 3	Organisations and Behaviour
Core Unit 4	Organisations, Competition and Environment
Core Unit 5	Quantitative Techniques for Business
Core Unit 6	Legal and Regulatory Framework
Core Unit 7	Management Information Systems
Core Unit 8	Business Strategy
Option Units 9-12	Business & Finance (1/01)
Option Units 13-16	Business & Management (1/01)
Option Units 17-20	Business & Marketing (1/01)
Option Units 21-24	Business & Personnel (1/01)

For more information, or to place an order, please call 020 8740 2211, or fill in the order form at the back of this book.

If you would like to send in your comments on this book, please turn to the review form on the last page.

EDEXCEL GUIDELINES FOR CORE UNIT 5 : QUANTITATIVE TECHNIQUES FOR BUSINESS

Description of the Unit

This unit develops the student's ability to deal with numerical and quantitative issues found in business. The student will be able to use statistical, graphical and algebraic techniques to address business problems using appropriate IT software where relevant. The reliable evaluation of numerical results, with and without the use of IT, will enable effective decisions to be made.

Outcomes and assessment criteria

Outcomes	Assessment criteria
	To achieve each outcome a student must demonstrate the ability to:
1 Use **statistical techniques** to collect and analyse data	• Prepare and implement a plan for the collection of primary and secondary information for a given business problem • Classify and record data • Solve problems involving the analysis and calculation of statistical quantities from frequency distributions
2 Produce forecasts based on **formalised procedures**	• Use formalised methods to forecast results • Assess the reliability of the forecasts made
3 Apply **quantitative techniques** to business situations	• Use the appropriate quantitative techniques to address business problems • Justify decisions made as a result of using the techniques

Generating evidence

Evidence of outcomes may be in the form of assignments specific to the unit, assignments which integrate this unit and others, class-based tests and examinations.

Implementation arrangements will involve the student in carrying out calculations associated with particular techniques and the use of 'practice' exercises will normally be used to develop the student's ability to complete work accurately.

It is important in completing such activities that the student is always aware of the business context in which the technique is being applied as well as the need for accuracy.

Other units within the HND/HNC programmes make use of Quantitative Techniques (see Links statement). This will have implications for the sequence in which units are delivered as well as providing opportunities for assessment evidence of the application of Techniques.

Evidence of achievement can be generated using IT to reflect the increasing use of computers in business. However, care must be exercised to ensure the capabilities of the 'package' are not allowed to mask any lack of capability of the student.

Content

1   **Statistical techniques**

Data sources: primary and secondary sources, survey methodology, sample frame, sampling methods, sample error, questionnaire design.

Interpretation of charts: graphical and diagrammatic presentation.

Frequency distributions: generation from raw data, grouping, class boundaries, irregular intervals, histograms, frequency polygons.

Representative values: mean, median and mode, calculation from raw data and frequency distributions, appropriate uses.

Cumulative frequency: tables and charts, calculation and use of interquartile range (IQR) and percentiles.

Measures of dispersion: definition and use of range, IQR and standard deviation, use of spreadsheets.

2   **Formalised procedure**

Time series analysis: derivation and use of moving averages, centred trend, seasonal variations and seasonally adjusted data using either the additive or multiplicative model.

Correlation: scatter graphs, positive and negative correlation, coefficient, significance.

Regression analysis: derivation of regression equation.

Forecasting analysis: preparation of forecasts using time series analysis and regression, reliability.

3   **Quantitative techniques**

Inventory control: periodic review, re-order level. Economic Order Quantity (EOQ), demand re-order timing.

Linear programming: formulating the problem, graphical solution, tight and slack constraints.

Networking: network diagrams, critical path, slack time, crashing activities, Gantt charts.

Indexes: simple, aggregate, retail price index (RPI), deflation.

Links

This unit is intended to provide underpinning knowledge for topics which are based on an understanding of quantitative techniques found in other units, in particular

'Management Accounting' (Unit 9), 'Financial Systems and Auditing' (Unit 10), 'Marketing Intelligence' (Unit 17), 'Sales Planning and Operations' (Unit 20), 'Purchasing' (Unit 25) and 'Quality Management' (Unit 26).

This unit offers opportunities for demonstrating Common Skill in Applying Numeracy and Applying Technology.

Resources

Appropriate application software such as spreadsheet, charting and word processing packages should be available. Additional mathematical support if required.

World Wide Web sites can be useful in providing information and case studies (eg www.bized.co.ac.uk which provides business case studies appropriate for educational purposes).

Delivery

Students should be exposed to a variety of case studies. Emphasis should be places on problem solving by the student, to gain coverage of different aspects of numerical and quantitative issues in business.

Suggested reading

There are a large number of textbooks available covering the areas contained within the unit. Examples are:

Bancroft and O'Sullivan – *Quantitative Methods for Accounting and Business Studies* – 3rd Ed. (McGraw-Hill, 1993)

Curwin and Slater – *Quantitative Methods for Business Decisions* – 4th Ed. (Chapman Hall, 1996)

Francis – *Business Mathematics and Statistics* – 4th Ed. (DP Publications, 1995)

Lucey – *Quantitative Techniques* – 5th Ed. (DP Publications, 1996)

STUDY GUIDE

This text gives full coverage of the Edexcel guidelines. This text also includes features designed specifically to make learning effective and efficient.

(a)   Each chapter begins with a summary diagram which maps out the areas covered by the chapter. There are detailed summary diagrams at the start of each main section of the chapter. You can use the diagrams during revision as a basis for your notes.

(b)   After the main summary diagram there is an introduction, which sets the chapter in context. This is followed by learning objectives, which show you what you will learn as you work through the chapter.

(c)   Throughout the text, there are special aids to learning. These are indicated by symbols in the margin,

Signposts guide you through the text, showing how each section connects with the next.

Definitions give the meanings of key terms. The *glossary* at the end of the text summarises these.

Activities help you to test how much you have learnt. Answers are given at the end of each chapter.

Examples relate what you have learnt to the outside world. Try to think up your own examples as you work through the text.

Chapter roundups present the key information from the chapter in a concise format. Useful for revision.

(d)   The wide **margin** on each page is for your notes. You will get the best out of this book if you interact with it. Write down your thoughts and ideas. Record examples, question theories, add references to other pages in the text and rephrase key points in your own words.

(e)   At the end of each chapter, there is a **chapter roundup**, a **quick quiz** and an **assignment**. Use these to revise and consolidate your knowledge. The chapter roundup summarises the chapter. The quick quiz tests what you have learnt. The assignment (with a time guide) allows you to put your knowledge into practice. Answer guidelines for the assignments are at the end of the text.

(f)   At the end of the text, there is a glossary of key terms and an index.

MATHEMATICAL TABLES

LOGARITHMS

	0	1	2	3	4	5	6	7	8	9	1	2	3	4	5	6	7	8	9
10	0000	0043	0086	0128	0170						4	9	13	17	21	26	30	34	38
						0212	0253	0294	0334	0374	4	8	12	16	20	24	28	32	37
11	0414	0453	0492	0531	0569						4	8	12	15	19	23	27	31	35
						0607	0645	0682	0719	0755	4	7	11	15	19	22	26	30	33
12	0792	0828	0864	0899	0934	0969					3	7	11	14	18	21	25	28	32
							1004	1038	1072	1106	3	7	10	14	17	20	24	27	31
13	1139	1173	1206	1239	1271						3	7	10	13	16	20	23	26	30
						1303	1335	1367	1399	1430	3	7	10	12	16	19	22	25	29
14	1461	1492	1523	1553							3	6	9	12	15	18	21	24	28
					1584	1614	1644	1673	1703	1732	3	6	9	12	15	17	20	23	26
15	1761	1790	1818	1847	1875	1903					3	6	9	11	14	17	20	23	26
							1931	1959	1987	2014	3	5	8	11	14	16	19	22	25
16	2041	2068	2095	2122	2148						3	5	8	11	14	16	19	22	24
						2175	2201	2227	2253	2279	3	5	8	10	13	15	18	21	23
17	2304	2330	2355	2380	2405	2430					3	5	8	10	13	15	18	20	23
							2455	2480	2504	2529	2	5	7	10	12	15	17	19	22
18	2553	2577	2601	2625	2648						2	5	7	9	12	14	16	19	21
						2672	2695	2718	2742	2765	2	5	7	9	11	14	16	18	21
19	2788	2810	2833	2856	2878						2	4	7	9	11	13	16	18	20
						2900	2923	2945	2967	2989	2	4	6	8	11	13	15	17	19
20	3010	3032	3054	3075	3096	3118	3139	3160	3181	3201	2	4	6	8	11	13	15	17	19
21	3222	3243	3263	3284	3304	3324	3345	3365	3385	3404	2	4	6	8	10	12	14	16	18
22	3424	3444	3464	3483	3502	3522	3541	3560	3579	3598	2	4	6	8	10	12	14	15	17
23	3617	3636	3655	3674	3692	3711	3729	3747	3766	3784	2	4	6	7	9	11	13	15	17
24	3802	3820	3838	3856	3874	3892	3909	3927	3945	3962	2	4	5	7	9	11	12	14	16
25	3979	3997	4014	4031	4048	4065	4082	4099	4116	4133	2	3	5	7	9	10	12	14	15
26	4150	4166	4183	4200	4216	4232	4249	4265	4281	4298	2	3	5	7	8	10	11	13	15
27	4314	4330	4346	4362	4378	4393	4409	4425	4440	4456	2	3	5	6	8	9	11	13	14
28	4472	4487	4502	4518	4533	4548	4564	4579	4594	4609	2	3	5	6	8	9	11	12	14
29	4624	4639	4654	4669	4683	4698	4713	4728	4742	4757	1	3	4	6	7	9	10	12	13
30	4771	4786	4800	4814	4829	4843	4857	4871	4886	4900	1	3	4	6	7	9	10	11	13
31	4914	4928	4942	4955	4969	4983	4997	5011	5024	5038	1	3	4	6	7	8	10	11	12
32	5051	5065	5079	5092	5105	5119	5132	5145	5159	5172	1	3	4	5	7	8	9	11	12
33	5185	5198	5211	5224	5237	5250	5263	5276	5289	5302	1	3	4	5	6	8	9	10	12
34	5315	5328	5340	5353	5366	5378	5391	5403	5416	5428	1	3	4	5	6	8	9	10	11
35	5441	5453	5465	5478	5490	5502	5514	5527	5539	5551	1	2	4	5	6	7	9	10	11
36	5563	5575	5587	5599	5611	5623	5635	5647	5658	5670	1	2	4	5	6	7	8	10	11
37	5682	5694	5705	5717	5729	5740	5752	5763	5775	5786	1	2	3	5	6	7	8	9	10
38	5798	5809	5821	5832	5843	5855	5866	5877	5888	5899	1	2	3	5	6	7	8	9	10
39	5911	5922	5933	5944	5955	5966	5977	5988	5999	6010	1	2	3	4	5	7	8	9	10
40	6021	6031	6042	6053	6064	6075	6085	6096	6107	6117	1	2	3	4	5	6	8	9	10
41	6128	6138	6149	6160	6170	6180	6191	6201	6212	6222	1	2	3	4	5	6	7	8	9
42	6232	6243	6253	6263	6274	6284	6294	6304	6314	6325	1	2	3	4	5	6	7	8	9
43	6335	6345	6355	6365	6375	6385	6395	6405	6415	6425	1	2	3	4	5	6	7	8	9
44	6435	6444	6454	6464	6474	6484	6493	6503	6513	6522	1	2	3	4	5	6	7	8	9
45	6532	6542	6551	6561	6571	6580	6590	6599	6609	6618	1	2	3	4	5	6	7	8	9
46	6628	6637	6646	6656	6665	6675	6684	6693	6702	6712	1	2	3	4	5	6	7	7	8
47	6721	6730	6739	6749	6758	6767	6776	6785	6794	6803	1	2	3	4	5	5	6	7	8
48	6812	6821	6830	6839	6848	6857	6866	6875	6884	6893	1	2	3	4	4	5	6	7	8
49	6902	6911	6920	6928	6937	6946	6955	6964	6972	6981	1	2	3	4	4	5	6	7	8

LOGARITHMS

	0	1	2	3	4	5	6	7	8	9	1	2	3	4	5	6	7	8	9
50	6990	6998	7007	7016	7024	7033	7042	7050	7059	7067	1	2	3	3	4	5	6	7	8
51	7076	7084	7093	7101	7110	7118	7126	7135	7143	7152	1	2	3	3	4	5	6	7	8
52	7160	7168	7177	7185	7193	7202	7210	7218	7226	7235	1	2	2	3	4	5	6	7	7
53	7243	7251	7259	7267	7275	7284	7292	7300	7308	7316	1	2	2	3	4	5	6	6	7
54	7324	7332	7340	7348	7356	7364	7372	7380	7388	7396	1	2	2	3	4	5	6	6	7
55	7404	7412	7419	7427	7435	7443	7451	7459	7466	7474	1	2	2	3	4	5	5	6	7
56	7482	7490	7497	7505	7513	7520	7528	7536	7543	7551	1	2	2	3	4	5	5	6	7
57	7559	7566	7574	7582	7589	7597	7604	7612	7619	7627	1	2	2	3	4	5	5	6	7
58	7634	7642	7649	7657	7664	7672	7679	7686	7694	7701	1	1	2	3	4	4	5	6	7
59	7709	7716	7723	7731	7738	7745	7752	7760	7767	7774	1	1	2	3	4	4	5	6	7
60	7782	7789	7796	7803	7810	7818	7825	7832	7839	7846	1	1	2	3	4	4	5	6	6
61	7853	7860	7868	7875	7882	7889	7896	7903	7910	7917	1	1	2	3	4	4	5	6	6
62	7924	7931	7938	7945	7952	7959	7966	7973	7980	7987	1	1	2	3	3	4	5	6	6
63	7993	8000	8007	8014	8021	8028	8035	8041	8048	8055	1	1	2	3	3	4	5	5	6
64	8062	8069	8075	8082	8089	8096	8102	8109	8116	8122	1	1	2	3	3	4	5	5	6
65	8129	8136	8142	8149	8156	8162	8169	8176	8182	8189	1	1	2	3	3	4	5	5	6
66	8195	8202	8209	8215	8222	8228	8235	8241	8248	8254	1	1	2	3	3	4	5	5	6
67	8261	8267	8274	8280	8287	8293	8299	8306	8312	8319	1	1	2	3	3	4	5	5	6
68	8325	8331	8338	8344	8351	8357	8363	8370	8376	8382	1	1	2	3	3	4	4	5	6
69	8388	8395	8401	8407	8414	8420	8426	8432	8439	8445	1	1	2	2	3	4	4	5	6
70	8451	8457	8463	8470	8476	8482	8488	8494	8500	8506	1	1	2	2	3	4	4	5	6
71	8513	8519	8525	8531	8537	8543	8549	8555	8561	8567	1	1	2	2	3	4	4	5	5
72	8573	8579	8585	8591	8597	8603	8609	8615	8621	8627	1	1	2	2	3	4	4	5	5
73	8633	8639	8645	8651	8657	8663	8669	8675	8681	8686	1	1	2	2	3	4	4	5	5
74	8692	8698	8704	8710	8716	8722	8727	8733	8739	8745	1	1	2	2	3	4	4	5	5
75	8751	8756	8762	8768	8774	8779	8785	8791	8797	8802	1	1	2	2	3	3	4	5	5
76	8808	8814	8820	8825	8831	8837	8842	8848	8854	8859	1	1	2	2	3	3	4	5	5
77	8865	8871	8876	8882	8887	8893	8899	8904	8910	8915	1	1	2	2	3	3	4	4	5
78	8921	8927	8932	8938	8943	8949	8954	8960	8965	8971	1	1	2	2	3	3	4	4	5
79	8976	8982	8987	8993	8998	9004	9009	9015	9020	9025	1	1	2	2	3	3	4	4	5
80	9031	9036	9042	9047	9053	9058	9063	9069	9074	9079	1	1	2	2	3	3	4	4	5
81	9085	9090	9096	9101	9106	9112	9117	9122	9128	9133	1	1	2	2	3	3	4	4	5
82	9138	9143	9149	9154	9159	9165	9170	9175	9180	9186	1	1	2	2	3	3	4	4	5
83	9191	9196	9201	9206	9212	9217	9222	9227	9232	9238	1	1	2	2	3	3	4	4	5
84	9243	9248	9253	9258	9263	9269	9274	9279	9284	9289	1	1	2	2	3	3	4	4	5
85	9294	9299	9304	9309	9315	9320	9325	9330	9335	9340	1	1	2	2	3	3	4	4	5
86	9345	9350	9355	9360	9365	9370	9375	9380	9385	9390	1	1	2	2	3	3	4	4	5
87	9395	9400	9405	9410	9415	9420	9425	9430	9435	9440	0	1	1	2	2	3	3	4	4
88	9445	9450	9455	9460	9465	9469	9474	9479	9484	9489	0	1	1	2	2	3	3	4	4
89	9494	9499	9504	9509	9513	9518	9523	9528	9533	9538	0	1	1	2	2	3	3	4	4
90	9542	9547	9552	9557	9562	9566	9571	9576	9581	9586	0	1	1	2	2	3	3	4	4
91	9590	9595	9600	9605	9609	9614	9619	9624	9628	9633	0	1	1	2	2	3	3	4	4
92	9638	9643	9647	9652	9657	9661	9666	9671	9675	9680	0	1	1	2	2	3	3	4	4
93	9685	9689	9694	9699	9703	9708	9713	9717	9722	9727	0	1	1	2	2	3	3	4	4
94	9731	9736	9741	9745	9750	9754	9759	9763	9768	9773	0	1	1	2	2	3	3	4	4
95	9777	9782	9786	9791	9795	9800	9805	9809	9814	9818	0	1	1	2	2	3	3	4	4
96	9823	9827	9832	9836	9841	9845	9850	9854	9859	9863	0	1	1	2	2	3	3	4	4
97	9868	9872	9877	9881	9886	9890	9894	9899	9903	9908	0	1	1	2	2	3	3	4	4
98	9912	9917	9921	9926	9930	9934	9939	9943	9948	9952	0	1	1	2	2	3	3	4	4
99	9956	9961	9965	9969	9974	9978	9983	9987	9991	9996	0	1	1	2	2	3	3	3	4

CORE UNIT 5

QUANTITATIVE TECHNIQUES FOR BUSINESS

Chapter 1 :
BASIC MATHEMATICS

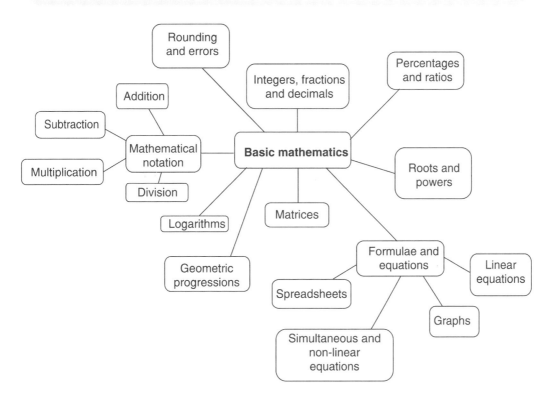

Introduction

The first part of this chapter introduces some mathematical tools which you will often have to use. For instance, percentages and ratios are found in business contexts, for example in quoting interest rates, and powers and roots are a convenient way of expressing problems where a number is to be multiplied by itself several times. Formulae and equations show how different amounts, such as the quantity of goods and the cost of making these goods, are related to each other. Computer spreadsheets are a quick and accurate way of performing calculations and preparing various types of table incorporating numerical data. The theory of geometric progressions underpins some of the techniques used to assess the viability of a capital investment.

The last three sections of the chapter examine approximation and rounding. Sometimes it is impossible to obtain an accurate value for a large number (such as the population of a town), and some figures may only be easily measurable to the nearest whole number (the speed of a car, for example). In some cases it may not be necessary or desirable to express data as accurately as it is possible to measure them. In such circumstances, numbers are rounded. When calculations are made using rounded data, errors may be introduced into the results of the calculations and any subsequent conclusions that may be drawn from them and so we will look at the types of error that can occur, and how we can take account of such errors in calculations using rounded data.

In Chapter 2 we will move on to specific quantitative methods, beginning with ways of presenting data.

Your objectives

After completing this chapter you should:

(a)   be able to deal with fractions, decimals, reciprocals, brackets, negative numbers and other mathematical symbols and be able to use your calculator to perform addition, subtraction, multiplication and division;

(b)   be able to perform calculations involving percentages and ratios;

(c)   understand the meaning of roots and powers and be able to calculate them;

(d)   know how to construct and solve various types of equation;

(e)   be able to draw the graph of both linear and non-linear equations;

(f)   know how to perform matrix calculations;

(g)   be able to construct formulae for spreadsheets;

(h)   understand the construction of a geometric progression;

(i)   be able to find the logarithm of a number;

(j)   be able to round numbers and determine maximum and relative errors.

1   INTEGERS, FRACTIONS AND DECIMALS

Definition

An *integer* is a whole number and can be either positive or negative.

1.1   The integers are therefore as follows.

...,–5, –4, –3, –2, –1, 0, 1, 2, 3, 4, 5,...

Definitions

Fractions (such as $^1/_2$, $^1/_4$, $^{19}/_{35}$, $^{101}/_{377}$, ...) and *decimals* (0.1, 0.25, 0.3135 ...) are both ways of showing parts of a whole.

1.2   Fractions can be turned into decimals by dividing the numerator by the denominator (in other words, dividing the top line by the bottom line). To turn decimals into fractions, all you have to do is remember that places after the decimal point stand for tenths, hundredths, thousandths and so on.

1.3   Sometimes a decimal number has too many digits in it for practical use. This problem can be overcome by rounding the decimal number to a specific number of significant digits by discarding digits using the following rule.

If the first digit to be discarded is greater than or equal to 5 then add 1 to the previous digit. Otherwise the previous digit is unchanged.

EXAMPLE: SIGNIFICANT DIGITS

(a)   187.392 correct to five significant digits is 187.39
        Discarding the 2 causes nothing to be added to the 9.

(b)   187.392 correct to four significant digits is 187.4
        Discarding the 9 causes 1 to be added to the 3.

(c)   187.392 correct to three significant digits is 187
        Discarding the 3 causes nothing to be added to the 7.

Activity 1

What is 17.385 correct to four significant digits?

2   MATHEMATICAL NOTATION

Brackets

2.1   Brackets are commonly used to indicate which parts of a mathematical expression should be grouped together, and calculated before other parts. In other words, brackets can indicate a priority, or an order in which calculations should be made. The rule is as follows.

(a)   Do things in brackets before doing things outside them.

(b)   Subject to rule (a), do things in this order.

    (i)   Powers and roots
    (ii)   Multiplications and divisions, working from left to right
    (iii)   Additions and subtractions, working from left to right

2.2   Thus brackets are used for the sake of clarity. Here are some examples.

(a) $3 + 6 \times 8 = 51$. This is the same as writing $3 + (6 \times 8) = 51$.

(b) $(3 + 6) \times 8 = 72$. The brackets indicate that we wish to multiply the sum of 3 and 6 by 8.

(c) $12 - 4 \div 2 = 10$. This is the same as writing $12 - (4 \div 2) = 10$ or $12 - (4/2) = 10$.

(d) $(12 - 4) \div 2 = 4$. The brackets tell us to do the subtraction first.

2.3   A figure outside a bracket may be multiplied by two or more figures inside a bracket, linked by addition or subtraction signs. Here is an example.

$5(6 + 8) = 5 \times (6 + 8) = 5 \times 6 + 5 \times 8 = 70$

This is the same as $5(14) = 5 \times 14 = 70$

The multiplication sign after the 5 can be omitted, as shown here $(5(6 + 8))$, but there is no harm in putting it in $(5 \times (6 + 8))$ if you want to.

Similarly:

$5(8 - 6) = 5(2) = 10$

or

$5 \times 8 - 5 \times 6 = 10$

2.4 When two sets of figures linked by addition or subtraction signs within brackets are multiplied together, each figure in one bracket is multiplied in turn by every figure in the second bracket. Thus:

$(8 + 4)(7 + 2) = (12)(9) = 108$

or

$8 \times 7 + 8 \times 2 + 4 \times 7 + 4 \times 2 = 56 + 16 + 28 + 8 = 108$

Negative numbers

2.5 When a negative number (–p) is added to another number (q), the net effect is to subtract p from q.

    (a) $10 + (-6) = 10 - 6 = 4$ (b) $-10 + (-6) = -10 - 6 = -16$

2.6 When a negative number (–p) is subtracted from another number (q), the net effect is to add p to q.

    (a) $12 - (-8) = 12 + 8 = 20$ (b) $-12 - (-8) = -12 + 8 = -4$

2.7 When a negative number is multiplied or divided by another negative number, the result is a positive number.

    (a) $-8 \times (-4) = +32$ (b) $-18/(-3) = +6$

2.8 If there is only one negative number in a multiplication or division, the result is negative.

    (a) $-8 \times 4 = -32$ (b) $3 \times (-2) = -6$
    (c) $12/(-4) = -3$ (d) $-20/5 = -4$

Activity 2

Work out the following.

(a) $(72 - 8) - (-2 + 1)$ (c) $8(2 - 5) - (4 - (-8))$

(b) $\dfrac{88 + 8}{12} + \dfrac{(29 - 11)}{-2}$ (d) $\dfrac{-36}{9 - 3} - \dfrac{84}{3 - 10} - \dfrac{-81}{3}$

Reciprocals

Definition

The *reciprocal* of a number is just 1 divided by that number.

2.9 For example, the reciprocal of 2 is 1 divided by 2, in other words $^1/_2$.

Extra symbols

2.10 We will come across several other mathematical signs in this book but there are five which you should learn right away.

(a) > means 'greater than'. So 46 > 29 is true, but 40 > 86 is false.
(b) ≥ means 'is greater than or equal to'. So 4 ≥ 3 and 4 ≥ 4.
(c) < means 'is less than'. So 29 < 46 is true, but 86 < 40 is false.
(d) ≤ means 'is less than or equal to'. So 7 ≤ 8 and 7 ≤ 7.
(e) ≠ means 'is not equal to'. So we could write 100.004 ≠ 100.

3 ADDITION, SUBTRACTION, MULTIPLICATION AND DIVISION

3.1 To ensure that you have understood how to deal with brackets and negative numbers and to check that you are able to use your calculator to perform addition, subtraction, multiplication and division, try the following activity.

Activity 3

Work out all answers to four decimal places, using a calculator.

(a) $(43 + 26.705) \times 9.3$

(b) $(844.2 \div 26) - 2.45$

(c) $\dfrac{45.6 - 13.92 + 823.1}{14.3 \times 112.5}$

(d) $\dfrac{303.3 + 7.06 \times 42.11}{1.03 \times 111.03}$

(e) $\dfrac{7.6 \times 1{,}010}{10.1 \times 76{,}000}$

(f) $(43.756 + 26.321) \div 171.036$

(g) $(43.756 + 26.321) \times 171.036$

(h) $171.45 + (-221.36) + 143.22$

(i) $66 - (-43.57) + (-212.36)$

(j) $\dfrac{10.1 \times 76{,}000}{7.6 \times 1{,}010}$

(k) $\dfrac{21.032 + (-31.476)}{3.27 \times 41.201}$

(l) $\dfrac{-33.33 - (-41.37)}{11.21 + (-24.32)}$

(m) $\dfrac{-10.75 \times (-15.44)}{-14.25 \times 17.15} + \left(\dfrac{16.23}{8.4 + 3.002}\right)$

(n) $\dfrac{-7.366 \times 921.3}{10{,}493 - 2{,}422.8} - \left(\dfrac{8.4 + 3.002}{16.23}\right)$

---

4 PERCENTAGES AND RATIOS

Definition

A *percentage* indicates the relative size or proportion of an item.

4.1   Percentages are used to indicate the *relative* size or proportion of items, rather than their absolute size. For example, if one office employs ten accountants, six secretaries and four supervisors, the *absolute* values of staff numbers and the *percentage* of the total work force in each type would be as follows.

	Accountants	Secretaries	Supervisors	Total
Absolute numbers	10	6	4	20
Percentages	50%	30%	20%	100%

4.2   The idea of percentages is that the whole of something can be thought of as 100%. The whole of a cake, for example, is 100%. If you share it out equally with a friend, you will get half each, or 100%/2 = 50% each.

4.3   To turn a percentage into a fraction or decimal you divide by 100. To turn a fraction or decimal back into a percentage you multiply by 100. Consider the following.

(a) $0.16 = 0.16 \times 100 = 16\%$

(b) $4/5 \times 100 = (400/5)\% = 80\%$

(c) $40\% = 40/100 = 2/5 = 0.4$

4.4   There are two main types of situation involving percentages.

(a)   You may be required to calculate a percentage of a figure, having been given the percentage.

Question: What is 40% of £64?
Answer: 40% of £64 = 0.4 × £64 = £25.60.

(b)   You may be required to state what percentage one figure is of another, so that you have to work out the percentage yourself.

Question: What is £16 as a percentage of £64?
Answer: £16 as a percentage of £64 = 16/64 × 100% = 1/4 × 100% = 25%

In other words, put the £16 as a fraction of the £64, and then multiply by 100%.

Discounts

4.5   To calculate discounts you have to be able to manipulate percentages. The following activities illustrate the technique.

Activity 4

A travel agent is offering a 17% discount on the brochure price of a particular holiday to America. The brochure price of the holiday is £795.

Required

Calculate the price being offered by the travel agent.

Activity 5

(a)   A television has been reduced from £490.99 to £340.99. What is the percentage reduction in price to three decimal places?

(b)   A stereo cost £757 in 20X3 and £892 one year later. What is the percentage increase in price to one decimal place?

BPP
PUBLISHING

Profits

4.6 In your examinations you may be required to calculate profit, selling price or cost of sale of an item or number of items from certain information. To do this you need to remember the following crucial formula.

	Example
	%
Cost of sales	100
Plus Profit	25
Equals Sales	125

Profit may be expressed either as a percentage of cost of sales (such as 25% (25/100) mark-up) or as a percentage of sales (such as 20% (25/125) margin).

EXAMPLE: PROFITS AND PERCENTAGES

Delilah's Dresses sells a dress at a 10% margin. The dress cost the shop £100.

Required

Calculate the profit made by Delilah's Dresses.

SOLUTION

The margin is 10% (ie (10/100))

Let selling price = 100%

Profit   = 10%

∴ Cost = 90% = £100
∴ 1%   = (£100/90)
∴ 10%   = profit = £100/90 × 10 = £11.11

EXAMPLE: PERCENTAGES AND PROFITS

Trevor's Trousers sells a pair of trousers for £80 at a 15% mark-up.

Required

Calculate the profit made by Delilah's Dresses.

SOLUTION

The mark-up is 15%.

Let cost of sales = 100%

Profit   = 15%

∴ Selling price = 115% = £80

∴ 1%   = £(80/115)

∴ 15%   = profit = £(80/115) × 15 = £10.43

Proportions

4.7   A proportion means writing a percentage as a proportion of 1 (that is, as a decimal).

100% can be thought of as the whole, or 1. 50% is half of that, or 0.5. Consider the following.

Question: There are 14 women in an audience of 70. What proportion of the audience are men?

Answer: Number of men = 70 – 14 = 56

Proportion of men $= \dfrac{56}{70} = \dfrac{8}{10} = 80\% = 0.8$

(a)   8/10 or 4/5 is the *fraction* of the audience made up of men.
(b)   80% is the *percentage* of the audience made up of men.
(c)   0.8 is the *proportion* of the audience made up of men.

Activity 6

There are 30 students in a classroom, 17 of whom have blonde hair. What proportion of the students do not have blonde hair?

Ratios

4.8   Suppose Tom has £12 and Dick has £8. The ratio of Tom's cash to Dick's cash is 12:8. This can be cancelled down, just like a fraction, to 3:2.

4.9   Often an examination question will pose the problem the other way around: Tom and Dick wish to share £20 out in the ratio 3:2. How much will each receive?

4.10   Because 3 + 2 = 5, we must divide the whole up into five equal parts, then give Tom three parts and Dick two parts.

(a)   £20 ÷ 5 = £4 (so each part is £4)

(b)   Tom's share = 3 × £4 = £12

(c)   Dick's share = 2 × £4 = £8

(d)   Check: £12 + £8 = £20 (adding up the two shares in the answer gets us back to the £20 in the question)

4.11   This method of calculating ratios as amounts works no matter how many ratios are involved. Here is another example.

Question: A, B, C and D wish to share £600 in the ratio 6 : 1 : 2 : 3. How much will each receive?

Answer: (a)   Number of parts   = 6 + 1 + 2 + 3 = 12

(b)   Value of each part = £600 ÷ 12 = £50

(c)   A: 6 × £50   = £300
B: 1 × £50   = £50
C: 2 × £50   = £100
D. 3 × £50   = £150

(d)   *Check*: £300 + £50 + £100 + £150 = £600

Activity 7

(a)   Tom, Dick and Harry wish to share out £800. Calculate how much each would receive if the ratio used was:

     (i)   3:2:5;

     (ii)   5:3:2;

     (iii) 3:1:1.

(b)   Lynn and Laura share out a certain sum of money in the ratio 4 : 5, and Laura ends up with £6.

     (i)   How much was shared out in the first place?

     (ii)   How much would have been shared out if Laura had got £6 and the ratio had been 5:4 instead of 4:5?

---

5   ROOTS AND POWERS

Definitions

The *square root* $\left(\sqrt{}\right)$ of a number is a value which, when multiplied by itself, equals the original number.

The *cube root* $\sqrt[3]{}$ of a number is the value which, when multiplied by itself twice, equals the original number.

5.1   For example,

$$\sqrt{9} = 3, \text{ since } 3 \times 3 = 9$$

Similarly,

$$\sqrt[3]{64} = 4, \text{ since } 4 \times 4 \times 4 = 64$$

5.2   The *nth root* of a number is a value which, when multiplied by itself (n – 1) times, equals the original number.

5.3   *Powers* work the other way round.

Thus the 6th power of $2 = 2^6 = 2 \times 2 \times 2 \times 2 \times 2 \times 2 = 64$.

Similarly, $3^4 = 3 \times 3 \times 3 \times 3 = 81$.

Since $\sqrt{9} = 3$, it also follows that $3^2 = 9$, and since $\sqrt[3]{64} = 4$, $4^3 = 64$.

5.4   When a number with an index (a 'to the power of' value) is multiplied by the same number with the same or a different index, the result is that number to the power of the sum of the indices.

    (a) $5^2 \times 5 = 5^2 \times 5^1 = 5^{(2+1)} = 5^3 = 125$

    (b) $4^3 \times 4^3 = 4^{(3+3)} = 4^6 = 4{,}096$

BPP PUBLISHING

5.5   Similarly, when a number with an index is divided by the same number with the same or a different index, the result is that number to the power of the first index minus the second index.

(a) $6^4 \div 6^3 = 6^{(4-3)} = 6^1 = 6$
(b) $7^8 \div 7^6 = 7^{(8-6)} = 7^2 = 49$

5.6   Any figure to the power of zero equals 1. $1^0 = 1$, $2^0 = 1$, $3^0 = 1$, $4^0 = 1$ and so on.

5.7   An index can be a fraction, as in $16^{1/2}$. What $16^{1/2}$ means is the square root of $16 (\sqrt{16}$ or 4$)$. If we multiply by $16^{1/2}$ we get $16^{(1/2 + 1/2)}$ which equals 16^1 and thus 16.

Similarly, $216^{1/3}$ is the cube root of 216 (which is 6) because $216^{1/3} \times 216^{1/3} \times 216^{1/3} = 216^{(1/3 + 1/3 + 1/3)} = 216^1 = 216$.

5.8   An index can be a negative value. The negative sign represents a reciprocal. Thus 2^{-1} is the reciprocal of, or 1 over, 2^1.

$$2^{-1} = \frac{1}{2^1} = \frac{1}{2}$$

Likewise

$$2^{-2} = \frac{1}{2^2} = \frac{1}{4} \; ; \; 2^{-3} = \frac{1}{2^3} = \frac{1}{8} \; ; \; 5^{-6} = \frac{1}{5^6} = \frac{1}{15,625}$$

5.9   When we multiply or divide by a number with a negative index, the rules previously stated still apply.

(a) $9^2 \times 9^{-2} = 9^{(2+(-2))} = 9^0 = 1$ (That is, $9^2 \times \frac{1}{9^2} = 1$)

(b) $4^5 \div 4^{-2} = 4^{(5-(-2))} = 4^7 = 16,384$

(c) $3^8 \times 3^{-5} = 3^{(8-5)} = 3^3 = 27$

(d) $3^{-5} \div 3^{-2} = 3^{-5-(-2)} = 3^{-3} = \frac{1}{3^3} = \frac{1}{27}$. (This could be re-expressed as

$$\frac{1}{3^5} \div \frac{1}{3^2} = \frac{1}{3^5} \times 3^2 = \frac{1}{3^3} .)$$

5.10   To calculate a power using a scientific calculator, you can use the [y^x] key.

For example, if you want to compute 7^4, put 7 in the display, then press the [y^x] key; next, key in 4 and then press the [$=$] key. The answer is then shown as 2,401.

ie 7[y^x] 4 [$=$] Answer: 2,401

Note. The [y^x] key is sometimes shown as the [x^y] key.

Activity 8

Work out the following, using your calculator as necessary.

(a) $(18.6)^{2.6}$

(b) $(18.6)^{-2.6}$

(c) $\sqrt[2.6]{18.6}$

(d) $(14.2)^4 \times (14.2)^{1/4}$

(e) $(14.2)^4 + (14.2)^{1/4}$

6 FORMULAE AND EQUATIONS

Variables

6.1 So far all our problems have been formulated entirely in terms of specific numbers. However, think back to when you were calculating powers with your calculator earlier in this chapter. You probably used the x^y key on your calculator. x and y stood for whichever numbers we happened to have in our problem, for example, 3 and 4 if we wanted to work out 3^4. When we use letters like this to stand for any numbers we call them variables. When we work out 3^4, x stands for 3. When we work out 7^2, x will stand for 7: its value can vary.

6.2 The use of variables enables us to state general mathematical truths.

For example:

$$x = x$$
$$x^2 = x \times x$$
If y $= 0.5 \times x$, then $x = 2 \times y$

These are true whatever values x and y have. For example, let $y = 0.5 \times x$

If $y = 3$, $x = 2 \times y = 6$
If $y = 7$, $x = 2 \times y = 14$
If $y = 1$, $x = 2 \times y = 2$, and so on for any other choice of a value for y.

Formulae

6.3 We can use variables to build up useful formulae and then put in values for the variables, and get out a value for something we are interested in.

6.4 Let us consider an example. For a business, profit = revenue – costs. Since revenue = selling price × units sold, we can say that

profit = selling price × units sold – costs.

'Selling price × units sold – costs' is a formula for profit.

6.5 We can use single letters to make the formula quicker to write.

Let x = profit
    p = selling price
    u = units sold
    c = cost

Then $x = p \times u - c$.

If we are then told that in a particular month, $p = £5$, $u = 30$ and $c = £118$, we can find out the month's profit.

Profit $= x = p \times u - c = £5 \times 30 - £118$
         $= £150 - £118 = £32$

It is usual when writing formulae to leave out multiplication signs between letters. Thus $p \times u - c$ can be written as $pu - c$. We will also write (for example) 2x instead of $2 \times x$.

Equations

Definition

An *equation* is an expression of the relationship between variables.

6.6 In the above example, pu – c was a formula for profit. If we write x = pu – c, we have written an equation. It says that one thing (profit, x) is equal to another (pu – c).

6.7 Sometimes, we are given an equation with numbers filled in for all but one of the variables. The problem is then to find the number which should be filled in for the last variable. This is called solving the equation.

6.8 (a) Returning to x = pu – c, we could be told that for a particular month p = £4, u = 60 and c = £208. We would then have the *equation* x = £4 × 60 – £208. We can solve this easily by working out £4 × 60 – £208 = £240 – £208 = £32. Thus x = £32.

(b) On the other hand, we might have been told that in a month when profits were £172, 50 units were sold and the selling price was £7. The thing we have not been told is the month's costs, c. We can work out c by writing out the equation.

£172 = £7 × 50 – c
£172 = £350 – c

We need c to be such that when it is taken away from £350 we have £172 left. By simple arithmetic, we can find that c = £178.

6.9 This method would take far too long in more complicated cases, however, and we will now go on to look at a rule for solving equations, which will take us directly to the answers we want.

The rule for solving equations

6.10 To solve an equation, we need to get it into the form:

Unknown variable = something with just numbers in it, which we can work out.

We therefore want to get the unknown variable on one side of the = sign, and everything else on the other side.

6.11 The rule is that you can do what you like to one side of an equation, so long as you do the same thing to the other side straightaway. The two sides are equal, and they will stay equal so long as you treat them in the same way.

6.12 For example, you can do any of the following.

Add 37 to both sides.
Subtract 3x from both sides.
Multiply both sides by –4.329.
Divide both sides by (x + 2).
Take the reciprocal of both sides.
Square both sides.
Take the cube root of both sides.

6.13 We can do any of these things to an equation either before or after filling in numbers for the variables for which we have values.

6.14 (a) In Paragraph 6.8 above, we had

£172 = £350 – c.
We can then get
£172 + c = £350   (add c to each side)
c = £350 – £172   (subtract £172 from each side)
c = £178   (work out the right hand side)

(b) $450 = 3x + 72$ (initial equation: x unknown)

    $450 – 72 = 3x$ (subtract 72 from each side)

    $\dfrac{450 - 72}{3} = x$ (divide each side by 3)

    $126 = x$ (work out the left hand side)

(c) $3y + 2 = 5y – 7$ (initial equation: y unknown)
    $3y + 9 = 5y$ (add 7 to each side)
    $9 = 2y$ (subtract 3y from each side)
    $4.5 = y$ (divide each side by 2)

(d) $\dfrac{\sqrt{3x^2 + x}}{2\sqrt{x}} = 7$ (initial equation: x unknown)

    $\dfrac{3x^2 + x}{4x} = 49$ (square each side)

    $(3x+1)/4 = 49$ (cancel x in the numerator and the denominator of the left hand side: this does not affect the value of the left hand side, so we do not need to change the right hand side)

    $3x + 1 = 196$ (multiply each side by 4)

    $3x = 195$ (subtract 1 from each side)

    $x = 65$ (divide each side by 3)

(e) Our example in Paragraph 6.6 was $x = pu – c$. We could change this, so as to give a formula for p.

    $x = pu – c$

    $x + c = pu$ (add c to each side)

    $\dfrac{x+c}{u} = p$ (divide each side by u)

    $p = \dfrac{x+c}{u}$ (swap the sides for ease of reading)

Given values for x, c and u we can now find p. We have rearranged the equation to give p in terms of x, c and u.

(f) Given that $y = \sqrt{3x + 7}$, we can get an equation giving x in terms of y.

    $y = \sqrt{3x + 7}$

    $y^2 = 3x + 7$ (square each side)

    $y^2 – 7 = 3x$ (subtract 7 from each side)

    $x = \dfrac{y^2 - 7}{3}$ (divide each side by 3, and swap the sides for ease of reading)

BPP
PUBLISHING

6.15 In equations, you may come across expressions such as 3(x + 4y – 2) (that is, 3 × (x + 4y – 2)). These can be rewritten in separate bits without the brackets, simply by multiplying the number outside the brackets by each item inside them. Thus 3(x + 4y – 2) = 3x + 12y – 6.

Activity 9

Question 1

Find the value of x in each of the following equations.

(a) 47x + 256 = 52x

(b) $4\sqrt{x} + 32 = 40.6718$

(c) $\dfrac{1}{3x + 4} = \dfrac{5}{2.7x - 2}$

(d) $x^3 = 4.913$

(e) 34x – 7.6 = (17x – 3.8) × (x + 12.5)

Question 2

(a) Rearrange $x = (3y - 20)^2$ to get an expression for y in terms of x.

(b) Rearrange $2(y - 4) - 4(x^2 + 3) = 0$ to get an expression for x in terms of y.

7 LINEAR EQUATIONS

Definition

A *linear equation* has the general form y = a + bx

where y is the dependent variable, depending for its value on the value of x;

x is the independent variable whose value helps to determine the corresponding value of y;

a is a constant, that is, a fixed amount;

b is also a constant, being the coefficient of x (that is, the number by which the value of x should be multiplied to derive the value of y).

7.1 Let us establish some basic linear equations. Suppose that it takes Joe Bloggs 15 minutes to walk 1 mile. How long does it take Joe to walk 2 miles? Obviously it takes him 30 minutes. How did you calculate the time? You probably thought that if the distance is doubled then the time must be doubled. How do you explain (in words) the relationships between the distance walked and the time taken? One explanation would be that every mile walked takes 15 minutes.

7.2 That is an explanation in words. Can you explain the relationship with an equation?

7.3　First you must decide which is the dependent variable and which is the independent variable. In other words, does the time taken depend on the number of miles walked or does the number of miles walked depend on the time it takes to walk a mile? Obviously the time depends on the distance. We can therefore let y be the dependent variable (time taken in minutes) and x be the independent variable (distance walked in miles).

7.4　We now need to determine the constants a and b. There is no fixed amount, so a = 0. To ascertain b, we need to establish the number of times by which the value of x should be multiplied to derive the value of y. Obviously y = 15x where y is in minutes. If y were in hours then y = $\frac{1}{4}$x.

EXAMPLE: DERIVING A LINEAR EQUATION

A salesman's weekly wage is made up of a basic weekly wage of £100 and commission of £5 for every item he sells.

Required

Derive an equation which describes this scenario.

SOLUTION

x = number of items sold and y = weekly wage
a = £100 and b = £5
∴y = 5x + 100

7.5　Note that the letters used in an equation do not have to be x and y. It may be sensible to use other letters, for example we could use p and q if we are describing the relationship between the price of an item and the quantity demanded.

8　LINEAR EQUATIONS AND GRAPHS

8.1　One of the clearest ways of presenting the relationship between two variables is by plotting a linear equation as a straight line on a graph.

The rules for drawing graphs

8.2　A graph has a horizontal axis, the x axis and a vertical axis, the y axis. The x axis is used to represent the independent variable and the y axis is used to represent the dependent variable.

8.3　If calendar time is one variable, it is always treated as the independent variable. When time is represented on the x axis of a graph, we have the graph of a time series.

8.4　(a)　If the data to be plotted are derived from calculations, rather than given in the question, make sure that there is a neat table in your working papers.

(b)　The scales on each axis should be selected so as to use as much of the graph paper as possible. Do not cramp a graph into one corner.

(c)　In some cases it is best not to start a scale at zero so as to avoid having a large area of wasted paper. This is perfectly acceptable as long as the scale adopted is clearly shown on the axis. One way of avoiding confusion is to break the axis concerned, as follows.

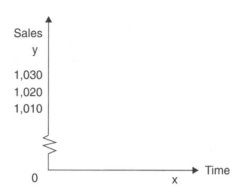

Figure 1.1 Graph with broken y axis

(d) The scales on the x axis and the y axis should be marked. For example, if the y axis relates to amounts of money, the axis should be marked at every £1, or £100 or £1,000 interval or at whatever other interval is appropriate. The axes must be marked with values to give the reader an idea of how big the values on the graph are.

(e) A graph should not be overcrowded with too many lines. Graphs should always give a clear, neat impression.

(f) A graph must always be given a title, and where appropriate, a reference should be made to the source of data.

EXAMPLE: DRAWING GRAPHS

Plot the graph for y = 4x + 5.

Consider the range of values from x = 0 to x = 10.

SOLUTION

The first step is to draw up a table for the equation. Although the problem mentions x = 0 to x = 10, it is not necessary to calculate values of y for x = 1, 2, 3 etc. A graph of a linear equation can actually be drawn from just two (x, y) values but it is always best to calculate a number of values in case you make an arithmetical error. We have calculated five values. You could settle for three or four.

x	y
0	5
2	13
4	21
6	29
8	37
10	45

Graph of y = 4x +5

The intercept and the slope

8.5 The graph of a linear equation is determined by two things, the gradient (or slope) of the straight line and the point at which the straight line crosses the y axis.

Definition

> The point at which the straight line crosses the y axis is known as the *intercept*.

8.6 Look back at the previous example. The intercept of $y = 4x + 5$ is $(0, 5)$. It is no coincidence that the intercept is the same as the constant represented by a in the general form of the equation $y = a + bx$. a is the value y takes when $x = 0$, in other words a constant, and so is represented on a graph by the point $(0, a)$.

Definition

> The *gradient* of the graph of a linear equation is $(y_2 - y_1)/(x_2 - x_1)$ where (x_1, y_1) and (x_2, y_2) are two points on the straight line.

8.7 The slope of $y = 4x + 5 = (21 - 13)/(4 - 2) = 8/2 = 4$ where $(x_1, y_1) = (2, 13)$ and $(x_2, y_2) = (4, 21)$

Activity 10

Find the gradient of $y = 10 - x$.

8.8 Note that the gradient of $y = 4x + 5$ is positive whereas the gradient of $y = 10 - x$ is negative. A positive gradient slopes upwards from left to right whereas a negative gradient slopes downwards from left to right. The greater the value of the gradient, the steeper the slope.

8.9 Just as the intercept can be found by inspection of the linear equation, so can the gradient. It is represented by the coefficient of x (b in the general form of the equation). The slope of the graph $y = 7x - 3$ is therefore 7 and the slope of the graph $y = 3,597 - 263x$ is -263.

Activity 11

Find the intercept and slope of the graph of $4y = 16x - 12$.

BPP
PUBLISHING

9 SIMULTANEOUS AND NON-LINEAR EQUATIONS

Simultaneous equations

Definition

> *Simultaneous equations* are two or more equations which are satisfied by the same variable values.

9.1 For example, we might have the following two linear equations.

$$y = 3x + 16$$
$$2y = x + 72$$

9.2 There are two unknown values, x and y, and there are two different equations which both involve x and y. There are as many equations as there are unknowns and so we can find the values of x and y.

Graphical solution

9.3 One way of finding a solution is by a graph. If both equations are satisfied together, the values of x and y must be those where the straight line graphs of the two equations intersect.

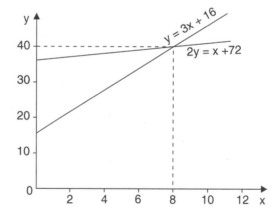

Figure 1.2 Finding a graphical solution

Since both equations are satisfied, the values of x and y must lie on both the lines. Since this happens only once, at the intersection of the lines, the value of x must be 8, and of y 40.

Algebraic solution

9.4 A more common method of solving simultaneous equations is by algebra.

(a) Returning to the original equations, we have:

$$y = 3x + 16 \qquad (1)$$
$$2y = x + 72 \qquad (2)$$

(b)   Rearranging these, we have:

$y - 3x = 16$ (3)
$2y - x = 72$ (4)

(c)   If we now multiply equation (4) by 3, so that the coefficient for x becomes the same as in equation (3), we get:

$6y - 3x \ = 216$ (5)
$y - 3x \ \ \ = 16$ (3)

(d)   Subtracting (3) from (5) we get:

$5y \qquad = 200$
$y \qquad = 40$

(e)   Substituting 40 for y in any equation, we can derive a value for x. Thus substituting in equation (4) we get:

$2(40) - x = 72$
$80 - 72 \ \ = x$
$8 \qquad \ \ = x$

(f)   The solution is $y = 40$, $x = 8$.

Activity 12

Solve the following simultaneous equations using algebra.

$5x + 2y = 34$

$x + 3y \ = 25$

Non-linear equations

9.5   In the previous sections we have been looking at equations in which the highest power of the unknown variable(s) is 1 (that is, the equation contains x, y but not x^2, y^3 and so on).

Definition

Non-linear equations are equations in which one variable varies with the nth power of another, where $n > 1$

9.6   We are now going to turn our attention to non-linear equations. The following are examples of non-linear equations.

$y = x^2$; $y = 3x^3 + 2$; $2y = 5x^4 - 6$; $y = -x^{12} + 3$

9.7   It is common for a non-linear equation to include a number of terms, all to different powers. Here are some examples.

$$y = x^2 + 6x + 10$$
$$2y = 3x^3 - 4x^2 - 8x + 10$$

$$y = -12x^9 + 3x^6 + 6x^3 + 2x^2 - 1$$
$$3y = 22x^8 + 7x^7 + 3x^4 - 12$$

9.8   Non-linear equations can be expressed in the form

$$y = ax^n + bx^{n-1} + cx^{n-2} + dx^{n-3} + \ldots + \text{constant}.$$

Consider the following equation.

$$y = -12x^9 + 3x^6 + 6x^3 + 2x^2 - 1$$

In this equation $a = -12$, $b = 0$, $c = 0$, $d = 3$, $e = 0$, $f = 0$, $g = 6$, $h = 2$, $i = 0$, constant $= -1$ and $n = 9$.

Graphing non-linear equations

9.9   The graph of a linear equation, as we saw earlier, is a straight line. The graph of a non-linear equation, on the other hand, is not a straight line. Let us consider an example.

EXAMPLE: GRAPHING NON-LINEAR EQUATIONS

Graph the equation $y = -2x^3 + x^2 - 2x + 10$

SOLUTION

The graph of this equation can be plotted in the same way as the graph of a linear equation is plotted. Take a selection of values of x, calculate the corresponding values of y, plot the pairs of values and join the points together. The joining must be done using as smooth a curve as possible.

x	–3	–2	–1	0	1	2	3
–2x	6	4	2	0	–2	–4	–6
x^2	9	4	1	0	1	4	9
$-2x^3$	54	16	2	0	–2	–16	–54
10	10	10	10	10	10	10	10
y	79	34	15	10	7	–6	–41

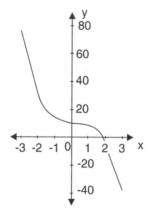

Quadratic equations

Definition

> *Quadratic equations* are a type of non-linear equation in which one variable varies with the square (or second power) of the other variable.

9.10 The following equations are all quadratic equations.

$$y = x^2 \qquad y = 5x^2 + 7 \qquad 2y = -2x^2 - 3 \qquad y = -x^2 + 3$$

9.11 A quadratic equation may include a term involving the square and also a term involving the first power of a variable. Here are some examples.

$$y = x^2 + 6x + 10 \qquad 2y = 3x^2 - 4x - 8 \qquad y = 2x^2 + 3x + 6$$

9.12 All quadratic equations can be expressed in the form $y = ax^2 + bx + c$. For instance, in the equation $y = 3x^2 + 2x - 6$, $a = 3$, $b = 2$, $c = -6$.

Graphing a quadratic equation

9.13 The graph of a quadratic equation can be plotted using the method illustrated in the previous example.

EXAMPLE: GRAPHING A QUADRATIC EQUATION

Graph the equation $y = -2x^2 + x - 3$

SOLUTION

x	−3	−2	−1	0	1	2	3
$-2x^2$	−18	−8	−2	0	−2	−8	−18
−3	−3	−3	−3	−3	−3	−3	−3
y	−24	−13	−6	−3	−4	−9	−18

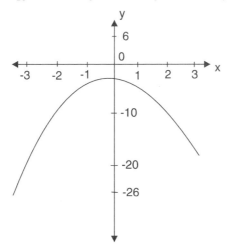

9.14 Graphs shaped like the one in the example are sometimes referred to as parabolas and they illustrate a number of points about the graph of the equation

$$y = ax^2 + bx + c.$$

(a) The constant term c determines the value of y at the point where the curve crosses the y axis (the intercept). In the graph above, c = –3 and the curve cross the y axis at y = –3.

(b) The sign of a determines the way up the curve appears. If a is positive, the curve is shaped like a ditch, but if a is negative, as in the example, the curve is shaped like a bell.

A ditch-shaped curve is said to have a *minimum* point, whereas a bell-shaped curve is said to have a *maximum* point.

(c) The graph enables us to find the values of x when y = 0 (if there are any). In other words the graph allows us to solve the quadratic equation $0 = ax^2 + bx + c$.

For the curve in the example above we see that there are no such values (that is, $0 = -2x^2 + x - 3$ cannot be solved).

Solving quadratic equations

9.15 The graphical method is not, in practice, the most efficient way to determine the solution of a quadratic equation. Many quadratic equations have two values of x (called solutions for x or roots of the equation) which satisfy the equation for any particular value of y. These values can be found using the following formula.

If $ax^2 + bx + c = 0$ then $x = \dfrac{-b \pm \sqrt{(b^2 - 4ac)}}{2a}$

EXAMPLE: QUADRATIC EQUATIONS

Solve $x^2 + x - 2 = 0$

SOLUTION

$$x = \frac{-1 \pm \sqrt{(1^2 - (4 \times 1 \times (-2)))}}{2 \times 1} = \frac{-1 \pm \sqrt{(1+8)}}{2} = \frac{-1 \pm 3}{2}$$

$\therefore x = \dfrac{-4}{2}$ or $\dfrac{2}{2}$ ie x = –2 or x = 1

Quadratic equations with a single value for x

9.16 Sometimes, $b^2 - 4ac = 0$, and so there is only one solution to the quadratic equation. Let us solve $x^2 + 2x + 1 = 0$.

$$x = \frac{-2 \pm \sqrt{(2^2 - (4 \times 1 \times 1))}}{2} = \frac{-2 \pm 0}{2} = -1$$

This quadratic equation can only be solved by one value of x.

Cost behaviour, equations and graphs

9.17 Problems often deal with cost behaviour based on both linear and non-linear functions. Attempt the following activities which represent common business problems.

Activity 13

A company manufactures a product. The total fixed costs are £75 and the variable cost per unit is £5.

Required

(a) Find an expression for total costs in terms of q, the quantity produced.

(b) Use your answer to (a) to determine the total costs if 100 units are produced.

(c) Prepare a graph of the expression for total costs.

(d) Use your graph to determine the total cost if 75 units are produced.

Activity 14

A company manufactures a product, the total cost function for the product being given by C = (25 – q)q, where q is the quantity produced and C is in £.

Required

Calculate the total costs if 15 units are produced.

10   MATRICES

Definition

A *matrix* (plural *matrices*) is an array or table of numbers or variables.

10.1   For example, the table below is a matrix.

	Skilled	Labour Semi-skilled	Unskilled
Factory P	100	75	250
Factory Q	40	40	200
Factory R	25	10	100

This table, showing the numbers of skilled, semi-skilled and unskilled workers in each of three factories, is a matrix with three rows and three columns; that is, its size is 3 × 3. A matrix with m rows and n columns is called an m × n matrix.

Definition

A table of numbers or variables which has just one row or column is called a *vector*.

10.2 A row vector is one row of numbers, and a column vector is a single column of numbers.

10.3 A matrix is usually shown in large brackets. The example above would be written as follows.

$$\begin{pmatrix} 100 & 75 & 250 \\ 40 & 40 & 200 \\ 25 & 10 & 100 \end{pmatrix}$$

This takes some time to write out in full, so we may refer to a matrix by a single letter. For example, we could call the matrix above X.

10.4 Each figure in a matrix is called an element. An element is identified by the row and column in which it falls. For example, in the above matrix X, the element X32 is that in the third row and the second column, namely the number of semi-skilled workers at factory R, which is 10.

Matrix addition

10.5 Two matrices may be added together (or subtracted) provided they are of the same size. The addition is performed by adding the corresponding elements together. Continuing our first example of workers in factories, we might have a matrix A showing the effects on staffing levels of changing to new working practices, and a matrix B showing the effects of changing from gas power to electric power. A + B would show the effects of changing working practices and changing to electric power, while A – B would show the effects of changing working practices and changing back from electric to gas power.

Thus if

$$A = \begin{pmatrix} 2 & 9 & -1 \\ 3 & -6 & -4 \\ -1 & 7 & 2 \end{pmatrix}$$

and

$$B = \begin{pmatrix} 3 & 6 & 2 \\ -1 & -5 & 9 \\ 7 & -2 & -1 \end{pmatrix}$$

then

$$A + B = \begin{pmatrix} 2+3 & 9+6 & -1+2 \\ 3-1 & -6-5 & -4+9 \\ -1+7 & 7-2 & 2-1 \end{pmatrix}$$

$$= \begin{pmatrix} 5 & 15 & 1 \\ 2 & -11 & 5 \\ 6 & 5 & 1 \end{pmatrix}$$

The revised matrix **X** for the total workforce, after both changes, would be

$$X + (A + B) = \begin{pmatrix} 105 & 90 & 251 \\ 42 & 29 & 205 \\ 31 & 15 & 101 \end{pmatrix}$$

BPP PUBLISHING

$$\mathbf{A} - \mathbf{B} \quad = \begin{pmatrix} 2-3 & 9-6 & -1-2 \\ 3+1 & -6+5 & -4-9 \\ -1-7 & 7+2 & 2+1 \end{pmatrix}$$

$$= \begin{pmatrix} -1 & 3 & -3 \\ 4 & -1 & -13 \\ -8 & 9 & 3 \end{pmatrix}$$

Matrix multiplication

10.6 Matrix multiplication is known as *scalar* multiplication. A scalar is an ordinary single number. If an entire matrix is multiplied by a scalar the effect is to multiply each element in the matrix by the scalar. Thus if:

$$\mathbf{A} \quad = \begin{pmatrix} 2 & 9 & -1 \\ 3 & -6 & -4 \\ -1 & 7 & 2 \end{pmatrix}$$

then

$$\mathbf{3A} \quad = \begin{pmatrix} 6 & 27 & -3 \\ 9 & -18 & -12 \\ -3 & 21 & 6 \end{pmatrix}$$

10.7 Two matrices can be multiplied together provided that the first matrix has the same number of columns as the second matrix has rows.

Thus if matrix **A** has four rows and two columns, and matrix **B** has two rows and three columns, the two can be multiplied together to get a product **AB**.

Since **A** is a 4×2 matrix and **B** is a 2×3 matrix, a product **AB** can be found, but a product matrix **BA** does not exist. **B** has three columns and **A** has four rows, therefore multiplication is impossible.

The elements in a product matrix are calculated as follows.

(a) Take the elements in the first row of the first matrix (say, matrix **A**) and multiply them by the corresponding elements in the first column of the second matrix (say, matrix **B**). The sum of the products then becomes the element in the first row and the first column of the product matrix.

(b) Similarly, the elements in row 2 of matrix **A** should be multiplied by the corresponding elements in column 1 of matrix **B**, and the sum of the products then becomes the element in row 2 and column 1 of the product matrix.

(c) This process must be repeated m × p times. The general rule is that the elements in row m of the first matrix should be multiplied by the corresponding elements in column p of the second matrix, and the sum of the products then becomes the element in row m and column p of the product matrix.

EXAMPLE: MATRIX MULTIPLICATION

Matrix **A** is a 2×3 matrix

$$\begin{pmatrix} 5 & 6 & 4 \\ 4 & 9 & 7 \end{pmatrix}$$

Matrix **B** is a 3×4 matrix

$$\begin{pmatrix} 3 & 5 & 5 & 5 \\ 6 & 4 & 4 & 0 \\ 0 & 3 & 5 & 5 \end{pmatrix}$$

Calculate matrix **C** where **C** = **AB**.

SOLUTION

Matrix C will be a 2×4 matrix. We use C_{12} to denote the number in row 1, column 2, and so on.

Element in matrix C	Elements in xth row of A	Elements in xth column of B	
C_{11}	1st	1st	$= (5 \times 3) + (6 \times 6) + (4 \times 0) = 51$
C_{12}	1st	2nd	$= (5 \times 5) + (6 \times 4) + (4 \times 3) = 61$
C_{13}	1st	3rd	$= (5 \times 5) + (6 \times 4) + (4 \times 5) = 69$
C_{14}	1st	4th	$= (5 \times 5) + (6 \times 0) + (4 \times 5) = 45$
C_{21}	2nd	1st	$= (4 \times 3) + (9 \times 6) + (7 \times 0) = 66$
C_{22}	2nd	2nd	$= (4 \times 5) + (9 \times 4) + (7 \times 3) = 77$
C_{23}	2nd	3rd	$= (4 \times 5) + (9 \times 4) + (7 \times 5) = 91$
C_{24}	2nd	4th	$= (4 \times 5) + (9 \times 0) + (7 \times 5) = 55$

Matrix C $= \begin{pmatrix} 51 & 61 & 69 & 45 \\ 66 & 77 & 91 & 55 \end{pmatrix}$

Activity 15

Let **A** = $\begin{pmatrix} 2 & 1 \\ 0 & 3 \end{pmatrix}$

B = $\begin{pmatrix} 5 & 1 & 0 \\ 2 & 3 & 1 \end{pmatrix}$

C = $\begin{pmatrix} 3 & 1 \\ 0 & 2 \\ 1 & 4 \end{pmatrix}$

Find **AB**, **CA**, **BC** and **CB**.

Null matrices

Definition

> A *null matrix* is one in which every element is 0.

10.8 The null matrix behaves like the number 0 in calculations. Thus, if any matrix is multiplied by a null matrix the solution will also be a null matrix.

$$\begin{pmatrix} 0 & 0 \\ 0 & 0 \end{pmatrix} \times \begin{pmatrix} 6 & -1 \\ 2 & 3 \end{pmatrix} = \begin{pmatrix} 0 & 0 \\ 0 & 0 \end{pmatrix}$$

Identity matrices

Definition

> An *identity* or *unit matrix* (often designated by **I**) is a square matrix which behaves like the number 1 in multiplication.

10.9 Each element on the main diagonal (top left to bottom right) of a unit matrix is 1 and all other elements are 0.

10.10 A unit matrix must be square, and the effect of multiplying a matrix by a unit matrix is to leave it unchanged.

$$\begin{pmatrix} 1 & 0 & 0 \\ 0 & 1 & 0 \\ 0 & 0 & 1 \end{pmatrix} \times \begin{pmatrix} 1 & 2 & 3 \\ 4 & 5 & 6 \\ 7 & 8 & 9 \end{pmatrix} = \begin{pmatrix} 1 & 2 & 3 \\ 4 & 5 & 6 \\ 7 & 8 & 9 \end{pmatrix}$$

$$\mathbf{I} \quad \times \quad \mathbf{A} \quad = \quad \mathbf{A}$$

Inverse of a matrix

10.11 The inverse of a square matrix A is represented by A^{-1} and can be defined by the equation:

$$\mathbf{AA^{-1}} = \mathbf{A^{-1}A} = \mathbf{I}$$

This means that if A is multiplied by its inverse or vice versa the product is an identity matrix.

The inverse of a 2×2 matrix can be found as follows.

$$\text{If } \mathbf{A} = \begin{pmatrix} a & b \\ c & d \end{pmatrix} \text{ then } \mathbf{A^{-1}} = \frac{1}{ad - bc} \begin{pmatrix} d & -b \\ -c & a \end{pmatrix}$$

Activity 16

Find the inverse of matrix A = $\begin{pmatrix} 7 & 9 \\ 3 & 2 \end{pmatrix}$

NOTES

Solving simultaneous equations using matrices

10.12 Matrices are widely used for solving simultaneous equations. The following example illustrates how this is done.

EXAMPLE: SOLVING SIMULTANEOUS EQUATIONS

Solve the equations

$5x + 9y = -30$
$6x - 2y = 28$

using matrix algebra.

SOLUTION

In a matrix format the equations can be stated as:

$$\begin{pmatrix} 5 & 9 \\ 6 & -2 \end{pmatrix}\begin{pmatrix} x \\ y \end{pmatrix} = \begin{pmatrix} -30 \\ 28 \end{pmatrix}$$

Invert the square matrix, to get:

$$\frac{1}{5\times(-2)-9\times6}\begin{pmatrix} -2 & -9 \\ -6 & 5 \end{pmatrix}$$

$$= \frac{-1}{64}\begin{pmatrix} -2 & -9 \\ -6 & 5 \end{pmatrix}$$

$$= \begin{pmatrix} 2/64 & 9/64 \\ 6/64 & -5/64 \end{pmatrix}$$

Multiply both sides of the equation by this inverse.

$$\begin{pmatrix} 2/64 & 9/64 \\ 6/64 & -5/64 \end{pmatrix}\begin{pmatrix} 5 & 9 \\ 6 & -2 \end{pmatrix}\begin{pmatrix} x \\ y \end{pmatrix} = \begin{pmatrix} 2/64 & 9/64 \\ 6/64 & -5/64 \end{pmatrix}\begin{pmatrix} -30 \\ 28 \end{pmatrix}$$

$$\begin{pmatrix} 1 & 0 \\ 0 & 1 \end{pmatrix}\begin{pmatrix} x \\ y \end{pmatrix} = \begin{pmatrix} 3 \\ -5 \end{pmatrix}$$

So $x = 3$ and $y = -5$.

11 FORMULAE FOR SPREADSHEETS

11.1 Spreadsheets are commonly used in a wide variety of courses and modules. If you haven't already met them, you undoubtedly will in the very near future. Building formulae in the cells of a spreadsheet is an important skill and should be acquired early on in your course.

11.2 A formula refers to other cells in the spreadsheet, and performs some sort of computation with them. For example, if cell C1 contains the formula +A1 –B1 this means that the contents of cell B1 should be subtracted from the contents of cell A1 and the result displayed in cell C1. Note that a formula starts with a '+' in most packages to distinguish it from text. In Lotus 1-2-3, a formula must start with one of the following characters: +, –, $ or @. In Excel, a formula must start with =.

11.3 By working through the following examples you will assimilate the knowledge required.

EXAMPLE: EASY SREADSHEET FORMULA

Below is a spreadsheet processing budgeted sales figures for three geographic areas for the first quarter of the year.

	A	**B**	**C**	**D**	**E**
1		JAN	FEB	MARCH	TOTAL
2	NORTH	2,431	3,001	2,189	7,621
3	SOUTH	6,532	5,826	6,124	18,482
4	WEST	895	432	596	1,923
5	TOTAL	9,858	9,259	8,909	28,026
6					
7					
8					

Required

What formula would you put in the following cells?

    (a)   Cell B5
    (b)   Cell E4
    (c)   Cell E5

SOLUTION

    (a)   + B2 + B3 + B4
    (b)   + B4 + C4 + D4
    (c)   Either + E2 + E3 + E4 or + B5 + C5 + D5

EXAMPLE: FORMULA IN A BALANCE SHEET MODEL

Consider the balance sheet model shown below.

	A	B	C	D	E
1			£'000	£'000	
2					
3	Fixed assets: cost				
4	Accumulated depreciation				
5	Net book value				
6	*Current assets:*				
7	Stocks				
8	Debtors				
9	Cash				
10					
11	*Current liabilities:*				
12	Overdraft				
13	Creditors				
14	Taxation				
15					
16	Net current assets				
17					
18	Net assets				

Required

Define the formulae required for the following operations.

(a) In cell C10: calculate the sum of the current assets
(b) In cell C15: calculate the sum of the current liabilities
(c) In cell D5: calculate cost of fixed assets less accumulated depreciation
(d) In cell D16: calculate current assets less current liabilities
(e) In cell D18: calculate the sum of fixed assets and net current assets

SOLUTION

(a) In cell C10: + C7 + C8 + C9
(b) In cell C15: + C12 + C13 + C14
(c) In cell D5: + D3 – D4
(d) In cell D16: + C10 – C15
(e) In cell D18: +D5 + D16 (alternatively + D5 + C10 – C15)

More complicated formulae

11.4 So far we have used a formula to add and subtract. Formulae can be used to perform a variety of calculations. Here are some examples.

(a) +C4*5. This formula multiplies the value in C4 by 5. The result will appear in the cell holding the formula.

(b) +C4*B10. This multiplies the value in C4 by the value in B10.

(c) +C4/E5. This divides the value in C4 by the value in E5. (Note that * means multiply and / means divide by.)

(d)   +C4*B10 − D1. This multiplies the value in C4 by that in B10 and then deducts the value in D1 from the result. Note that generally the computer will perform multiplication before addition or subtraction.

(e)   +C4+17.5%. This adds 17.5% to the value in C4. It could be used to calculate a price including 17.5% VAT.

(f)   + (C4+C5+C6)/3. This, in effect, calculates the average of the values in C4, C5 and C6. Note that the brackets tell the computer to perform the addition first. Without the brackets the computer would first divide the value in C6 by 3 and then add the result to the total of the values in C4 and C5.

(g)   If may be quicker, when totalling a long row or column of figures, to use the formula @ SUM (B2..B12).

EXAMPLE: MORE COMPLICATED FORMULAE

The following four insurance salesmen earn a basic salary of £14,000 pa. They also earn a commission of 2% of sales. The following spreadsheet has been created to process their commission and total earnings.

	A	B	C	D	E
1	*Salesmen:*	*Salary and commission*			
2	*Name*	*Sales*	*Salary*	*Commission*	*Total earnings*
3					
4	Ken	284,000	14,000	5,680	19,680
5	Mike	193,000	14,000	3,860	17,860
6	Alf	12,000	14,000	240	14,240
7	Jack	152,000	14,000	3,040	17,040
8					
9	Total	641,000	56,000	12,820	68,820

Required

Give an appropriate formula for the following cells.

(a)   Cell D4
(b)   Cell E6
(c)   Cell D9
(d)   Cell E9

SOLUTION

(a)   +B4*0.02

(b)   +C6+D6

(c)   +D4+D5+D6+D7; or @SUM(D4..D7)

(d)   One of the following would be suitable.

      (i)   +E4+E5+E6+E7
      (ii)   @SUM(E4..E7)
      (iii) +C9+D9

11.5 Note that a formula which calculates a percentage of a value, such as commission as a percentage of sales, could be used in preparing a payroll. For example, National Insurance or pension contributions may be a set percentage of salary.

11.6 A business will often need to compare its results with budgets or targets to see how far it has exceeded, or fallen short of, its expectations. It is useful to express variations as a percentage of the original target, for example sales may be 10% higher than predicted.

EXAMPLE: SPREADSHEET FORMULAE INVOLVING PERCENTAGE DIFFERENCES

Continuing the example of the insurance salesmen, a spreadsheet could be set up as follows showing differences between actual sales and target sales, and expressing the difference as a percentage of target sales.

	A	B	C	D	E	F
1	*Salesmen:*	*Actual sales v target sales*				
2	*Name*	*Target sales*	*Actual sales*	*Difference*	*Difference as a % of target*	
3						
4	Ken	275,000	284,000	9,000	3.27	
5	Mike	200,000	193,000	−7,000	−3.50	
6	Alf	10,000	12,000	2,000	20.00	
7	Jack	153,000	152,000	−1,000	−0.65	
8						
9	Total	638,000	641,000	3,000	0.47	
10						
11						

Required

Give a suitable formula for the following cells.

  (a)   Cell D4
  (b)   Cell E6
  (c)   Cell E9

SOLUTION

  (a)   +C4 – B4

  (b)   (D6/B6)*100. With some spreadsheets, for example Lotus 1-2-3, you do not need to use brackets because the formula automatically operates from left to right where you have both multiplication and division. The formula would thus be +D6/B6*100.

  (c)   (D9/B9)*100 or +D9/B9*100. Note that in (c) you cannot simply add up the individual percentage differences. This is because the percentages are based on very different quantities. For example, Alf has exceeded his target by 20%, but this is only £2,000, while Ken's 3.27% difference is actually £9,000. You should always use your common sense in thinking about any formula you choose to put in.

Spreadsheets and budgets

11.7 It is useful to have an awareness of budgeting. Read through the following example to give you an idea of how to set up a spreadsheet which will assist in the budgeting process.

11.8 The cost accountant of a small company wishes to computerise the cash flow projections using a spreadsheet package. The cash flow projection is to provide a monthly cash flow analysis over a five-year period. The following data is relevant.

    (a)   Initial cash held by the company on 1 January 20X1 is expected to be £15,000.

    (b)   Sales in January are expected to be £25,000, and a growth rate of 2% per month in sales is predicted throughout the forecast period.

    (c)   The company buys stock one month in advance and pays in cash.

    (d)   On average, payment is received from customers as follows.

        (i)   60% one month in arrears
        (ii)   40% two months in arrears

    All sales are on credit. There are no bad debts.

    (e)   The cost of sales is 65% of sales value. Overhead costs (cash expenses) are expected to be £6,500 per month, rising by 5% at the start of each new calendar year.

    (f)   Purchases of capital equipment and payments of tax, interest charges and dividends must also be provided for within the model. The interest rate on bank overdrafts is expected to be 1% per month.

Inserting text

11.9 The first job is to put in the various headings that you want on the model. There is a facility within the program that enables you to specify the text for any column, combined columns or rows of data. (It is usually convenient to start the tabulation at row 1 and column A, although this is not essential.)

11.10 The cost accountant might decide to label the spreadsheet rows and columns as follows.

	: A :	B :	C :	D :	E :	F :
1:		20X1				
2:		Jan	Feb	March	April	May
3:		£	£	£	£	£
4:	Sales					
5:	Cash receipts					
6:	One months in arrears					
7:	Two months in arrears					
8:	Three months in arrears					
9:	Total receipts					
10:						
11:	Cash payments					
12:	Stock					
13:	Overheads					
14:	Interest					
15:	Tax					
16:	Dividends					
17:	Capital purchases					
18:	Total payments					
19:						
20:	Cash receipts less payments					
21:	Balance b/f					
22:	Balance c/f					

Inserting formulae

11.11 The next stage in constructing a model is to put in the calculations you want the computer to carry out, expressed as formulae. The formulae required can be constructed in a variety of ways. One way would be to insert some 'constant' values into cells of the spreadsheet.

	Column	
Row	*A*	*B*
23:	Sales growth factor per month	1.02
24:	Interest rate per month	0.01
25:	Debts paid within 1 month	0.6
26:	Debts paid within 2 months	0.4
27:	Debts paid within 3 months	0
28:	Bad debts	0
29:	Cost of sales as proportion of sales	0.65

Alternatively, these values could be specified in the formulae in the spreadsheet.

11.12 Unlike the text, these formulae will not be shown on the spreadsheet itself, but at the bottom of the screen. So at this stage, the spreadsheet looks just the same as it did after setting up the headings – but when the cursor is on a cell where a formula has been input, then that formula is shown at the bottom of the screen.

11.13 Examples of constructing formulae for the spreadsheet are as follows.

(a) The formulae for sales in February 20X1, in this example, would be (+B4*B23), in March 20X1 (+ C4*B23), in April 20X1 (+ D4*B23) and so on. Replication of the formula could be used to save input time.

(b) The formula for cash receipts in April 20X1 would be:

E6 = +D4*B25
E7 = +C4*B26
E8 = +B4*B27
E9 = +E6 + E7 + E8

(c) Cash payments for stock would be expressed as the cost of sales in the previous month; for February 20X1, this would be:

C12 = +B4*B29

(d) Total cash payments in May 20X1 would be the sum of cells F12 to F17.

F18 = @ SUM (F12..F17)

Inserting numerical data

11.14 The last stage in setting up a spreadsheet is to input data. Input data would include the opening cash balance on 1 January 20X1, dividend and tax payments, capital purchases, sales in January 20X1, the constant values (in our example in column B, rows 23 to 29) and the other data needed to establish cash receipts and payments in the first month or so of the forecast period (for example, receipts in January 20X1 will depend on sales in November and December 20X0, which the simplified model shown here has not provided for). With this input data, and the spreadsheet formulae, a full cash flow projection for the five-year period can be produced and, if required, printed out.

12 GEOMETRIC PROGRESSIONS

Definition

> A *geometric progression* is a sequence of numbers in which there is a common or constant ratio between adjacent terms.

12.1 Some examples of geometric progressions are as follows.

(a) 2, 4, 8, 16, 32, where there is a common ratio of 2.

(b) 121, 110, 100, 90.91, 82.64, where (allowing for rounding differences in the fourth and fifth terms) there is a common ratio of $1/1.1 = 0.9091$.

12.2 An algebraic representation of a geometric progression is as follows.

$A, AR, AR^2, AR^3, AR^4, ..., AR^{n-1}$

where   A   is the first term
        R   is the common ratio
        n   is the number of terms

EXAMPLE: A GEOMETRIC PROGRESSION

A sales manager has reported that sales in the next year will amount to 5,000 units of product. He also estimates that sales will then increase in volume by 40% a year until year 6. What sales volume would be expected in year 6?

SOLUTION

We require the sixth term in the geometric progression.

A   = year 1 sales = 5,000

R   = rate of growth = 140% (Note that R = 140% or 1.4, not 40% or 0.4.)

n   = 6

T_6 = $5,000 \times 1.4^{(6-1)}$

   = $5,000 \times 5.37824$

   = 26,891.2 units (say 26,891 units)

The sum of a geometric progression

12.3 It is sometimes necessary to calculate the sum of the terms in a geometric progression. For example, suppose that a factory expects to produce 4,000 units in week 1 and to increase output by 20% each week for three more weeks.

Total output in the four weeks = 4,000 + 4,800 + 5,760 + 6,912 = 21,472 units

12.4 The calculation is relatively straightforward when the progression consists of a small number of terms. However, when we wish to calculate the sum of longer geometric progressions, it is easier to use a formula.

12.5 The formula for the sum (S) of a geometric progression is derived as follows.

$S = A + AR + AR^2 + AR^3 + ... + AR^{n-1}$ (1)

Multiply both sides of the equation by R to give:

$RS = AR + AR^2 + AR^3 + ... + AR^n$ (2)

Subtract (1) from (2).

$RS - S = AR^n - A$

$\therefore S(R - 1) = A(R^n - 1)$

$\therefore S = \dfrac{A(R^n - 1)}{R - 1}$

12.6 In the example above, we have the following.

$S = 4,000 + 4,000 \times 1.2 + 4,000 \times 1.2^2 + 4,000 \times 1.2^3$

$1.2S = 4,000 \times 1.2 + 4,000 \times 1.2^2 + 4,000 \times 1.2^3 + 4,000 \times 1.2^4$

$1.2S - S = (4,000 \times 1.2^4) - 4,000$

$S = \dfrac{4,000(1.2^4 - 1)}{(1.2 - 1)}$

= +21,472 units

Geometric progressions are particularly important in financial mathematics.

13 LOGARITHMS

Definition

> The *logarithm* of a number is the power to which 10 must be raised to equal that number.

13.1 Your calculator might well enable you to work out complex values with little difficulty. For example, if you want the value of 1.12^{15} it could be a simple matter of entering two values into your calculator to obtain an answer.

13.2 However, when sophisticated calculators are unavailable, logarithms are one way of doing compounding arithmetic relatively easily. Furthermore, knowledge of logarithms enables us to ascertain the rate of change of a variable over time. Let us start by seeing what logarithms actually are.

13.3 The figure 10 can be expressed as 10^1. Similarly,

1	can be expressed as 10^0
100	can be expressed as 10^2
1,000	can be expressed as 10^3
10,000	can be expressed as 10^4

and so on.

To multiply 100 by 1,000, one way of expressing the calculation is

$$100 \times 1,000 = 10^2 \times 10^3 = 10^{(2+3)}$$
$$= 10^5$$
$$= 100,000$$

13.4 Logarithms work on the same principle.

Every number can be converted into 10 to a certain power. For example:

2	$= 10^{0.3010}$
20	$= 10^{1.3010}$
200	$= 10^{2.3010}$

How do we know this?

(a) Any value between 1 (10^0) and 10 (10^1) must have a 'to a certain power' value between 0 and 1.

(b) Similarly, any value between 10 (10^1) and 100 (10^2) must have a 'to a certain power' value between 1 and 2.

(c) Again, any value between 100 (10^2) and 1,000 (10^3) must have a 'to a certain power' value between 2 and 3.

This explains the figures to the left of the decimal points.

The value to the right of the decimal points, for 2, 20, 200 and indeed for 2,000, 20,000, 0.2, 0.02 and so on, is the same, and it is found by looking it up in logarithm tables. Tables are given at the front of this Course Book. For 2, we look at row 20, column 0 and find .3010.

13.5 Here are some more examples to illustrate the use of logarithm tables.

    (a)   (i)   The logarithm of 2.4 is 0.3802.

            The value to the left of the decimal point is 0 because we want the logarithm of a figure between 1 and 10.

            The value to the right of the decimal point is found from the tables, row 24, column 0.

        (ii)   The logarithm of 24 is 1.3802.

        (iii)   The logarithm of 240 is 2.3802.

    (b)   The logarithm of 2.45 is 0.3892. The value to the right of the decimal point is found from the tables, row 24, column 5.

    (c)   The logarithm of 24.8 is 1.3945. The value to the right of the decimal point is found from the tables, row 24, column 8.

    (d)   What about the logarithm of 2.026? The value to the right of the decimal point is found from the tables by starting at row 20 column 2 (0.3054) and then looking at the columns 1–9 on the far right of the table for the value in column 6, which is 13. This is added to the 3054 to get 3067, and the logarithm of 2.026 is 0.3067.

13.6 To convert a logarithm answer back to a 'normal' number, we can again use tables.

    (a)   There are antilogarithm tables, similar to logarithm tables, but which are used to convert logarithms back to normal numbers.

    (b)   Alternatively, you can find the solution by looking for the logarithm within the logarithm tables.

Logarithms of values between 0 and 1

13.7 We know that $10^0 = 1$ and $10^{-1} = 0.1$.

It follows that numbers between 0.1 and 1 ought to have logarithms between 0 and –1.

Similarly, since $10^{-2} = 0.01$, it follows that numbers between 0.01 and 0.1 ought to have logarithms between –1 and –2.

13.8 This is so. The logarithm of 0.2 is written $\bar{1}$.3010, pronounced 'bar one point 3010'.

The bar means minus and so $= \bar{1} = -1$, $\bar{2} = -2$ and so on. So the logarithm of 0.2, which is $\bar{1}$.3010, is minus 1 *plus* 0.3010.

    (a)   Any figure from 0.1 up to just less than 1 has a logarithm with $\bar{1}$ to the left of the decimal point.

    (b)   Any figure from 0.01 up to just less than 0.1 has a logarithm with $\bar{2}$ to the left of the decimal point.

    (c)   Similarly, any figure from 0.001 up to just less than 0.01 has a logarithm with $\bar{3}$ to the left of the decimal point.

Logarithms and the examination

13.9 Logarithm tables are usually provided in examinations and we have worked through this section using tables since this provides a greater understanding of how logarithms are devised.

In the examination you can, of course, use your calculator. Most calculators do not use the, $\overline{1}, \overline{2}$ system but give you negative numbers where appropriate (–0.3979 for log 0.4).

14 ROUNDING

14.1 There are three methods of rounding and these will be illustrated using the figure 18,600.

(a) *Rounding up:* 18,600 would be expressed as 19,000 to the nearest thousand above.

(b) *Rounding down:* 18,600 would be expressed as 18,000 to the nearest thousand below.

(c) *Rounding to the nearest round amount:* 18,600 would be expressed as 19,000 to the nearest thousand.

Method (c) is the most commonly used.

In rounding to the nearest unit, a value ending in 0.5 is usually rounded up. Thus 3.5 rounded to the nearest unit would be 4.

14.2 Rounding can be specified to the nearest whole unit (as above), by the number of decimal places (3.94712 to two decimal places is 3.95), or by the number of significant digits.

Activity 17

(a) What is £482,365.15 to the nearest:

   (i)   £1
   (ii)   £100
   (iii) £1,000
   (iv)   £10,000?

(b) What is 843.668 correct to:

   (i)   one decimal place
   (ii)   two decimal places?

(c) What is 628.0273 to:

   (i)   five significant figures
   (ii)   four significant figures?

Spurious accuracy

14.3 Spurious accuracy arises when a statistic gives the impression that it is more accurate than it really is. For example we might see stated '24.68% of women over the age of 30 are smokers'. This result is probably based on a sample and so we know that it cannot be as accurate as it seems: the two decimal places have arisen simply because of the arithmetic of the calculations. It would be less misleading to state 'approximately 25% of women over the age of 30 are smokers'. This removes the spurious accuracy implied by the decimal places.

15   MAXIMUM ERRORS

Absolute errors

15.1   Suppose that the population of a country is stated as 40 million. It is quite likely that this figure has been rounded to the nearest million. We could therefore say that the country's population is

40 million ± 500,000

where 40 million is the *estimate* of the population and 500,000 is the *maximum absolute error*.

15.2   In general terms an estimate with a maximum absolute error can be expressed as

a ± b.

Relative errors

15.3   The error in the population of the country could also be expressed as

40 million ± 1.25%

where 500,000 is 1.25% of 40 million. In this instance the maximum error is a maximum relative error and is calculated as

$$\frac{\text{maximum absolute error}}{\text{estimate}} \times 100\%.$$

16   ERRORS AND CALCULATIONS

16.1   If calculations are made using values that have been rounded then the results of such calculations will only be approximate. However, provided that we are aware of the maximum errors that can occur, we can still draw conclusions from the results of the calculations.

16.2   There are two rules to remember when performing calculations involving rounded or approximate numbers.

(a)   *Addition/subtraction*

When two or more rounded or approximate numbers are added or subtracted the maximum absolute error in the result equals the sum of the individual maximum absolute errors.

(b)   *Multiplication/division*

When two or more rounded or approximate numbers are multiplied or divided, the approximate maximum relative error in the result is obtained by adding the individual maximum relative errors.

We will use an example to illustrate these rules.

EXAMPLE: ERRORS

A chemical producer plans to sell 50,000 litres (to the nearest 1,000 litres) of a particular chemical at a price of £10 (to the nearest pound) per litre.

The cost of materials used to produce the chemicals is expected to be £100,000 but depending on wastage levels this is subject to an error of ± 5%. Labour costs are estimated to be £300,000 ± 10%, depending on overtime working and pay negotiations.

Required

Calculate the maximum absolute error and the maximum relative error in revenue and costs of production.

SOLUTION

	Estimate	*Maximum absolute error*	*Maximum relative error* %
Quantity sold	50,000 litres	500 litres	1
Price	£10	£0.50	5
Materials	£100,000	£5,000	5
Labour	£300,000	£30,000	10

(a) Revenue = quantity sold × price
  = (50,000 ± 1%) × (£10 ± 5%)
  = (50,000 × £10) ± (1% + 5%)
  = £500,000 ± 6%
  = £500,000 ± £30,000
  ∴ Approximate maximum absolute error = £30,000
  ∴ Approximate maximum relative error = 6%

Note that we need to use relative errors when doing multiplication/division calculations.

(b) Costs of production = material + labour
  = (£100,000 ± £5,000) + (£300,000 ± £30,000)
  = (£100,000 + £300,000) ± (£5,000 + £30,000)
  = £400,000 ± £35,000
  = £400,000 ± 8.75 %

  ∴ Maximum absolute error = £35,000
  ∴ Maximum relative error = 8.75%

Note that we need to use absolute errors when doing addition/subtraction calculations.

16.3 The rule in Paragraph 16.2(b) only gives an approximate maximum relative error. Let's see what the actual error would have been in the example above.

Maximum revenue = maximum quantity × maximum price
  = (50,000 + 1%) × (£10 + 5%)
  = 50,500 × £10.50
  = £530,250

∴ Our approximation of the maximum absolute error was correct to within £(530,250 − 530,000) = £250.0

NOTES

Activity 18

Suppose that $A = \dfrac{J \times B}{M}$

where J and B are subject to a maximum relative error of 10% and M to a maximum relative error of 20%.

Required

(a) Calculate the approximate maximum relative error in A (using the rule in Paragraph 16.2(b))

(b) Calculate the actual maximum relative error.

In this chapter we have introduced some of the mathematical tools that you will be required to use in Unit 5: Quantitative Techniques for Business. The next chapter begins our study of quantitative techniques by looking at the collection of data.

Chapter roundup

* This chapter has covered the basic mathematics which you will need to understand before attempting the remainder of this Course Book.

* Brackets indicate a priority or an order in which calculations should be made.

* The negative number rules are as follows.

$$-p + q = q - p$$
$$q - (-p) = q + p$$
$$-p \times -q = pq \text{ and } -p/-q = p/q$$
$$-p \times q = -pq \text{ and } -p/q = -p/q$$

* The reciprocal of a number is 1 divided by that number.

* Percentages are used to indicate the relative size or proportion of items, rather than their absolute size. To turn a percentage into a fraction or decimal you divide by 100%. To turn a fraction or decimal back into a percentage you multiply by 100%.

* A percentage increase or reduction is calculated as (difference ÷ initial value) × 100%.

* A proportion means writing a percentage as a proportion of 1 (that is, as a decimal).

* Ratios show relative shares of a whole.

* The nth root of a number is a value which, when multiplied by itself (n − 1) times, equals the original number. Powers work the other way round.

* When we use letters to stand for any numbers we call them variables. The use of variables enables us to state general truths about mathematics.

* The general rule for solving equations is that you can do what you like to one side of an equation, so long as you do the same thing to the other side straightaway.

PUBLISHING

- A linear equation has the general form y = a + bx, where x is the independent variable and y the dependent variable, and a and b are fixed amounts.

- Make sure that you are aware of the rules for drawing graphs.

- The graph of a linear equation is a straight line. The intercept of the line on the y axis is a in y = a + bx and the slope of the line is b.

- Simultaneous equations are two or more equations which are satisfied by the same variable values. They can be solved graphically or algebraically.

- In non-linear equations, one variable varies with the nth power of another, where n > 1. The graph of a non-linear equation is not a straight line.

- Quadratic equations are non-linear equations in which one variable varies with the square of the other variable.

- Formulae for spreadsheets follow a particular format. Ensure that you are able to construct formulae which incorporate addition, subtraction, multiplication, division and percentage differences.

- A geometric progression is a sequence of numbers in which there is a common ratio between adjacent terms.

- The logarithm of a number is the power to which 10 has to be raised to get that number.

- Approximation arises if it is not possible to obtain an accurate figure or if a number has been rounded. Rounding can be specified to the nearest whole unit, by the number of decimal places or by the number of significant figures.

- Spurious accuracy arises when a statistic gives the impression that it is more accurate than it really is.

- Maximum errors can be absolute or relative.

- When two or more rounded or approximate numbers are multiplied or divided, the approximate maximum relative error in the result is obtained by adding the individual relative errors.

- You can determine the actual error in calculations involving only a few values/variables without using the two rules.

- Make sure that you have worked through all of the examples in this chapter since it provides the foundation for the remainder of the Course Book.

Quick quiz

1 Is $3^3/_4$ an integer?

2 What is 1004.002955 to nine significant digits?

3 What is the product of a negative number and a negative number?

4 $217 \leq 217$. True or false?

5 How do you turn a fraction into a percentage?

6 Define the nth root of a number.

7 What is the difference between a formula and an equation?

8 What is a linear equation?

9 What are the rules for drawing graphs?

10 What is the intercept?

11 What are quadratic equations?

12 What quick formula could you use to total the values in cells F15 to F27 in a spreadsheet?

13 What is geometric progression?

14 What is the formula for the sum of a geometric progression?

15 What is the logarithm of 550.77? (Use your calculator)

16 What is spurious accuracy?

17 How is a maximum relative error calculated?

18 What are the two rules to remember when performing calculations using rounded or approximate numbers?

Answers to activities

1   17.39

2   (a) $64 - (-1) = 64 + 1 = 65$ (c) $-24 - (12) = -36$

    (b) $8 + (-9) = -1$ (d) $-6 - (-12) - (-27) = -6 + 12 + 27 = 33$

3   (a) 648.2565   (h) 93.31

    (b) 30.0192   (i) −102.79

    (c) 0.5313   (j) 100 (Note that this question is the reciprocal of part (e), and so the answer is the reciprocal of the answer to part (e).)

    (d) 5.2518   (k) −0.0775

    (e) 0.01   (l) −0.6133

    (f) 0.4097   (m) 0.7443

    (g) 11,985.69   (n) −1.5434

4   Let 100% = £795

    $\therefore 1\% = \dfrac{100\%}{100} = \dfrac{£795}{100} = £7.95$

    $\therefore 17\% = 17 \times 1\% = 17 \times £7.95 = £135.15$

    $\therefore$ Price offered = £(795 − 135.15) = £659.85

Alternatively

Price offered = £795 × (100 − 17)% = £795 × 83% = £795 × 0.83 = £659.85

5   (a) Difference in price = £(490.99 − 340.99) = £150.00

        Percentage reduction = $\dfrac{150}{490.99} \times 100\% = 30.551\%$

    (b) Difference in price = £(892 − 757) = £135

        Percentage increase = $\dfrac{135}{757} \times 100\% = 17.8\%$

6   (30 − 17)/30 × 100% = 43.33% = 0.4333

7   (a)   (i)   Total parts = 10

                Each part is worth £800 ÷ 10 = £80
                Tom gets   3 × £80 = £240
                Dick gets   2 × £80 = £160
                Harry gets   5 × £80 = £400

        (ii)   Same parts as (i) but in a different order.
                Tom gets   £400
                Dick gets   £240
                Harry gets   £160

        (iii)   Total parts = 5
                Each part is worth £800 ÷ 5 = £160
                Therefore Tom gets £480
                Dick and Harry each get £160

    (b)   (i)   Laura's share = £6 = 5 parts
                Therefore one part is worth £6 ÷ 5 = £1.20
                Total of 9 parts shared out originally
                Therefore total was 9 × £1.20 = £10.80

        (ii)   Laura's share = £6 = 4 parts
                Therefore one part is worth £6 ÷ 4 = £1.50
                Therefore original total was 9 × £1.50 = £13.50

8   (a) $(18.6)^{2.6} = 1{,}998.64$

    (b) $(18.6)^{-2.6} = \left(\dfrac{1}{18.6}\right)^{2.6} = 0.0005$

    (c) $\sqrt[2.6]{18.6} = 3.078$

    (d) $(14.2)^4 + (14.2)^{1/4} = (14.2)^{4.25} = 78{,}926.98$

    (e) $(14.2)^4 + (14.2)^{1/4} = 40{,}658.69 + 1.9412 = 40{,}660.6312$

9   **Solution 1**

    (a) $47x + 256 = 52x$
                    $256 = 5x$ (subtract 47x from each side)
                    $51.2 = x$ (divide each side by 5)

    (b) $4\sqrt{x} + 32 = 40.6718$
             $4\sqrt{x} = 8.6718$ (subtract 32 from each side)
             $\sqrt{x} = 2.16795$ (divide each side by 4)
             $x = 4.7$ (square each side).

    (c) $\dfrac{1}{3x+4} = \dfrac{5}{2.7x-2}$

        $3x + 4 = \dfrac{2.7x-2}{5}$ (take the reciprocal of each side)

        $15x + 20 = 2.7x - 2$ (multiply each side by 5)

        $12.3x = -22$ (subtract 20 and subtract 2.7x from each side)

        $x = -1.789$ (divide each side by 12.3).

    (d) $x^3 = 4.913$

        $x = 1.7$ (take the cube root of each side).

(e) $34x - 7.6 = (17x - 3.8) \times (x + 12.5)$

This one is easy if you realise that $17 \times 2 = 34$ and $3.8 \times 2 = 7.6$, so $2(17x - 3.8) = 34x - 7.6$

We can then divide each side by $17x - 3.8$ to get

$2 \qquad = x + 12.5$

$-10.5 = x$ \qquad\qquad\qquad (subtract 12.5 from each side).

Solution 2

(a) $x = (3y - 20)^2$

$\sqrt{x} = 3y - 20$ \qquad (take the square root of each side)

$20 + \sqrt{x} = 3y$ \qquad (add 20 to each side)

$y = \dfrac{20 + \sqrt{x}}{3}$ \qquad (divide each side by 3, and swap the sides for ease of reading)

(b) $2(y - 4) - 4(x^2 + 3) = 0$

$2(y - 4) = 4(x^2 + 3)$ \quad (add $4(x^2 + 3)$ to each side)

$0.5(y - 4) = x^2 + 3$ \quad (divide each side by 4)

$0.5(y - 4) - 3 = x^2$ \quad (subtract 3 from each side)

$x = \sqrt{0.5(y - 4) - 3}$ \quad (take the square root of each side, and swap the sides for ease of reading)

$x = \sqrt{0.5y - 5}$

10   Gradient $= -1$

11    $4y = 16x - 12$

The equation must be of the form $y = a + bx$

$y = -\dfrac{12}{4} + \dfrac{16}{4}x = -3 + 4x$

Intercept $= a = -3$, ie $(0, -3)$

Slope $= 4$

12
$5x + 2y$	$=$	34	(1)	
$x + 3y$	$=$	25	(2)	
$5x + 15y$	$=$	125	(3)	$5 \times (2)$
$13y$	$=$	91	(4)	$(3) - (1)$
y	$=$	7		
$x + 21$	$=$	25		Substitute into (2)
x	$=$	$25 - 21$		
x	$=$	4		

The solution is $x = 4$, $y = 7$.

13   (a)   Let C = total costs
                    C = total variable costs + total fixed costs
                    C = $5q + 75$

(b)   If $q = 100$, $C = (5 \times 100) + 75 = £575$

(c)   If q = 0,   C = £75
       If q = 100,   C = £575

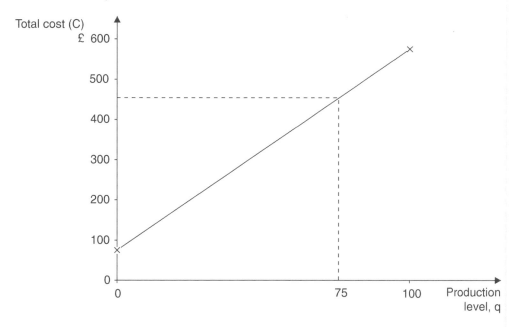

(d)   From the graph above, if q = 75, C = £450

14   C = (25 − q)q

If q = 15, C = (25 − 15) × 15 = 10 × 15 = £150

15    $AB = \begin{pmatrix} ((2\times5)+(1\times2)) & ((2\times1)+(1\times3)) & ((2\times0)+(1\times1)) \\ ((0\times5)+(3\times2)) & ((0\times1)+(3\times3)) & ((0\times0)+(3\times1)) \end{pmatrix}$

$= \begin{pmatrix} 12 & 5 & 1 \\ 6 & 9 & 3 \end{pmatrix}$

$CA = \begin{pmatrix} ((3\times2)+(1\times0)) & ((3\times1)+(1\times3)) \\ ((0\times2)+(2\times0)) & ((0\times1)+(2\times3)) \\ ((1\times2)+(4\times0)) & ((1\times1)+(4\times3)) \end{pmatrix}$

$= \begin{pmatrix} 6 & 6 \\ 0 & 6 \\ 2 & 13 \end{pmatrix}$

$BC = \begin{pmatrix} ((5\times3)+(1\times0)+(0\times1)) & ((5\times1)+(1\times2)+(0\times4)) \\ ((2\times3)+(3\times0)+(1\times1)) & ((2\times1)+(3\times2)+(1\times4)) \end{pmatrix}$

$= \begin{pmatrix} 15 & 7 \\ 7 & 12 \end{pmatrix}$

$CB = \begin{pmatrix} ((3\times5)+(1\times2)) & ((3\times1)+(1\times3)) & ((3\times0)+(1\times1)) \\ ((0\times5)+(2\times2)) & ((0\times1)+(2\times3)) & ((0\times0)+(2\times1)) \\ ((1\times5)+(4\times2)) & ((1\times1)+(4\times3)) & ((1\times0)+(4\times1)) \end{pmatrix}$

$$= \begin{pmatrix} 17 & 6 & 1 \\ 4 & 6 & 2 \\ 13 & 13 & 4 \end{pmatrix}$$

16 $A^{-1} = \dfrac{1}{((7\times2)-(9\times3))} \begin{pmatrix} 2 & -9 \\ -3 & 7 \end{pmatrix}$

$$= -\dfrac{1}{13} \begin{pmatrix} 2 & -9 \\ -3 & 7 \end{pmatrix} = \begin{pmatrix} -2/13 & 9/13 \\ 3/13 & -7/13 \end{pmatrix}$$

17 (a) (i)   £482,365   (b) (i)   843.7 (c) (i)   628.03
        (ii) £482,400   (ii) 843.67   (ii) 628.0
        (iii) £482,000
        (iv) £480,000

18 (a) Approximate maximum relative error = 10% + 10% + 20% = 40%

    (b) A is at a maximum when the numerator is big and the denominator small, that is when J and B are at a maximum and M at a minimum.

    Maximum A = $\dfrac{1.1J\times1.1B}{0.8M} = \dfrac{1.5125JB}{M}$

    ∴ Actual maximum positive relative error = 51.25%.

    A is at a minimum when the numerator is small and the denominator big, that is when J and B are at a minimum and M at a maximum.

    Minimum A = $\dfrac{0.9J\times0.9B}{1.2M} = \dfrac{0.675JB}{M}$

    ∴ Actual maximum negative relative error = 32.5%

Assignment 1   (45 minutes)

(a) The total cost of producing a batch of a given product is assumed to follow a quadratic relationship. Batches of 10, 20 and 40 units of the product cost £700, £400 and £1,600 respectively.

    (i)   Determine the precise form of the relationship.

    (ii)   Draw a graph of the total cost function for batches of sizes 0 to 50 units.

    (iii) From the graph, determine the batch size that minimises total cost.

(b) The product sells for £30 per unit.

    (i)   Draw, on the same graph as before, the revenue function.

    (ii)   Find from the graph the range of batch sizes over which the product makes a profit.

    (iii) Determine the precise form of the profit function.

Chapter 2 :
THE COLLECTION OF DATA

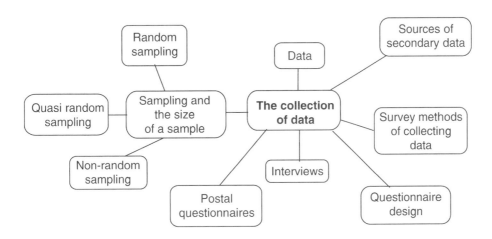

Introduction

The words 'quantitative methods' often strike terror into the hearts of students. They conjure up images of complicated mathematical formulae, scientific analysis of reams of computer output and the drawing of strange graphs and diagrams. Such images are wrong. Quantitative methods simply involve collecting data, presenting them in a useful form and interpreting them.

You will soon discover that quantitative methods are nothing to be afraid of and that a knowledge of them will be extremely advantageous in your studies. The main advantage of quantitative techniques is that they offer a way to make sense of numbers. In a business environment, for example, a manager may collect all sorts of data on production levels, costs and sales, but the numbers on their own are unlikely to mean very much. By using quantitative techniques, a manager can try to make sense out of the numbers, which in turn should help in making sensible business decisions.

In this chapter we will be looking at data collection. In Chapter 3 we will consider how data should be presented once they have been collected.

Your objectives

After completing this chapter you should:

(a)   be aware of the various types of data;

(b)   know about the sources of secondary data;

(c)   be able to design questionnaires;

(d)   be aware of the advantages and disadvantages of interviews and postal questionnaires;

(e)   know the appropriate sampling method to use in particular circumstances.

1 DATA

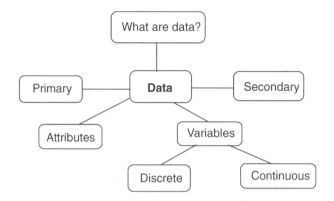

What are data?

1.1. 'Data' is a term that you will come across time and time again in your study of quantitative methods, but what does it mean?

Definition

> *Data* is simply a 'scientific' term for facts, 'figures, information and measurements.

Data therefore include the number of people with red hair who pass their driving test each year, the number of goals scored by each football team in the second division in the current season to date, and the profit after tax for the past ten years of the four biggest supermarket chains.

Types of data

1.2 Data may be of several types. The first distinction to make is between attributes and variables.

Attributes and variables

Definition

> An *attribute* is something an object has either got or not got.

1.3 An attribute cannot be measured. For example, an individual is either male or female. There is no measure of *how* male or *how* female somebody is: the sex of a person is an attribute.

Definition

> A *variable* is something which can be measured.

1.4   For example, the height of a person is a variable which can be measured according to some scale (such as centimetres).

Discrete and continuous variables

1.5   Variables can be further classified as discrete or continuous.

(a)   Discrete variables can only take a finite or countable number of values within a given range. Examples of such variables include 'goals scored by Chachont United against Willford City', 'shoe size' and 'number of people entering SupaSave SupaMarket in Rutminster between 9.05am and 9.10am on a particular day'. If we arbitrarily chose a range of 0 – 10, 2 goals could be scored but not $2^1/_2$, a (British) shoe size could be $5^1/_2$ but not 5.193 and 9 people could enter the supermarket but not 9.999.

(b)   Continuous variables may take on any value. They are measured rather than counted. For example, it may be considered sufficient to measure the heights of a number of people to the nearest centimetre but there is no reason why the measurements should not be made to the nearest 1/100 cm. Two people who are found to have the same height to the nearest centimetre could almost certainly be distinguished if more precise measurements were taken.

Activity 1

Look through the following list of surveys and decide whether each is collecting data on attributes, discrete variables or continuous variables.

(a)   A survey of statistics textbooks, to determine how many diagrams they contain.

(b)   A survey of cans in a shop, to determine whether or not each has a price sticker.

(c)   A survey of athletes to find out how long they take to run a mile.

(d)   A survey of the heights of telegraph poles in England.

Primary data and secondary data

1.6   The data used in a statistical survey, whether variables or attributes, can be either primary data or secondary data.

Definitions

Primary data are data collected especially for the purpose of whatever survey is being conducted.

Raw data are primary data which have not been processed at all, but are still just (for example) a list of numbers.

Secondary data are data which have already been collected elsewhere, for some other purpose, but which can be used or adapted for the survey being conducted.

1.7　An advantage of using primary data is that the investigator knows where the data came from, the circumstances under which they were collected, and any limitations or inadequacies in the data.

1.8　In contrast, note the following inadequacies of secondary data.

(a)　Any limitations in the data might not be known to the investigator, because he or she did not collect them.

(b)　The data might not be entirely suitable for the purpose they are being used for.

Secondary data are sometimes used despite their inadequacies, simply because they are available cheaply whereas the extra cost of collecting primary data would far outweigh their extra value.

Now that we have some idea of the different types of data, we can address ourselves to the problem of getting hold of them.

2　SOURCES OF SECONDARY DATA

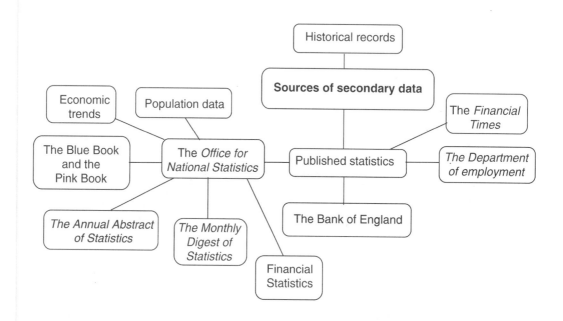

2.1　Secondary data are data that were originally collected as primary data for a particular purpose or for general use, but are now being used for another purpose. The Government, for example, collects data to help with making decisions about running the country, and makes these data available to the public.

2.2　Examples of secondary data include the following.

(a)　*Published statistics*. For example, the Government publishes statistics through the Office for National Statistics (ONS) (formed by the merger of the Central Statistical Office and the Office of Population Censuses and Surveys in April 1996). The European Union and the United Nations also publish statistics. So do various newspapers.

(b)　*Historical records*. The type of historical record used for a survey obviously depends on what survey is being carried out. An accountant producing an estimate of future company sales might use historical records of past sales.

Sources of published statistics

2.3 You may be expected to identify the sources of certain published statistics. As you will probably be aware, the range of published economic, business and accounting data is very wide, and a comprehensive knowledge of sources is impracticable. In this chapter the better known sources will be described.

2.4 All published statistics are a source of secondary data. Great care must be taken in using them, since the data may not be obtained or classified in precisely the same way as primary data collected *specifically* for the purpose of the current statistical analysis would be.

2.5 Despite the general shortcomings of secondary data there are many circumstances in which published statistics can be of great value. Many Government statistics are compiled at least partly for the purpose of being used in further analysis and explanatory notes are given so that people using the data know to what extent they are relevant to their needs and what level of confidence they can have in the results of their analysis.

The Office for National Statistics (ONS) and other bodies

2.6 The ONS publishes the following.

(a) The *Monthly Digest of Statistics* (which gives data for the recent past)

(b) The *Annual Abstract of Statistics* (which gives data over a much longer period)

(c) *Economic Trends* (published monthly)

(d) *Financial Statistics* (published monthly)

2.7 The European Union has a Statistical Office of the European Community (SOEC) which gathers statistics from each of the member countries. The SOEC has several statistical publications, including *Basic Statistics of the Community*.

2.8 The United Nations also publishes some statistics on the world economy (for example the statistical yearbook), and a yearbook of labour statistics is published by the International Labour Organisation.

2.9 In the remainder of this section, we shall concentrate on statistical publications in the UK.

The Department of Employment Gazette

2.10 The Department of Employment publishes statistics monthly about employment and unemployment, and about retail prices. The statistics which are published monthly in the *Department of Employment Gazette* include, for example, statistics on the following.

(a) Retail prices
(b) Employment
(c) Unemployment
(d) Unfilled job vacancies
(e) Wage rates
(f) Overtime
(g) Stoppages at work

2.11 Retail prices are very important to a wide variety of users.

(a) For the Government, the Retail Prices Index (RPI) indicates the degree of success there has been in fighting inflation.

(b) For employees, the RPI may give an indication of how much wages need to rise to keep pace with inflation.

(c) For consumers, the RPI indicates the increases to be expected in the prices of goods in shops.

(d) For businesses, the RPI may give a broad indication of how much costs should have been expected to rise over recent years and months.

(e) For pensioners and social security recipients, the movement in the RPI is used to update benefit levels.

The Bank of England Quarterly Bulletin

2.12 The Bank of England issues a quarterly publication which includes data on banks in the UK, the money supply and Government borrowing and financial transactions.

Population data

2.13 Data on the UK population, such as population numbers in total and by region, births, deaths and marriages, are produced monthly by ONS in a publication entitled *Population Trends*.

The ONS also produces an annual statistical review.

Every ten years, there is a full census of the whole population, and results of the census are published. The most recent census was in April 1991.

The Blue Book and the Pink Book

2.14 *The Blue Book on National Income and Expenditure* is published annually by the ONS, giving details of:

(a) gross national product (analysed into sections of the economy such as transport and communication, insurance, banking and finance, public administration and defence);

(b) gross national income (analysed into income from self-employment, income from employment, profits of companies, income from abroad and so on);

(c) gross national expenditure (analysed into expenditure on capital goods, expenditure by consumers and by public authorities, imports and so on).

2.15 This information is augmented by more detailed statistics, also provided in the Blue Book. There is also an annual *Pink Book, The UK Balance of Payments* which analyses the UK's external trade, external capital transactions (inflows and outflows of private capital) and official financing.

The Annual Abstract of Statistics

2.16 Most government statistics of economic and business data are brought together into a main reference book, the *Annual Abstract of Statistics*, which is published by the ONS. Notes about the data and definitions of the data provided are contained in the book.

The Monthly Digest of Statistics

2.17 The ONS's *Monthly Digest of Statistics* is an abbreviated version of the *Annual Abstract*, updated and published monthly. A January supplement provides definitions. The information included in the *Monthly Digest* covers a wide range of topics, such as industrial output, production costs, prices and wages, social services, law enforcement, national income, external trade, retailing, transport, construction, agriculture and food.

Financial statistics

2.18 The ONS publishes a monthly compilation of financial data in *Financial Statistics*. This gives statistics on a variety of financial topics.

    (a)   Government income, expenditure and borrowing

    (b)   Assets and liabilities of banks and statistics on other financial institutions, such as building societies, unit trusts, investment trusts, insurance companies and pension funds

    (c)   Companies (profits, sources and uses of capital funds, acquisitions and mergers, share trading and so on)

    (d)   Personal sector finance (loans for home buying, consumer credit, personal income expenditure and saving and so on)

    (e)   The overseas sector

    (f)   The money supply

    (g)   Issues of capital and Stock Exchange transactions

    (h)   Exchange rates, interest rates and share prices

Economic Trends

2.19 Like the *Monthly Digest of Statistics and Financial Statistics, Economic Trends* is a monthly publication of the ONS. As its name implies, its main purpose is to indicate trends, and the publication includes graphs as well as numerical statistics.

The Financial Times

2.20 The *Financial Times* and other newspapers and investment journals provide statistics about the Stock Market. These include the following.

    (a)   The FT-Actuaries All-Share Index (compiled jointly by the Financial Times, the Institute of Actuaries in London and the Faculty of Actuaries in Edinburgh). This is an index of share prices quoted on the Stock Exchange.

    (b)   The FTSE 100 index. This is a stock market index of 100 leading shares, compiled by the *Financial Times* and the Stock Exchange.

The *Financial Times* also includes various other items of daily information on financial matters.

    (a)   Foreign exchange rates
    (b)   Interest rates
    (c)   Gilts and other stock prices

3   SURVEY METHODS OF COLLECTING DATA

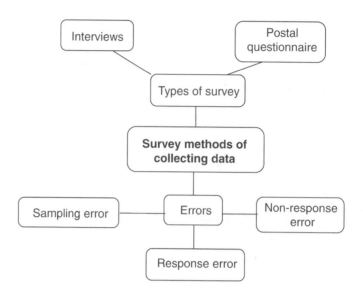

3.1   There are two basic methods of collecting primary data from individuals: you can ask people questions or observe their behaviour. The latter method of collection is called observation and is outside the scope of this Course Book; the former involves the collection of data using surveys.

3.2   There are two main types of survey.

   (a)   Interviews
   (b)   Postal questionnaires

3.3   We will be looking at each type, and their respective advantages and disadvantages, in later sections.

3.4   Although surveys offer a quick, efficient and cost-effective way of obtaining the required data, they are not straightforward. Without skill, tact and expertise the results may easily become contaminated with bias and error and the conclusions subsequently drawn will be useless.

3.5   A famous example of this occurred years ago in the United States, when somebody was asked to conduct an opinion poll (which is a form of survey) on whether the next president was likely to be Democrat or Republican. The survey was carried out, but in an inappropriate way. The survey officer *telephoned* people, and in those days far more Republican than Democrat voters had telephones. The survey was useless, because it had not been planned properly.

3.6   The reason why the opinion poll turned out so badly was that the population for the survey had not been defined properly. In data collection, the word 'population' refers to the entire collection of items being considered. The opinion poll should have used the population 'all Americans of voting age', whereas it actually used the population 'all Americans with a telephone'.

Errors in survey methods of collecting data

3.7   There are three main types of error that can appear in survey methods of collecting data.

   (a)   *Sampling error* arises when the sample of the population surveyed (if the entire population is not being investigated) is not representative of the population from which it is drawn. For example, if a sample of the population of a city was composed entirely of babies less than three months old, the sample would obviously not be representative of the population of the city.

(b)   *Response error* can occur even when all members of the population are surveyed and arises because respondents are either unable (through ignorance, forgetfulness or inarticulateness) or unwilling (due to time pressure, desire for privacy, guessing and so on) to respond.

(c)   *Non-response error* can occur either if respondents refuse to take part in the survey or are 'not at home'.

3.8   Non-response in survey methods of data collection is a particular problem if those who refuse to take part in the survey are likely to be in some way different from those who do take part. The easiest way to reduce the effect of this situation is to try and increase the percentage of those taking part (responding).

(a)   *Reducing non-response for interviews*

(i)   The success of interviews relies on the quality of interaction between respondent and interviewer. Interviewers who give the impression of being pleasant, interesting and interested in respondents and who convincingly persuade them that their views are important will produce lower rates of refusal.

(ii)   If someone is 'not at home' the interviewer should call back.

(iii) Respondents can be promised gifts or monetary reward.

(b)   *Reducing non-response for postal questionnaires*

(i)   Contact respondents prior to despatching the questionnaire to ask whether they would be prepared to aid the study by completing a questionnaire.

(ii)   Include a covering letter to explain why the data are being collected and to put the respondent in the appropriate frame of mind.

(iii) Include a freepost or stamped addressed envelope for ease of reply.

(iv)   Provide a gift or monetary incentive upon questionnaire completion.

(v)   Address the respondent by name. This not only increases the response rate but will encourage the named person to complete the questionnaire personally.

(vi)   Use postal or telephone follow up reminders.

(vii) Carefully select a target audience who have particular interest in the topic.

4 QUESTIONNAIRE DESIGN

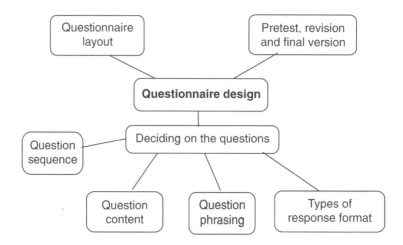

Deciding on the questions

Question content

4.1 When deciding on question content it is vital to think about the following.

(a) Is the question necessary?

(b) Will the respondent understand the question?

The language used should be that of the respondent group. Think about the different language used by managing directors and teenagers.

(c) Will the question elicit the required data?

A survey often fails to generate the required data because of badly phrased questions or questions that are too ambiguous to elicit specific information. Double-barrelled questions ('Do you often go to pubs and restaurants?') should be split, and words describing frequency ('often', 'slightly', 'somewhat') should be avoided as they have a wide range of interpretation.

> **Activity 2**
>
> What might be a better way of asking 'Do you often go to the cinema?'

(d) Does the respondent have the necessary data to be able to answer the question?

The ability of the respondent to answer will depend on three factors.

(i) If respondents do not know the answer to a question they may try to bluff their way out of what they see as an embarrassing situation by guessing. Such answers lead to errors in the conclusions drawn from the data collected. Questions should therefore be phrased so that it does not appear that the interviewer is suggesting that the respondent should know the answer.

(ii) Questions relating to unimportant/ infrequent events or to events some time in the past are likely to tempt respondents to guess. This may introduce error and so it is better to 'jog' respondents' memories in some way.

(iii) Even the most articulate of respondents may find it difficult to be verbally adept about their feelings, beliefs, opinions and motivations.

(e) Is the respondent willing and able to answer the questions?

A respondent may refuse to answer one or more questions on a questionnaire (non-response) or many 'refuse' by providing a wrong or distorted answer. Certain techniques can be employed to eliminate distorted, wrong or inaccurate answers.

(i) Assess whether the question is really necessary (especially if it will cause embarrassment or a loss of prestige).

(ii) Reassure respondents of the importance of the question and of the value of their response.

(iii) Begin a 'difficult' question with a statement which implies the topic of the question is common or quite usual.

(iv) Imply that the behaviour in which you are interested is an attribute of a third party (someone other than the respondent).

(v) Provide respondents with a card listing possible responses, identified by a letter or a number, to potentially embarrassing questions. Respondents need only provide the appropriate letter or number as their answer.

(vi) When analysing the data, replies to questions related to image or prestige should be upgraded or downgraded as necessary.

Activity 3

How might the question be rephrased?

'Do you visit the pub to get drunk?'

Question phrasing

4.2 Given below is a checklist of factors to consider when translating data requirements into words.

(a) Use a style of language appropriate to the target population.

(b) Avoid long questions.

(c) Avoid vague and ambiguous words.

(d) Avoid biased words and leading questions.

(e) Do not use double-barrelled questions.

(f) Avoid negative questions.

(g) Do not encourage respondents to guess.

(h) Avoid questions which assume respondents possess all the relevant information pertaining to the question.

Types of response format

4.3   Questions can be open or closed. Open questions are difficult to analyse. An open question might be worded like this.

'How did you travel to work today?'

The responses may be so numerous that analysis becomes onerous and time consuming. The designer of the questionnaire should instead try to offer a full range of possible responses to the question, perhaps like this.

'Please indicate how you travelled to work today.'

By bus

By train

By private car

On foot

By bicycle/motorcycle

I did not go to work today (illness, holidays etc)

I work at home

I do not work

Other (please give details) ....'

The responses from this closed question will be much easier to analyse. It is important, however, to avoid putting such lists of responses in order of supposed popularity.

Activity 4

What types of problem can you envisage arising from the use of multiple choice questions? How can such problems be overcome?

Question sequence

4.4   (a)   Start with quota control questions to determine right away whether the interviewee is the right type of person. Quota control questions might identify whether the interviewee is employed or unemployed, under 40 over 40 and so on. Such questions enable you to terminate worthless interviews as early as possible.

(b)   Move on to questions which will engage interest, reassure and give a foretaste of what is to follow.

(c)   Questions should be in logical order as far as possible, but if difficult questions are necessary it may be more appropriate to put them at the end.

(d)   Avoid questions which suggest the answers to later questions. This will cause bias.

Questionnaire layout

4.5 (a) Use good quality paper.

(b) The questionnaire should be as short as possible. Questionnaires that are too long may discourage the respondent from even starting.

(c) If respondents have to complete the questionnaire themselves, it must be as approachable as possible. Consider the use of lines, boxes, different typefaces or print sizes and small pictures. Use plenty of space.

(d) Make sure that the instructions which guide the respondent through the questionnaire are as user friendly as possible and are kept to a minimum.

(e) Explain the purpose of the survey at the beginning of the questionnaire and, where possible, guarantee confidentiality. Emphasise the date by which it must be returned.

(f) At the end of the questionnaire, thank the respondent and make it clear what they should do with the completed questionnaire.

Pretest, revision and final version of the questionnaire

4.6 Pretesting the questionnaire will uncover faults in its design before it is too late and should therefore ensure that the final version of the questionnaire gathers the required data.

5 INTERVIEWS

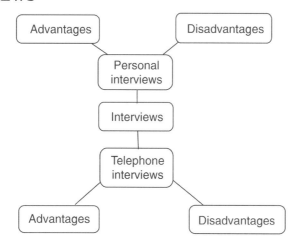

5.1 There are basically two types of interview that can be used to collect data, the personal (face to face) interview and the telephone interview.

Personal interviews

Advantages of personal interviews

5.2 (a) The interviewer is able to reduce respondent anxiety and allay potential embarrassment, thereby increasing the response rate and decreasing the potential for error.

(b) the interviewer's experience makes the routing of questions easier (for example, 'if yes go to question 7, if no go to question 10').

(c) Interviewers can ask, within narrow limits, for a respondent's answer to be clarified.

(d) The questions can be given in a fixed order with a fixed wording and the answers can be recorded in a standard manner. This will reduce variability if there is more than one interviewer involved in the survey.

(e) Standardised questions and ways of recording the responses mean that less skilled interviewers may be used, thereby reducing the cost of the survey.

(f) Pictures, signs and objects can be used.

Disadvantages of personal interviews

5.3 (a) They can be time consuming.

(b) The cost per completed interview can be higher than with other survey methods.

(c) Questionnaires can be difficult to design.

(d) Fully-structured interviews have particular disadvantages.

(i) Questions must be kept relatively simple, thus restricting the depth of data collected.

(ii) Questions must normally be closed because of the difficulties of recording answers to open questions.

(iii) Interviewers cannot probe vague or ambiguous replies.

Telephone interviews

5.4 Telephone interviews are a relatively fast and low-cost means of gathering data compared to personal interviews. They are most useful when only a small amount of information is required. They also benefit the respondent in terms of the short amount of time taken up by the interview.

5.5 CATI (computer-assisted telephone interviewing) has been used successfully by insurance services and banks as well as consumer research organisations. The telephone interviewer calls up a questionnaire on screen and reads questions to the respondent. Answers are then recorded instantly on computer. Complex questions with questionnaire routing may be handled in this way.

Advantages of telephone interviews

5.6 (a) The response is rapid.

(b) A wide geographical area can be covered fairly cheaply from a central location. There is no need for the interviewer to travel between respondents.

(c) It may be easier to ask sensitive or embarrassing questions.

Disadvantages of telephone interviews

5.7 (a) A biased sample may result from the fact that a proportion of people do not have telephones and many of those who do are ex-directory.

(b) It is not possible to use 'showcards' or pictures.

(c) The refusal rate is much higher than with face-to-face interviews.

(d)   It is not possible to see the interviewee's expression or to develop the rapport that is possible with personal interviews.

(e)   The interview must be short.

(f)   Respondents may be unwilling to participate for fear of being sold something.

6   POSTAL QUESTIONNAIRES

6.1   If the size of interviewer-induced error is likely to be large, or its magnitude cannot be predicted with any degree of accuracy, and if cost is an important factor when deciding on the data collection method, postal questionnaires should be seriously considered.

6.2   Because there is no one to clear up ambiguity in questions, the wording and sequence of the questionnaire must be carefully thought out before it is used.

Advantages of postal questionnaires

6.3   Postal questionnaires have the following advantages over personal interviews.

(a)   The cost per person is likely to be less, so more people can be sampled.

(b)   It is usually possible to ask more questions because the people completing the forms (the respondents) can do so in their own time.

(c)   All respondents are presented with questions in the same way. There is no opportunity for an interviewer to influence responses (interviewer bias) or to misrecord them.

(d)   It may be easier to ask personal or embarrassing questions in a postal questionnaire than in a personal interview.

(e)   Respondents may need to look up information for the questionnaire. This will be easier if the questionnaire is sent to their home or place of work.

Disadvantages of postal questionnaires

6.4   On the other hand, the use of personal interviews does have certain advantages over the use of postal questionnaires.

(a)   Large numbers of postal questionnaires may not be returned or may be returned only partly completed. This may lead to biased results if those replying are not representative of all people in the survey. Response rates are likely to be higher with personal interviews, and the interviewer can encourage people to answer all questions. Low response rates are a major problem with postal questionnaires.

(b)   Misunderstanding is less likely with personal interviews because the interviewer can explain questions which the interviewee does not understand.

(c)   Personal interviews are more suitable when deep or detailed questions are to be asked, since the interviewer can take the time required with each interviewee to explain the implications of the question. Also, the interviewer can probe for further information and encourage the respondent to think deeper.

7   SAMPLING

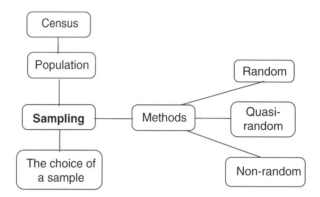

Definition

Sampling involves selecting a sample of items from a population.

7.1   Sampling is one of the most important subjects in quantitative methods. In most practical situations the population will be too large to carry out a complete survey and only a sample will be examined. A good example of this is a poll taken to try to predict the results of an election. It is not possible to ask everyone of voting age how they are going to vote: it would take too long and cost too much. So a sample of voters is taken, and the results from the sample are used to estimate the voting intentions of the whole population.

7.2   Occasionally a population is small enough that all of it can be examined: for example, the examination results of one class of students. This type of survey is quite rare, however, and usually the investigator has to choose some sort of sample.

Definition

When all of the population is examined, the survey is called a *census*.

7.3   You may think that using a sample is very much a compromise, but you should consider the following points.

(a)   In practice, a 100% survey (a census) never achieves the completeness required.

(b)   A census may require the use of semi-skilled investigators, resulting in a loss of accuracy in the data collected.

(c)   It can be shown mathematically that once a certain sample size has been reached, very little extra accuracy is gained by examining more items.

(d)   It is possible to ask more questions with a sample.

(e)   The higher cost of a census may exceed the value of results.

(f)   Things are always changing. Even if you took a census it could well be out of date by the time you completed it.

The choice of a sample

7.4   One of the most important requirements of sample data is that they should be complete. That is, the data should cover all areas of the population to be examined. If this requirement is not met, then the sample will be biased.

7.5   For example, suppose you wanted to survey the productivity of workers in a factory, and you went along every Monday and Tuesday for a few months to measure their output. Would these data be complete? The answer is no. You might have gathered very thorough data on what happens on Mondays and Tuesdays, but you would have missed out the rest of the week. It could be that the workers, keen and fresh after the weekend, work better at the start of the week than at the end. If this is the case, then your data will give you a misleadingly high productivity figure. Careful attention must therefore be given to the sampling method employed to produce a sample.

7.6   Sampling methods fall into three main groups.

(a)   Random sampling
(b)   Quasi-random sampling
(c)   Non-random sampling

8   RANDOM SAMPLING

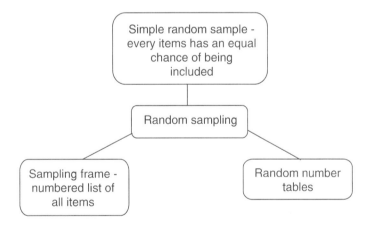

8.1   To ensure that the sample selected is free from bias, random sampling must be used. Inferences about the population being sampled can then be made validly.

Definition

A simple *random sample* is a sample selected in such a way that every item in the population has an equal chance of being included.

8.2   For example, if you wanted to take a random sample of library books, it would not be good enough to pick them off the shelves, even if you picked them at random. This is because the books which were out on loan would stand no chance of being chosen. You would either have to make sure that all the books were on the shelves before taking your sample, or find some other way of sampling (for example, using the library index cards).

8.3   A random sample is not necessarily a perfect sample. For example, you might pick what you believe to be a completely random selection of library books, and find that every one of them is a detective thriller. It is a remote possibility, but it could happen. The only way to eliminate the possibility altogether is to take 100% survey (a census) of the books, which, unless it is a tiny library, is impractical.

Sampling frames

Definition

> A *sampling frame* is a numbered list of all the items in the population.

8.4   If random sampling is used then it is necessary to construct a sampling frame. Once this has been made, it is easy to select a random sample, simply by generating a list of random numbers.

8.5   For instance, if you wanted to select a random sample of children from a school, it would be useful to have a list of names:

0   J Absolam
1   R Brown
2   S Brown
       ...

Now the numbers 0, 1, 2 and so on can be used to select the random sample. It is normal to start the numbering at 0, so that when 0 appears in a list of random numbers it can be used.

8.6   Sometimes it is not possible to draw up a sampling frame. For example, if you wanted to take a random sample of Americans, it would take too long to list all Americans.

8.7   A sampling frame should have the following characteristics.

(a)   *Completeness*. Are all members of the population included on the list?

(b)   *Accuracy*. Is the information correct?

(c)   *Adequacy*. Does it cover the entire population?

(d)   *Up to dateness*. Is the list up to date?

(e)   *Convenience*. Is the sampling frame readily accessible?

(f)   *Non-duplication*. Does each member of the population appear on the list only once?

8.8   Two readily available sampling frames for the human population of Great Britain are the council tax register (list of dwellings) and the electoral register (list of individuals).

Random number tables

8.9 Assuming that a sampling frame can be drawn up, then a random sample can be picked from it by one of the following methods.

(a) The lottery method, which amounts to picking numbered pieces of paper out of a box

(b) The use of random number tables

8.10 Set out below is part of a typical random number table.

93716	16894	98953	73231
32886	59780	09958	18065
92052	06831	19640	99413
39510	35905	85244	35159
27699	06494	03152	19121
92962	61773	22109	78508
10274	12202	94205	50380
75867	20717	82037	10268
85783	47619	87481	37220

You should note the following points.

(a) The sample is found by selecting groups of random numbers with the number of digits depending on the total population size, as follows.

Total population size	Number of random digits
1 – 10	1
1 – 100	2
1 – 1,000	3

The items selected for the sample are those corresponding to the random numbers selected.

(b) The starting point on the table should be selected at random. After that, however, numbers must be selected in a consistent manner. In other words, you should use the table row by row or column by column. By jumping around the table from place to place, personal bias may be introduced.

(c) In many practical situations it is more convenient to use a computer to generate a list of random numbers, especially when a large sample is required.

EXAMPLE: RANDOM NUMBER TABLES

An investigator wishes to select a random sample from a population of 800 people, who have been numbered 000, 001, ..., 799. As there are three digits in 799 the random numbers will be selected in groups of three. Working along the first line of the table given earlier, the first few groups are as follows.

937   161   689   498   953   732

Numbers over 799 are discarded. The first four people in the sample will therefore be those numbered 161, 689, 498 and 732.

Drawbacks of random sampling

8.11 (a) The selected items are subject to the full range of variation inherent in the population.

(b) An unrepresentative sample may result.

(c) The members of the population selected may be scattered over a wide area, adding to the cost and difficulty of obtaining the data.

(d) An adequate sampling frame might not exist.

(e) The numbering of the population might be laborious.

Quasi- and non-random sampling

8.12 In many situations it might be too expensive to obtain a random sample, in which case quasi-random sampling is necessary, or else it may not be possible to draw up a sampling frame. In such cases, non-random sampling has to be used.

9 QUASI-RANDOM SAMPLING

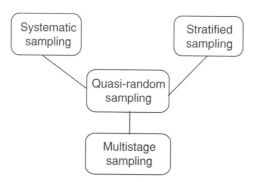

9.1 Quasi-random sampling, which provides a good approximation to random sampling, necessitates the existence of a sampling frame.

The main methods of quasi-random sampling are as follows.

(a) Systematic sampling
(b) Stratified sampling
(c) Multistage sampling

Systematic sampling

9.2 Systematic sampling may provide a good approximation to random sampling. It works by selecting every nth item after a random start. For example, if it was decided to select a sample of 20 from a population of 800, then every 40th (800 ÷ 20) item after a random start in the first 40 should be selected. The starting point could be found using the lottery method or random number tables. If (say) 23 was chosen, then the sample would include the 23rd, 63rd, 103rd, 143rd, ..., 783rd items.

The gap of 40 is known as the sampling interval.

The investigator must ensure that there is no regular pattern to the population which, if it coincided with the sampling interval, might lead to a biased sample. In practice, this problem is often overcome by choosing multiple starting points and using varying sampling intervals whose size is selected at random.

9.3 If the sampling frame is in random order (such as an alphabetical list of students) a systematic sample is essentially the same as a simple random sample.

A systematic sample does not fully meet the criterion of randomness since some samples of the given size have zero probability of being chosen. However, the method is easy and cheap, and hence is widely used.

Stratified sampling

9.4 In many situations stratified sampling is the best method of choosing a sample. The population must be divided into strata or categories.

If we took a random sample of all cost and management accountants in the country, it is conceivable that the entire sample might consist of members of the CIMA working in public companies. Stratified sampling removes this possibility as random samples could be taken from each type of employment, the number in each sample being proportional to the total number of cost and management accountants in each type (for example those in partnerships, those in public companies and those in private companies).

EXAMPLE: STRATIFIED SAMPLING

The number of accountants in each type of work in a particular country are as follows.

Partnerships	500
Public companies	500
Private companies	700
Public practice	800
	2,500

If a sample of 20 was required the sample would be made up as follows.

		Sample
Partnerships	$\dfrac{500}{2,500} \times 20$	4
Public companies	$\dfrac{500}{2,500} \times 20$	4
Private companies	$\dfrac{700}{2,500} \times 20$	6
Public practice	$\dfrac{800}{2,500} \times 20$	6
		20

9.5 The strata frequently involve multiple classifications. In social surveys, for example, there is usually stratification by age, sex and social class. This implies that the sampling frame must contain information on these three variables before the threefold stratification of the population can be made.

9.6 Advantages of stratification are as follows.

(a) It ensures a representative sample since it guarantees that every important category will have elements in the final sample.

(b) The structure of the sample will reflect that of the population if the same proportion of individuals is chosen from each stratum.

(c)   Each stratum is represented by a randomly chosen sample and therefore inferences can be made about each stratum.

(d)   Precision is increased. Sampling takes place within strata and, because the range of variation is less in each stratum than in the population as a whole and variation between strata does not enter as a chance effect, higher precision is obtainable. (For this to occur, the items in each stratum must be as similar as possible and the difference between the individual strata must be as great as possible.)

9.7   Note, however, that stratification requires prior knowledge of each item in the population. Sampling frames do not always contain this information. Stratification from the electoral register as to age structure would not be possible because the electoral register does not contain information about age.

Multistage sampling

9.8   Multistage sampling is normally used to cut down the number of investigators and the costs of obtaining a sample. An example will show how the method works.

EXAMPLE: MULTISTAGE SAMPLING

A survey of spending habits is being planned to cover the whole of Britain. It is obviously impractical to draw up a sampling frame, so random sampling is not possible and multistage sampling is to be used instead.

The country is divided into a number of areas and a small sample of these is selected at random. Each of the areas selected is subdivided into smaller units and again a smaller number of these is selected at random. This process is repeated as many times as necessary and, finally, a random sample of the relevant people living in each of the smallest units is taken. A fair approximation to a random sample can be obtained.

Thus, we might choose a random sample of eight areas, and from each of these areas, select a random sample of five towns. From each town, a random sample of 200 people might be selected so that the total sample size is $8 \times 5 \times 200 = 8,000$ people.

9.9   The main advantage of this method is one of cost saving but there are a number of disadvantages.

(a)   There is the possibility of bias if, for example, only a small number of regions are selected.

(b)   The method is not truly random as once the final sampling areas have been selected the rest of the population cannot be in the sample.

(c)   If the population is heterogeneous, the areas chosen should reflect the full range of the diversity. Otherwise, choosing some areas and excluding others (even if it is done randomly) will result in a biased sample.

9.10   The sampling methods looked at so far have necessitated the existence of a sampling frame (or in multistage sampling, sampling frames of areas, sub-areas and items within selected sub-areas). It is often impossible to identify a satisfactory sampling frame and, in such instances, other sampling methods have to be employed.

10   NON-RANDOM SAMPLING

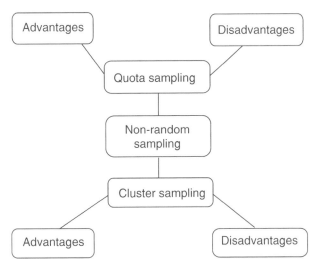

10.1   There are two main methods of non-random sampling, used when a sampling frame cannot be established.

(a)   Quota sampling
(b)   Cluster sampling

Quota sampling

10.2   In quota sampling, randomness is forfeited in the interests of cheapness and administrative simplicity. Investigators are told to interview all the people they meet up to a certain quota. A large degree of bias could be introduced accidentally. For example, an interviewer in a shopping centre may fill her quota by meeting only people who can go shopping during the week. In practice, this problem can be partly overcome by subdividing the quota into different types of people, for example on the basis of age, sex and income, to ensure that the sample mirrors the structure or stratification of the population. The interviewer is then told to interview, for example, 30 males between the ages of 30 and 40 from social class C1. The actual choice of the individuals to be interviewed, within the limits of the *quota controls*, is left to the field worker.

Advantages of quota sampling

10.3   (a)   It is cheap and administratively easy.

(b)   A much larger sample can be studied, and hence more information can be gained at a faster speed for a given outlay than when compared with a fully randomised sampling method.

(c)   Although a fairly detailed knowledge of the characteristics of a population is required, no sampling frame is necessary because the interviewer questions every person she meets up to the quota.

(d)   Quota sampling may be the only possible approach in certain situations, such as television audience research.

(e)   Given suitable, trained and properly briefed field workers, quota sampling yields enough accurate information for many forms of commercial market research.

Disadvantages of quota sampling

10.4 (a) The method can result in certain biases (although these can often be allowed for or may be unimportant for the purpose of the research).

(b) The non-random nature of the method rules out any valid estimate of the sampling error in estimates derived from the sample.

Conclusion

10.5 Quota sampling cannot be regarded as ultimately satisfactory in research where it is important that theoretically valid results should be obtained. It can be argued, however, that when other large sources of error, such as non-response, exist, it is pointless to worry too much about sampling error.

EXAMPLE: QUOTA SAMPLING

Consider the figures in the stratified sampling example above, but with the following additional information relating to the sex of the accountants.

	Male	*Female*
Partnerships	300	200
Public companies	400	100
Private companies	300	400
Public practice	300	500

An investigator's quotas might be as follows.

	Male	*Female*	*Total*
Partnerships	30	20	50
Public companies	40	10	50
Private companies	30	40	70
Public practice	30	50	80
			250

Using quota sampling, the investigator would interview the first 30 male cost and management accountants in partnerships that he met, the first 20 female cost and management accountants in partnerships that he met and so on.

Cluster sampling

10.6 Cluster sampling involves selecting one definable subsection of the population as the sample, that subsection taken to be representative of the population in question. The pupils of one school might be taken as a cluster sample of all children at school in one county.

Cluster sampling benefits from low costs in the same way as multistage sampling.

10.7 The advantages of cluster sampling are that it is a good alternative to multistage sampling if a satisfactory sampling frame does not exist and it is inexpensive to operate because little organisation or structure is involved. There is, however, the potential for considerable bias.

Activity 5

Describe four methods a brewery could employ to test the market for a new canned beer. Discuss the relative advantages and disadvantages of each method chosen.

---

11 THE SIZE OF A SAMPLE

11.1 As well as deciding on the appropriateness of a particular sampling method for a given situation, the size of the sample actually selected must also be given consideration.

11.2 Although, in certain circumstances, statistical processes can be used to calculate sample sizes, there is no universal law for determining the size of the sample. Two general considerations should, however, be borne in mind.

    (a)   The larger the size of the sample, the more accurate the results.

    (b)   There reaches a point after which there is little to be gained from increasing the size of the sample.

11.3 Despite these principles other, more administration-type factors, play a role in determining sample size.

    (a)   *Money and time available.*

    (b)   *Degree of precision required.* A survey may have the aim of discovering residents' reaction to a road widening scheme and hence a fairly small sample, producing imprecise results, would be acceptable. An enquiry into the safety of a new drug would, on the other hand, require an extremely large sample so that the information gained was as precise as possible.

    (c)   *Number of subsamples required.* If a complicated sampling method such as stratified sampling is to be used, the overall sample size will need to be large so as to ensure adequate representation of each subgroup (in this case, each stratum).

In this chapter we have looked at the different ways in which data can be collected – once the data has been collected, it must be presented in a useful form. The next chapter will look in detail at the different ways in which data can be presented.

Chapter roundup

- This chapter has concentrated on the practical problems of collecting data.

- An attribute is something an object has either got or not got. It cannot be measured. A variable is something which can be measured.

- Variables can be discrete (may take specific values) or continuous (may take any value).

- Data may be primary (collected specifically for the current purpose) or secondary (collected already).

- Examples of secondary data include published statistics and historical records.

- Primary data can be collected using surveys. There are two main types of survey: interviews and postal questionnaires. Interviews can be face to face or performed over the telephone.

- Questionnaire design involves considering question content, question phrasing, types of response format, questions required and layout. Questionnaires should be pretested.

- Data are often collected from a sample rather than from a population. A sample can be selected using random sampling (using random number tables or the lottery method), quasi-random sampling (systematic, stratified and multistage sampling) or non-random sampling (quota and cluster sampling). Ensure that you know the characteristics, advantages and disadvantages of each sampling method.

- Once data have been collected they need to be presented and analysed. It is important to remember that if the data have not been collected properly, no amount of careful presentation or interpretation can remedy the defect.

Quick quiz

1   What is a discrete variable?

2   What are secondary data?

3   List some of the UK sources of published statistics.

4   What types of error can appear in survey methods of collecting data?

5   What factors relating to question sequence should be considered when designing a questionnaire?

6   What are the advantages and disadvantages of personal interviews?

7   List the arguments in favour of using a sample.

8   What is a simple random sample?

9   What is stratified sampling?

10 List three administrative factors which may affect the size of a sample.

Answers to activities

1   (a)   The number of diagrams in a textbook is a discrete variable, because it can only be counted in whole number steps. You cannot, for example, have $26\frac{1}{4}$ diagrams or 47.32 diagrams in a book.

    (b)   Whether or not a can possesses a sticker is an attribute. It is not something which can be measured. A can either possesses the attribute or it does not.

    (c)   How long an athlete takes to run a mile is a continuous variable, because the time recorded can, in theory, take any value, for example 4 minutes 2.0643 seconds.

    (d)   The height of a telegraph pole is a continuous variable.

2   'Do you go to the cinema (a) once a week, (b) once a month, (c) twice a year?'

3   'Do you think that people go to the pub simply to get drunk?'

4 Here are some ideas. You may have thought of others.

(a) Capturing a full range of possible responses to a question such as 'In which store do you buy the majority of your clothes?' can be impractical.

This problem can be overcome by listing the most popular stores and using an 'other (please specify)' option

(b) The position of the alternative responses may introduce bias.

This problem can be overcome (but not entirely) by producing different versions of the questionnaire.

(c) An unbalanced set of alternative responses could be provided such as the following.

Q: What do you think of TV programme 'XXX'?

A: 1   2   3
Too boring   Very dull   Indifferent

Obviously such response sets should not be used.

5 (a) The brewery could try to supply the beer to a random sample of beer drinkers, and then ask for their views. Such samples are taken in such a way that every member of the population (in this case, all beer drinkers and perhaps all potential beer drinkers) has an equal chance of being selected for the sample. The main advantage of random sampling is that it allows mathematical analysis of the data to be carried out. The main disadvantage is that a random sample can be difficult and expensive to collect. The brewery may well find that it is impossible to compile a list of all beer drinkers from which to select a sample.

(b) Stratified sampling may well be appropriate. The population would first be divided into groups, perhaps by age or by weekly beer consumption, and then samples would be selected from each group (reflecting the proportion of the population in the group). The main advantage of stratified sampling is that it ensures that each group is represented in the sample. The main disadvantage is that preliminary work is needed to determine which groupings are likely to be useful and the proportion of the population in each group.

(c) Cluster sampling may well be a practical alternative, giving some of the benefits of both random sampling and stratified sampling. The population could be divided geographically into beer drinkers at public houses in different regions of the country and beer purchasers at off-licences within these regions. A sample of regions could be selected, and a sample of public houses and off-licences in each selected region could be chosen. All consumers at the chosen public houses and off-licences would then form the sample. The main advantage of cluster sampling is its relative cheapness. The main disadvantage is that the sample obtained will not be truly random, so some forms of statistical analysis will not be possible.

(d) Quota sampling has the advantage of being even cheaper than cluster sampling, but the disadvantage of producing a sample which is even further from being random. Researchers would simply visit a selection of public houses and off-licences and interview the first beer drinkers they met until they had fulfilled some quota (say ten men and ten women).

Assignment 2 (45 minutes)

A local weekly newspaper sells about half a million copies in a week in a region of about 100 square miles. Market research indicates that the readership profile is as follows.

Age	%	Annual income £'000	%	Sex	%
Under 25	10	Under 10	10	Male	50
25 – 34	15	10 – 15	10	Female	50
35 – 44	20	15 – 20	25		
45 – 54	20	20 – 25	25	Region	%
55 – 64	20	25 – 30	20	Rural	10
65 +	15	Over 30	10	Suburban	30
Total	100	Total	100	Town	60

You are working with a marketing colleague on the design of a sample survey to find out (i) current strengths and weaknesses of the paper and (ii) whether the introduction of colour, leisure and/or business supplements and so on would increase sales and by how much.

Required

Considering the information requirements, recommend a method for collecting the data (such as by post, telephone, personal interviews and so on), giving reasons.

Design and explain a suitable practical sampling scheme that would achieve the objectives.

Do not attempt to write a questionnaire.

Chapter 3 :
DATA PRESENTATION

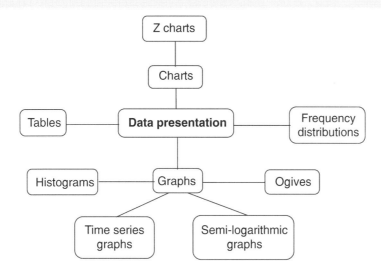

Introduction

You now know how to collect data. So what do you do with them next? You have to present the data you have collected so that they can be of use. This chapter begins by looking at how data can be presented in tables and charts. Such methods are helpful in presenting key data in a concise and easy to understand way. They are, however, purely descriptive and offer little opportunity for further detailed numerical analysis of a situation.

Data that are a mass of numbers can usefully be summarised into a frequency distribution (effectively a table which details the frequency with which a particular value occurs). Histograms and ogives are the pictorial representation of grouped and cumulative frequency distributions and provide the link between the purely descriptive approach to data analysis and the numerical approach covered in Chapter 5.

Data recorded over time can be presented as time series graphs. Z charts and semi-logarithmic graphs are special types of time series graph.

Your objectives

After completing this chapter you should:

(a)   be able to present data using tables, pie charts and bar charts;

(b)   be able to construct frequency distributions;

(c)   be able to prepare histograms;

(d)   be able to draw ogives, time series graphs, Z charts and semi-logarithmic graphs;

(e)   know the circumstances in which each data presentation format should be used.

1 TABLES

Definition

> A *table* is a matrix of data in rows and columns, with the rows and the columns having titles.

1.1 Raw data (the list of results from a survey) need to be summarised and analysed, to give them meaning. This chapter is concerned with several different ways of presenting data to convey their meaning. We will start with one of the most basic ways, the preparation of a table.

1.2 Tabulation means putting data into tables.

1.3 Since a table is two-dimensional, it can only show two variables. For example, the resources required to produce items in a factory could be tabulated, with one dimension (rows or columns) representing the items produced and the other dimension representing the resources.

Resources for production: all figures in pounds

	Product items				
	A	*B*	*C*	*D*	*Total*
Resources					
Direct material A	X	X	X	X	X
Direct material B	X	X	X	X	X
Direct labour grade 1	X	X	X	X	X
Direct labour grade 2	X	X	X	X	X
Supervision	X	X	X	X	X
Machine time	X	X	X	X	X
Total	X	X	X	X	X

1.4 To tabulate data, you need to recognise what the two dimensions should represent, prepare rows and columns accordingly with suitable titles, and then insert the data into the appropriate places in the table.

Guidelines for tabulation

1.5 The table in Paragraph 1.3 illustrates certain guidelines which you should apply when presenting data in tabular form. These are as follows.

(a) The table should be given a clear title.

(b) All columns should be clearly labelled.

(c) Where appropriate, there should be clear sub-totals.

(d) A total column may be presented; this is usually the right-hand column.

(e) A total figure is often advisable at the bottom of each column of figures.

(f) Tables should not be packed with so much data that reading the information is difficult.

(g) Eliminate non-essential information, rounding large numbers to two or three significant figures.

(h) Do not hide important figures in the middle of the table. Consider ordering columns or rows by order of importance or magnitude.

EXAMPLE: TABLES

The total number of employees in a certain trading company is 1,000. They are employed in three departments: production, administration and sales. There are 600 people employed in the production department and 300 in administration. There are 110 male juveniles in employment, 110 female juveniles, and 290 adult females. The remaining employees are adult males.

In the production department there are 350 adult males, 150 adult females and 50 male juveniles, whilst in the administration department there are 100 adult males, 110 adult females and 50 juvenile males.

Required

Draw up a table to show all the details of employment in the company and its departments and provide suitable secondary statistics to describe the distribution of people in departments.

SOLUTION

The basic table required has the following two dimensions.

(a) Departments
(b) Age/sex analysis

Secondary statistics (not the same thing as secondary data) are supporting figures that are supplementary to the main items of data, and which clarify or amplify the main data. A major example of secondary statistics is percentages. In this example, we could show one of the following.

(a) The percentage of the total work force in each department belonging to each age/sex group

(b) The percentage of the total of each age/sex group employed in each department

In this example, (a) has been selected but you might consider that (b) would be more suitable. Either could be suitable, depending of course on what purposes the data are being collected and presented for.

Analysis of employees

	Production		Administration		Sales		Total	
	No	%	No	%	No	%	No	%
Adult males	350	58.4	100	33.3	**40	40	*490	49
Adult females	150	25.0	110	36.7	**30	30	290	29
Male juveniles	50	8.3	50	16.7	**10	10	110	11
Female juveniles	*50	8.3	*40	13.3	**20	20	110	11
Total	600	100.0	300	100.0	100	100	1,000	100

* Balancing figure to make up the column total
** Balancing figure then needed to make up the row total

Rounding errors

1.6 Rounding errors may become apparent when, for example, a percentages column does not add up to 100%. Any rounding should therefore be to the nearest unit and the potential size of errors should be kept to a tolerable level by rounding to a small enough unit (for example to the nearest £10, rather than to the nearest £1,000).

2 CHARTS

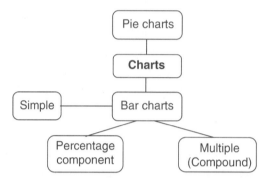

2.1 Instead of presenting data in a table, it might be preferable to give a visual display in the form of a chart.

2.2 The purpose of a chart is to convey the data in a way that will demonstrate its meaning or significance more clearly than a table of data would. Charts are not always more appropriate than tables, and the most suitable way of presenting data will depend on the following.

   (a) What the data are intended to show. Visual displays usually make one or two points quite forcefully, whereas tables usually give more detailed information.

   (b) Who is going to use the data. Some individuals might understand visual displays more readily than tabulated data.

Pie charts

Definition

> A *pie chart* is used to show pictorially the relative sizes of component elements of a total.

2.3 Such charts are called pie charts because they are circular, and so have the shape of a pie in a round pie dish and because the 'pie' is then cut into slices. Each slice represents a part of the total.

2.4 Pie charts have sectors of varying sizes, and you need to be able to draw sectors fairly accurately. To do this, you need a protractor. Working out sector sizes involves converting parts of the total into equivalent degrees of a circle.

EXAMPLE: PIE CHARTS

The costs of production at Factory A and Factory B during March 20X2 were as follows.

	Factory A		Factory B	
	£'000	%	£'000	%
Direct materials	70	35	50	20
Direct labour	30	15	125	50
Production overhead	90	45	50	20
Office costs	10	5	25	10
	200	100	250	100

Required

Show the costs for the factories in pie charts.

SOLUTION

To convert the components into degrees of a circle, we can use either the percentage figures or the actual cost figures.

(a) Using the percentage figures, the total percentage is 100%, and the total number of degrees in a circle is 360°. To convert from one to the other, we multiply each percentage value by 360/100 = 3.6.

	Factory A		Factory B	
	%	Degrees	%	Degrees
Direct materials	35	126	20	72
Direct labour	15	54	50	180
Production overhead	45	162	20	72
Office costs	5	18	10	36
	100	360	100	360

(b) Using the actual cost figures, we would multiply each cost by

$\dfrac{\text{Number of degrees}}{\text{Total cost}}$	Factory A $\dfrac{360}{200} = 1.8$	Factory B $\dfrac{360}{250} = 1.44$

	Factory A		Factory B	
	£'000	Degrees	£'000	Degrees
Direct materials	70	126	50	72
Direct labour	30	54	125	180
Production overhead	90	162	50	72
Office costs	10	18	25	36
	200	360	250	360

A pie chart could be drawn for each factory, as follows. A protractor is used to measure the degrees accurately to obtain the correct sector sizes.

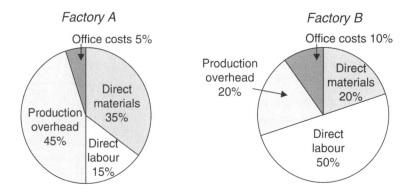

2.5 The advantages of pie charts are as follows.

(a) They give a simple pictorial display of the relative sizes of elements of a total.

(b) They show clearly when one element is much bigger than others.

(c) They can sometimes clearly show differences in the elements of two different totals. In the example above, the pie charts for factories A and B show how factory A's costs mostly consist of production overhead and direct materials, whereas at factory B, direct labour is the largest cost element.

2.6 The disadvantages of pie charts are as follows.

(a) They show only the relative sizes of elements. In the example of the two factories, for instance, the pie charts do not show that costs at Factory B were £50,000 higher in total than at Factory A.

(b) They involve calculating degrees of a circle and drawing sectors accurately, and this can be time consuming.

(c) It is sometimes difficult to compare sector sizes accurately by eye.

Bar charts

Definition

> A *bar chart* is a chart in which quantities are shown in the form of bars.

2.7 The bar chart is one of the most common methods of presenting data in a visual form.

2.8 There are three main types of bar chart.

(a) Simple bar charts
(b) Component bar charts, including percentage component bar charts
(c) Multiple (or compound) bar charts

Simple bar charts

2.9 A simple bar chart is a chart consisting of one or more bars, in which the length of each bar indicates the magnitude of the corresponding data item.

EXAMPLE: A SIMPLE BAR CHART

A company's total sales for the years from 20X1 to 20X6 are as follows.

Year	*Sales* £'000
20X1	800
20X2	1,200
20X3	1,100
20X4	1,400
20X5	1,600
20X6	1,700

The data could be shown on a simple bar chart as follows.

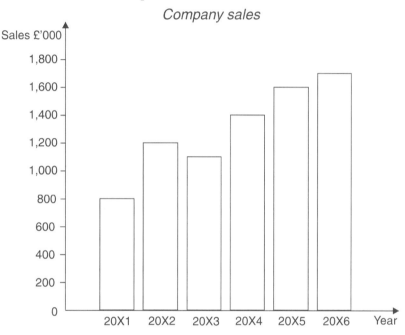

Each axis of the chart must be clearly labelled, and there must be a scale to indicate the magnitude of the data. Here, the y axis includes a scale for the amount of sales, and so readers of the bar chart can see not only that sales have been rising year by year (with 20X3 being an exception) but also what the actual sales have been each year.

2.10 Simple bar charts serve two purposes.

  (a) They show the actual magnitude of each item.

  (b) They enable one to compare magnitudes, by comparing the lengths of bars on the chart.

Component bar charts

2.11 A component bar chart is a bar chart that gives a breakdown of each total into its components.

EXAMPLE: A COMPONENT BAR CHART

Charbart plc's sales for the years from 20X7 to 20X9 are as follows.

	20X7	20X8	20X9
	£'000	£'000	£'000
Product A	1,000	1,200	1,700
Product B	900	1,000	1,000
Product C	500	600	700
Total	2,400	2,800	3,400

A component bar chart would show the following.

(a)   How total sales have changed from year to year
(b)   The components of each year's total

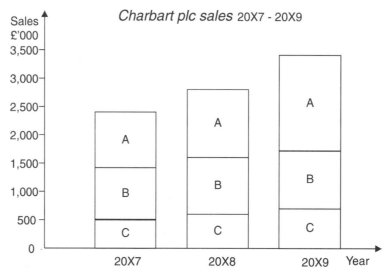

In this diagram the growth in sales is illustrated and the significance of growth in product A sales as the reason for the total sales growth is also fairly clear. The growth in product A sales would have been even clearer if product A had been drawn as the bottom element in each bar instead of the top one.

Percentage component bar charts

2.12   The difference between a component bar chart and a percentage component bar chart is that with a component bar chart, the total length of each bar (and the length of each component in it) indicates magnitude. A bigger amount is shown by a longer bar. With a percentage component bar chart, total magnitudes are not shown. If two or more bars are drawn on the chart, the total length of each bar is the same. The only varying lengths in a percentage component bar chart are the lengths of the sections of a bar, which vary according to the relative sizes of the components.

EXAMPLE: A PERCENTAGE COMPONENT BAR CHART

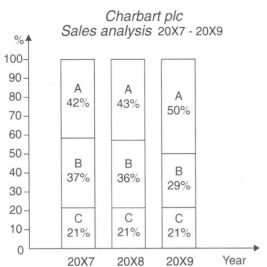

The information in the previous example of sales of Charbart plc could have been shown in a percentage component bar chart as follows.

Working

	20X7		20X8		20X9	
	£'000	%	£'000	%	£'000	%
Product A	1,000	42	1,200	43	1,700	50
Product B	900	37	1,000	36	1,000	29
Product C	500	21	600	21	700	21
Total	2,400	100	2,800	100	3,400	100

This chart shows that sales of C have remained a steady proportion of total sales, but the proportion of A in total sales has gone up quite considerably, while the proportion of B has fallen correspondingly.

Multiple bar charts (compound bar charts)

2.13   A multiple bar chart (or compound bar chart) is a bar chart in which two or more separate bars are used to present sub-divisions of data.

EXAMPLE: A MULTIPLE BAR CHART

The data on Charbart plc's sales could be shown in a multiple bar chart as follows.

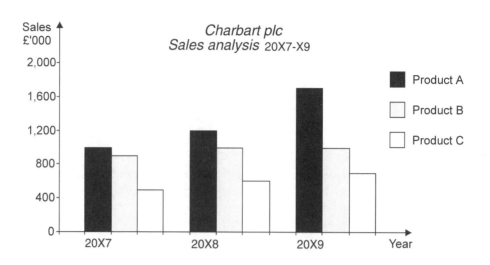

2.14 A multiple bar chart uses several bars for each total. In the above example, the sales in each year are shown as three separate bars, one for each product, A, B and C.

Multiple bar charts are sometimes drawn with the bars horizontal instead of vertical.

2.15 Multiple bar charts present similar information to component bar charts, except for the following.

(a) Multiple bar charts do not show the grand total (in the above example, the total output each year) whereas component bar charts do.

(b) Multiple bar charts illustrate the comparative magnitudes of the components more clearly than component bar charts.

Activity 1

Income for Lemmi Bank in 20X0, 20X1 and 20X2 is made up as follows.

	20X0	20X1	20X2
	£'000	£'000	£'000
Interest income	3,579	2,961	2,192
Commission income	857	893	917
Other income	62	59	70

Required

Using the above data, draw the following.

(a) A simple bar chart
(b) A component bar chart
(c) A percentage component bar chart
(d) A compound bar chart

---

3 FREQUENCY DISTRIBUTIONS

3.1 Frequently the data collected from a statistical survey or investigation are simply a mass of numbers.

65	69	70	71	70	68	69	67	70	68
72	71	69	74	70	73	71	67	69	70

3.2 The raw data above yield little information as they stand; imagine how much more difficult it would be if there were hundreds or even thousands of data items. The data could, of course, be arranged in order size (an array) and the lowest and highest data items, as well as typical items, could be identified.

Definitions

> A *frequency distribution* (or *frequency table*) records the number of times each value occurs (the *frequency*).

3.3 Many sets of data, however, contain a limited number of data values, even though there may be many occurrences of each value. It can therefore be useful to organise the data into a frequency distribution recording the number of times each value occurs. A frequency distribution for the data in Paragraph 3.1 (the output in units of 20 employees during one week) is as follows.

Output of employees in one week in units

Output Units	*Number of employees (frequency)*
65	1
66	0
67	2
68	2
69	4
70	5
71	3
72	1
73	1
74	1
	$\overline{\underline{20}}$

3.4 When the data are arranged in this way it is immediately obvious that 69 and 70 units are the most common volumes of output per employee per week.

Grouped frequency distributions

3.5 If there is a large set of data or if every (or nearly every) data item is different, it is often convenient to group frequencies together into bands or classes. For example, suppose that the output produced by another group of 20 employees during one week was as follows, in units.

1,087	850	1,084	792
924	1,226	1,012	1,205
1,265	1,028	1,230	1,182
1,086	1,130	989	1,155
1,134	1,166	1,129	1,160

3.6 The range of output from the lowest to the highest producer is 792 to 1,265, a range of 473 units. This range could be divided into classes of say, 100 units (the class width or class interval), and the number of employees producing output within each class could then be grouped into a single frequency, as follows.

Output Units	Number of employees (frequency)
700 – 799	1
800 – 899	1
900 – 999	2
1,000 – 1,099	5
1,100 – 1,199	7
1,200 – 1,299	4
	20

3.7 Note, however, that once items have been 'grouped' in this way their individual values are lost.

Grouped frequency distributions of continuous variables

3.8 As well as being used for discrete variables (as above), grouped frequency distributions (or grouped frequency tables) can be used to present data for continuous variables.

EXAMPLE: A GROUPED FREQUENCY DISTRIBUTION FOR A CONTINUOUS VARIABLE

Suppose we wish to record the heights of 50 different individuals. The information might be presented as a grouped frequency distribution, as follows.

Height (cm)	Number of individuals (frequency)
Up to and including 154	1
Over 154, up to and including 163	3
Over 163, up to and including 172	8
Over 172, up to and including 181	16
Over 181, up to and including 190	18
Over 190	4
	50

Note the following points.

(a) It would be wrong to show the ranges as 0–154, 154–163, 163–172 and so on, because 154 cm and 163 cm would then be values in two classes, which is not permissible. Although each value should only be in one class, we have to make sure that each possible value can be included. Classes such as 154–162, 163–172 would not be suitable since a height of 162.5 cm would not belong in either class. Such classes could be used for discrete variables, however.

(b) There is an *open-ended* class at each end of the range. This is because heights up to 154 cm and over 190 cm are thought to be uncommon, so that a single 'open-ended' class is used to group all the frequencies together.

Preparing grouped frequency distributions

3.9 To prepare a grouped frequency distribution, a decision must be made about how wide each class should be. In an examination, you might be told how many classes to use, or what the class interval should be. You should, however, generally observe the following guidelines.

(a) The size of each class should be appropriate to the nature of the data being recorded, and the most appropriate class interval varied according to circumstances.

(b) The upper and lower limits of each class interval should be suitable 'round' numbers for class intervals which are in multiples of 5, 10, 100, 1,000 and so on. For example, if the class interval is 10, and data items range in value from 23 to 62 (discrete values), the class intervals should be 20–29, 30–39, 40–49, 50–59 and 60–69, rather than 23–32, 33–42, 43–52 and 53–62.

(c) With continuous variables, either:

(i) the upper limit of a class should be 'up to and including ...' and the lower limit of the next class should be 'over ...'; or

(ii) the upper limit of a class should be 'less than...', and the lower limit of the next class should be 'at least ...'.

Activity 2

The commission earnings for May 20X3 of the assistants in a department store were as follows (in pounds).

60	35	53	47	25	44	55	58	47	71
63	67	57	44	61	48	50	56	61	42
43	38	41	39	61	51	27	56	57	50
55	68	55	50	25	48	44	43	49	73
53	35	36	41	45	71	56	40	69	52
36	47	66	52	32	46	44	32	52	58
49	41	45	45	48	36	46	42	52	33
31	36	40	66	53	58	60	52	66	51
51	44	59	53	51	57	35	45	46	54
46	54	51	39	64	43	54	47	60	45

Required

Prepare a grouped frequency distribution classifying the commission earnings into categories of £5 commencing with '£25 and under £30'.

3.10 You should be able to interpret a grouped frequency distribution and express an interpretation in writing. In the example following Paragraph 3.8, an interpretation of the data is fairly straightforward.

(a) Most heights fell between 154 cm and 190 cm.

(b) Most heights were in the middle of this range, with few people having heights in the lower and upper ends of the range.

Cumulative frequency distributions

Definition

A *cumulative frequency distribution* (or *cumulative frequency table*) can be used to show the total number of times that a value above or below a certain amount occurs.

3.11 There are two possible cumulative frequency distributions for the grouped frequency distribution in Paragraph 3.6.

	Cumulative frequency			Cumulative frequency
≥ 700	20		< 800	1
≥ 800	19		< 900	2
≥ 900	18		<1,000	4
≥1,000	16		<1,100	9
≥1,100	11		<1,200	16
≥1,200	4		<1,300	20

Notes

(a) The symbol > means 'greater than' and ≥ means 'greater than or equal to'. The symbol < means 'less than' and ≤ means 'less than or equal to'. These symbols provide a convenient method of stating classes.

(b) The first cumulative frequency distribution shows that of the total of 20 employees, 19 produced 800 units or more, 18 produced 900 units or more, 16 produced 1,000 units or more and so on.

(c) The second cumulative frequency distribution shows that, of the total of 20 employees, one produced under 800 units, two produced under 900 units, four produced under 1,000 units and so on.

4 HISTOGRAMS

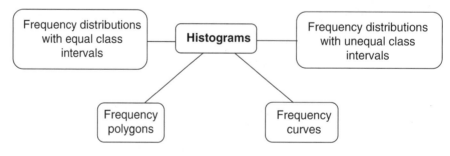

Definitions

A *histogram* is the pictorial representation of a frequency distribution.

4.1 It is often simpler to interpret data after they have been presented pictorially rather than as a table of figures. A frequency distribution can be represented pictorially by means of a histogram. Histograms look rather like bar charts except that the bars are joined together and whereas frequencies are represented by the height of bars on a bar chart, frequencies are represented by the *area* covered by bars on a histogram.

Histograms of frequency distributions with equal class intervals

4.2 If all the class intervals are the same, as in the frequency distribution in Paragraph 3.6, the bars of the histogram all have the same width and the heights will be proportional to the frequencies. The histogram looks almost identical to a bar chart except that the bars are joined together. Because the bars are joined together, when presenting discrete data the data must be treated as continuous so that there are no gaps between class intervals. For example, for a cricketer's scores in various games the classes would have to be ≥0 but <10, ≥10 but <20 and so on, instead of 0–9, 10–19 and so on.

4.3 A histogram of the distribution in Paragraph 3.6 would be drawn as follows.

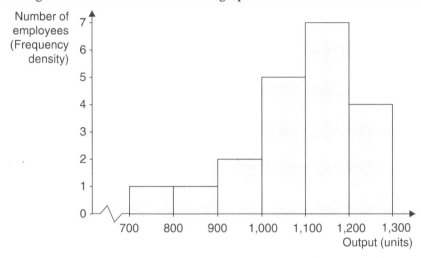

4.4 Note that the discrete data have been treated as continuous, the intervals being changed to >700 but ≤ 800, >800 but ≤ 900 and so on.

Histograms of frequency distributions with unequal class intervals

4.5 If a distribution has unequal class intervals, the heights of the bars have to be adjusted for the fact that the bars do not have the same width.

EXAMPLE: A HISTOGRAM WITH UNEQUAL CLASS INTERVALS

The weekly wages of employees of Salt Lake Ltd are as follows.

Wages per employee	*Number of employees*
Up to and including £60	4
>£60 ≤ £80	6
>£80 ≤ £90	6
>£90 ≤ £120	6
>£120	3

The class intervals for wages per employee are not all the same, and range from £10 to £30.

A histogram is drawn as follows.

(a)   The width of each bar on the chart must be proportionate to the corresponding class interval. In other words, the bar representing wages of $>£60 \leq £80$, a range of £20, will be twice as wide as the bar representing wages of $>£80 \leq £90$, a range of only £10.

(b)   A standard width of bar must be selected. This should be the size of class interval which occurs most frequently. In our example, class intervals £10, £20 and £30 each occur once. An interval of £20 will be selected as the standard width.

(c)   Open-ended classes must be closed off. It is usual for the width of such classes to be the same as that of the adjoining class. In this example, the class 'up to and including £60' will become $>£40 \leq £60$ and the class 'more than £120' will become $>£120 \leq £150$.

(d)   Each frequency is then multiplied by (standard class width ÷ actual class width) to obtain the height of the bar in the histogram.

(e)   The height of bars no longer corresponds to *frequency* but rather to *frequency density* and hence the vertical axis should be labelled frequency density.

(f)   Note that the data is considered to be continuous since the gap between, for example, £79.99 and £80.00 is so small.

Class interval	Size of interval	Frequency	Adjustment	Height of bar
$>£40 \leq £60$	20	4	$\times 20/20$	4
$>£60 \leq £80$	20	6	$\times 20/20$	6
$>£80 \leq £90$	10	6	$\times 20/10$	12
$>£90 \leq £120$	30	6	$\times 20/30$	4
$>£120 \leq £150$	30	3	$\times 20/30$	2

(a)   The first two bars will be of normal height.

(b)   The third bar will be twice as high as the class frequency (6) would suggest, to compensate for the fact that the class interval, £10, is only half the standard size.

(c)   The fourth and fifth bars will be two thirds as high as the class frequencies (6 and 3) would suggest, to compensate for the fact that the class interval, £30, is 150% of the standard size.

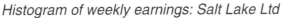

Histogram of weekly earnings: Salt Lake Ltd

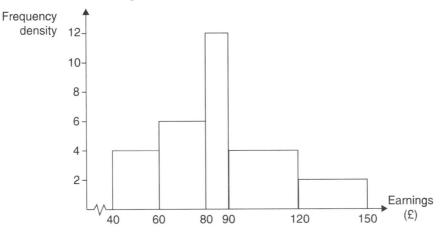

Activity 3

The sales force of a company have just completed a successful sales campaign. The performances of individual sales staff have been analysed as follows, into a grouped frequency distribution.

Sales	Number of sales staff
Up to £10,000	1
>£10,000 ≤ £12,000	10
>£12,000 ≤ £14,000	12
>£14,000 ≤ £18,000	8
>£18,000 ≤ £22,000	4
>£22,000	1

Required

Draw a histogram from this information.

Frequency polygons

4.6 A histogram is not a particularly accurate method of presenting a frequency distribution because, in grouping frequencies together in a class interval, it is assumed that these frequencies occur evenly throughout the class interval, which is unlikely. To overcome this criticism, we can convert a histogram into a frequency polygon, which is drawn on the assumption that, within each class interval, the frequency of occurrence of data items is not evenly spread. There will be more values at the end of each class interval nearer the histogram's peak (if any), and so the flat top on a histogram bar should be converted into a rising or falling line.

4.7 A frequency polygon is drawn from a histogram, in the following way.

(a) Mark the mid-point of the top of each bar in the histogram.
(b) Join up all these points with straight lines.

4.8 The ends of the diagram (the mid-points of the two end bars) should be joined to the base line at the mid-points of the next class intervals outside the range of observed data. These intervals should be taken to be of the same size as the last class intervals for observed data.

EXAMPLE: A FREQUENCY POLYGON

The following grouped frequency distribution relates to the number of occasions during the past 40 weeks that a particular cost has been a given amount.

Cost £	Number of occasions
> 800 ≤ 1,000	4
>1,000 ≤ 1,200	10
>1,200 ≤ 1,400	12
>1,400 ≤ 1,600	10
>1,600 ≤ 1,800	4
	40

Required

Prepare a frequency polygon.

SOLUTION

A histogram is first drawn, in the way described earlier. All classes are of the same width.

The mid-points of the class intervals outside the range of observed data are 700 and 1,900.

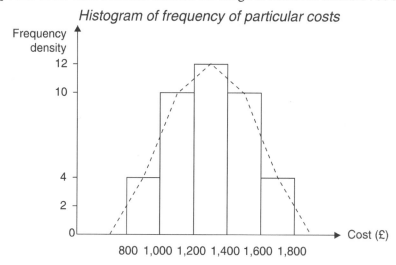

Frequency curves

4.9 Because a frequency polygon has straight lines between points, it too can be seen as an inaccurate way of presenting data. One method of obtaining greater accuracy would be to make the class intervals smaller. If the class intervals of a distribution were made small enough the frequency polygon would become very smooth. It would become a curve.

5 OGIVES

Definition

> An *ogive* shows the cumulative number of items with a value less than or equal to, or alternatively greater than or equal to, a certain amount.

NOTES

5.1 Just as a grouped frequency distribution can be graphed as a histogram, a cumulative frequency distribution can be graphed as an ogive.

EXAMPLE: OGIVES

Consider the following frequency distribution.

Number of faulty units rejected on inspection	Frequency	Cumulative frequency
>0 ≤ 1	5	5
>1 ≤ 2	5	10
>2 ≤ 3	3	13
>3 ≤ 4	1	14
	14	

An ogive would be drawn as follows.

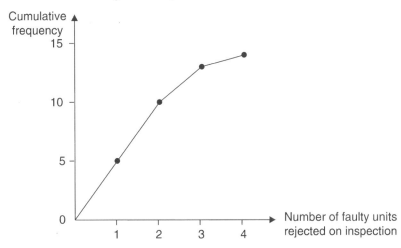

Ogive of rejected items

5.2 The ogive is drawn by plotting the cumulative frequencies on the graph, and joining them with straight lines. Although many ogives are more accurately curved lines, you can use straight lines in drawing an ogive in an examination. An ogive drawn with straight lines may be referred to as a cumulative frequency *polygon* (or cumulative frequency *diagram*) whereas one drawn as a curve may be referred to as a cumulative frequency *curve*.

5.3 For grouped frequency distributions, where we work up through values of the variable, the cumulative frequencies are plotted against the *upper* limits of the classes. For example, for the class 'over 2, up to and including 3', the cumulative frequency should be plotted against 3.

PUBLISHING

Activity 4

A grouped frequency distribution for the volume of output produced at a factory over a period of 40 weeks is as follows.

Output (units)	Number of times output achieved
>0 ≤ 200	4
>200 ≤ 400	8
>400 ≤ 600	12
>600 ≤ 800	10
>800 ≤ 1,000	6
	40

Required

Draw an appropriate ogive, and estimate the number of weeks in which output was 550 units or less.

5.4   We can also draw ogives to show the cumulative number of items with values greater than or equal to some given value.

EXAMPLE: DOWNWARD-SLOPING OGIVES

Output at a factory over a period of 80 weeks is shown by the following frequency distribution.

Output per week Units	Number of times output achieved
> 0 ≤ 100	10
>100 ≤ 200	20
>200 ≤ 300	25
>300 ≤ 400	15
>400 ≤ 500	10
	80

If we want to draw an ogive to show the number of weeks in which output exceeded a certain value, the cumulative total should begin at 80 and drop to 0. In drawing an ogive when we work down through values of the variable, the descending cumulative frequency should be plotted against the lower limit of each class interval.

Lower limit of interval	Frequency	Cumulative ('more than') frequency
0	10	80
100	20	70
200	25	50
300	15	25
400	10	10
500	0	0

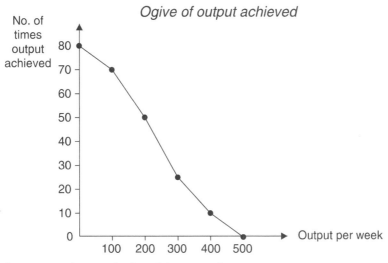

Ogive of output achieved

Make sure that you understand what this curve shows.

For example, 350 on the x axis corresponds with about 18 on the y axis. This means that output of 350 units or more was achieved 18 times out of the 80 weeks.

Activity 5

If you wanted to produce an ogive showing the cumulative number of students in a class with an exam mark of 55% or more, would you need an upward-sloping or a downward-sloping ogive?

6 TIME SERIES GRAPHS

Definitions

A *time series* is a series of figures or values recorded over time such as monthly sales over the last two years. A graph of a time series is called a *historigram*. (Note the 'ri'; this is not the same as a histogram).

6.1 The horizontal axis of a historigram is always chosen to represent time and the vertical axis represents the values of the data recorded. The graph will give some indication of the trend in the data over time.

6.2 A *component time* series is data in which various classifications (for example sales in the four branches of a retail organisation each month) can be thought of as the components of a meaningful total (the total monthly sales of the retail organisation). A *multiple time series*, on the other hand, is data which have classifications for each time period which cannot be added to form meaningful totals. An example would be prices of selected food items (such as tea (per packet), bread (per loaf) and caviare (per jar)).

EXAMPLE: TIME SERIES

The following data show the sales of a product in the period 20X6–X8.

Year	Quarter 1 '000	Quarter 2 '000	Quarter 3 '000	Quarter 4 '000
20X6	86	42	57	112
20X7	81	39	55	107
20X8	77	35	52	99

Required

Plot a time series of the above data.

SOLUTION

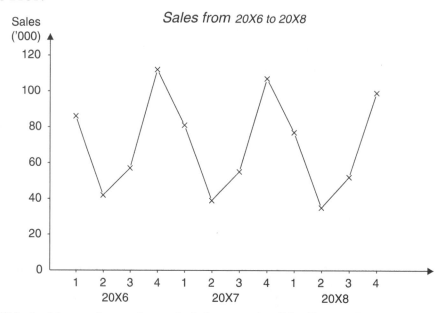

We will be looking at time series analysis in some detail in Chapter 7.

7   Z CHARTS

Definition

> A *Z chart* is a form of time series graph.

7.1   A Z chart can be very useful for presenting business data. It shows the following.

(a)   The value of a variable plotted against time over the year
(b)   The cumulative sum of values for that variable over the year to date
(c)   The annual moving total for that variable

The annual moving total is the sum of values of the variable for the 12-month period up to the end of the month under consideration.

EXAMPLE: Z CHARTS

The sales figures for a company for 20X2 and 20X3 are as follows.

	20X2 sales	20X3 sales
	£m	£m
January	7	8
February	7	8
March	8	8
April	7	9
May	9	8
June	8	8
July	8	7
August	7	8
September	6	9
October	7	6
November	8	9
December	8	9
	90	97

Required

Draw a Z chart to represent these data.

SOLUTION

The first thing to do is to calculate the cumulative sales for 20X3 and the annual moving total for the year.

	Sales 20X2	Sales 20X3	Cumulative sales 20X3	Annual moving total
	£m	£m	£m	£m
January	7	8	8	91
February	7	8	16	92
March	8	8	24	92
April	7	9	33	94
May	9	8	41	93
June	8	8	49	93
July	8	7	56	92
August	7	8	64	93
September	6	9	73	96
October	7	6	79	95
November	8	9	88	96
December	8	9	97	97

The first figure in the annual moving total is arrived at by taking the sales for the year ended December 20X2, adding those for January 20X3 and subtracting those for January 20X2. This gives the sales for a 12-month period to the end of January 20X3 as 90 + 8 – 7 = 91.

A similar approach is used for the rest of the year, by adding on the new 20X3 month and deducting the corresponding 20X2 month.

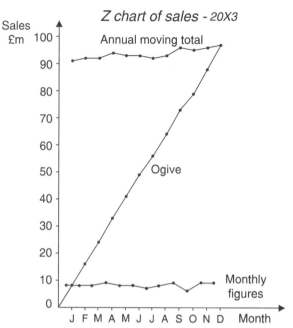

You will notice that while the values of the annual moving total and the cumulative values are plotted on month-end positions, the values for the current monthly figures are plotted on mid-month positions. This is because the monthly figures represent achievement over a particular month whereas the annual moving totals and the cumulative values represent achievement up to a particular month end.

The interpretation of Z charts

7.2 The popularity of Z charts in practical applications derives from the wealth of information which they can contain.

(a) *Monthly totals* show the monthly results at a glance, together with any seasonal variations.

(b) *Cumulative totals* show the performance to date, and can be easily compared with planned or budgeted performance by superimposing a budget line.

(c) *Annual moving totals* compare the current levels of performance with those of the previous year. If the line is rising then this year's monthly results are better than the results of the corresponding month last year. The opposite applies if the line is falling. The annual moving total line indicates the long-term trend in values of the variable, whether rising, falling or steady.

7.3 You should note that Z charts do not have to cover 12 months of a year. They could also be drawn for (for example) four quarters of a year, or seven days of a week. The method would be exactly the same.

Activity 6

Why does the annual moving total line on a Z chart show the long-term trend, unaffected by seasonal effects such as sales being higher in summer than winter?

8   SEMI-LOGARITHMIC GRAPHS

8.1   A variation of the time series graph is the semi-logarithmic graph.

Definition

> A *semi-logarithmic graph* is plotted on special semi-logarithmic (log-linear) graph paper. This has a normal horizontal axis against which time is plotted but, on the vertical axis, equal intervals represent equal proportional changes in the variable. For example, the distance on the axis between y = 10 and y = 30 is the same as the distance between y = 30 and y = 90 (both represent a three-fold increase).

8.2   Sections of a semi-logarithmic graph having equal slope represent equal proportional changes in the variable. A straight line therefore indicates that a variable is increasing or decreasing at a constant rate whereas a curve indicates that a variable is increasing or decreasing at an increasing or decreasing rate. The steeper the line, the higher the rate of increase or decrease.

8.3   The principal relationships likely to be shown on semi-logarithmic graphs are as follows.

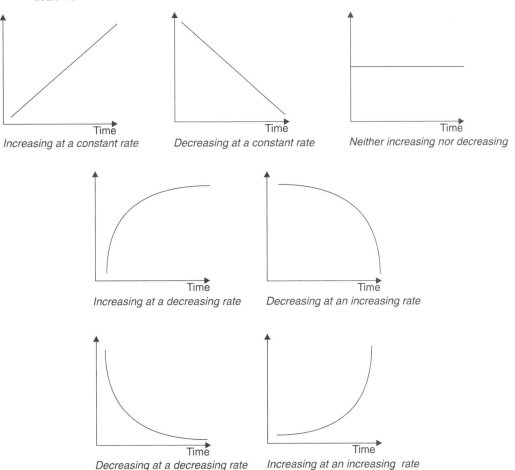

Figure 3.1 Semi-logarithmic graphs

8.4   An alternative to using semi-logarithmic paper is to plot the logarithms of the values of the variable on the vertical axis against time on the horizontal axis.

8.5 Because only proportional changes are of interest, time series measured in different units can be compared on the same semi-logarithmic graph.

8.6 Such graphs are also useful in situations where the dependent variable covers a great range of values. In such a case, use of an ordinary graph would require such a small scale on the vertical axis that significant changes would be obscured.

8.7 Although semi-logarithmic graphs can be useful, they do have a number of disadvantages. Any variables having zero or negative values cannot be plotted. Perhaps more importantly, however, most people are used to interpreting normal graphs and may therefore misread semi-logarithmic graphs. It must therefore be clear if graphs have been drawn on a logarithmic basis. There is a case for not actually labelling the vertical axis since it is the slope of lines that are important, not values.

EXAMPLE: SEMI-LOGARITHMIC GRAPHS

The annual production volumes of a particular company over the last ten years are shown below.

Year	Production volume	Log	Year	Production volume	Log
1	1,014	3.0060	6	10,630	4.0265
2	1,622	3.2101	7	17,009	4.2307
3	2,595	3.4141	8	27,214	4.4348
4	4,152	3.6183	9	43,543	4.6389
5	6,644	3.8224	10	69,669	4.8430

(a) The production volumes cover a very large range. To plot them on a conventional graph would require such a small scale as to make changes in early years impossible to decipher.

(b) It is difficult to determine how production volumes have changed over the period simply by looking at the figures.

If we plot the logarithms of the production volumes against time (as in diagram (a) below) or plot the volumes against time on semi-logarithmic graph paper (as in diagram (b) below) we are able to view changes in volume across the entire 10 year period, and ascertain that the production volume has been increasing at a fairly constant rate.

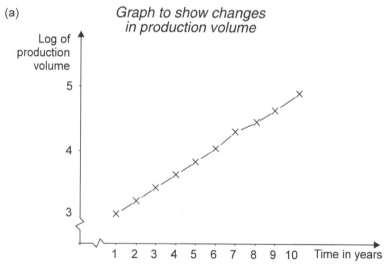

(a) Graph to show changes in production volume

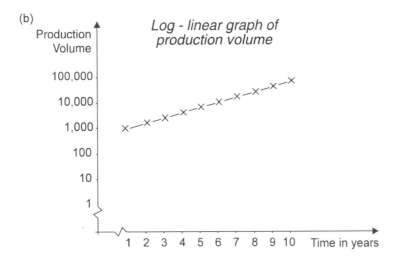

(b)

Log - linear graph of production volume

This chapter has looked at the different ways in which data can be presented in various useful forms.

Sometimes we might wish to obtain more information from our data, for example we might wish to identify trends using statistical rather than usual means. One of the ways in which this may be achieved is by the construction of a set of index numbers. Index numbers are the subject of the next chapter.

Chapter roundup

- This chapter has considered a number of ways of presenting data.

- Tables are a simple way of presenting information about two variables.

- Charts often convey the meaning or significance of data more clearly than would a table.

- There are three main types of bar chart: simple, component (including percentage component) and multiple (or compound).

- Frequency distributions are used if values of particular variables occur more than once. Make sure that you know the difference between grouped frequency and cumulative frequency distributions.

- A frequency distribution can be represented pictorially by means of a histogram. The number of observations in a class is represented by the area covered by the bar, rather than by its height. Frequency polygons and frequency curves are perhaps more accurate methods of data presentation than the standard histogram.

- An ogive shows the cumulative number of items with a value less than or equal to, or alternatively greater than or equal to, a certain amount.

- The graph of a time series is called a historigram.

- A Z chart shows the value of a variable plotted against time over the period, the cumulative sum of values for that variable over the period to date and the period moving total for that variable.

- Semi-logarithmic graphs are useful if the dependent variable covers a great range of values.

- Make sure that you are able to present data in all of the formats covered in this chapter and that you are aware of the information available from each method of presentation. When selecting a method of data presentation remember to

NOTES

consider the type of information which must be shown and the presentation which the ultimate user of the information will find most helpful.

Quick quiz

1   What are the main guidelines for tabulation?

2   What are the disadvantages of pie charts?

3   Name the three main types of bar chart.

4   How would you prepare a grouped frequency distribution?

5   What is a cumulative frequency distribution?

6   What are the computations needed to draw a histogram?

7   How would you draw a frequency polygon from a histogram?

8   How would you draw an ogive?

9   What is a historigram?

10   What three lines are drawn on a Z chart?

11   What is log-linear paper?

Answers to activities

1	(a)	20X0	20X1	20X2
		£'000	£'000	£'000
		3,579	2,961	2,192
		857	893	917
		62	59	70
		4,498	3,913	3,179

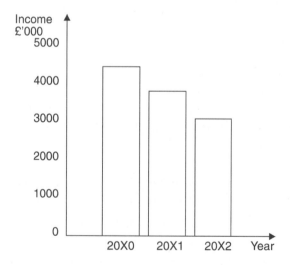

(b)

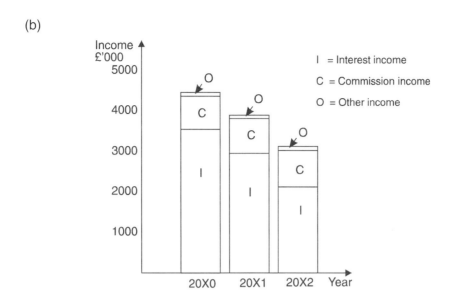

(c)

	20X0		20X1		20X2	
	£'000	%	£'000	%	£'000	%
	3,579	80	2,961	76	2,192	69
	857	19	893	23	917	29
	62	1	59	1	70	2
	4,498	100	3,913	100	3,179	100

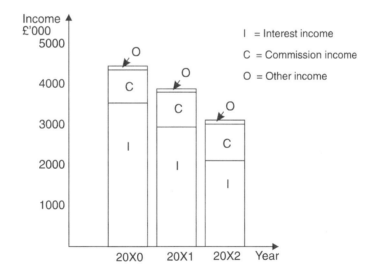

PUBLISHING

(d)

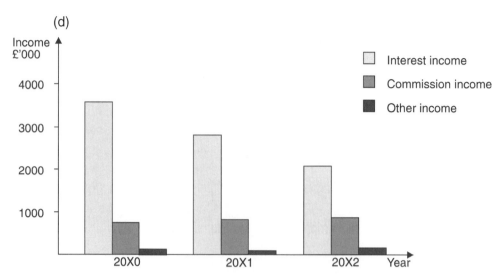

2   We are told what classes to use, so the first step is to identify the lowest and highest values in the data. The lowest value is £25 (in the first row) and the highest value is £73 (in the fourth row). This means that the class intervals must go up to '£70 and under £75'.

We can now set out the classes in a column, and then count the number of items in each class using tally marks.

Class interval	Tally marks	Total
£25 and less than £30	///	3
£30 and less than £35	HIT	4
£35 and less than £40	HIT HIT	10
£40 and less than £45	HIT HIT HIT	15
£45 and less than £50	HIT HIT HIT ///	18
£50 and less than £55	HIT HIT HIT HIT	20
£55 and less than £60	HIT HIT ///	13
£60 and less than £65	HIT ///	8
£65 and less than £70	HIT /	6
£70 and less than £75	///	3
	Total	100

3   Before drawing the histogram, we must decide on the following.

(a)   A standard class width: £2,000 will be chosen.

(b)   An open-ended class width. In this example, the open-ended class width will therefore be £2,000 for class '≤ £10,000' and £4,000 for the class '>£22,000'.

Class interval	Size of width £	Frequency	Adjustment	Height of block
≤ £10,000	2,000	1	× 2/2	1
>£10,000 ≤ £12,000	2,000	10	× 2/2	10
>£12,000 ≤ £14,000	2,000	12	× 2/2	12
>£14,000 ≤ £18,000	4,000	8	× 2/4	4
>£18,000 ≤ £22,000	4,000	4	× 2/4	2
>£22,000	4,000	1	× 2/4	$^1/_2$

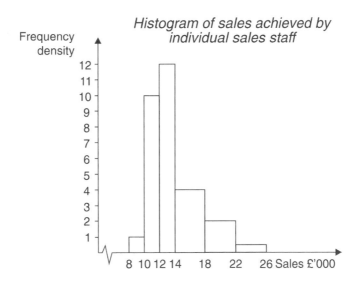

Histogram of sales achieved by individual sales staff

4

Upper limit of interval	Frequency	Cumulative frequency
200	4	4
400	8	12
600	12	24
800	10	34
1,000	6	40

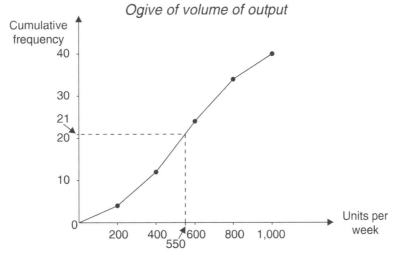

Ogive of volume of output

The dotted lines indicate that output of up to 550 units was achieved in 21 out of the 40 weeks.

5   A downward-sloping ogive

6   One example of each month is included in the annual moving total. Thus although July might be a very good month, but January a very bad month, there will be one July and one January in the total, balancing each other.

Assignment 3   **(45 minutes)**

The unit sales of a brand for 20X1 and 20X2 were as follows.

	Jan	Feb	Mar	Apr	May	Jun	Jul	Aug	Sept	Oct	Nov	Dec
20X1	29	30	30	34	37	39	40	40	40	45	49	52
20X2	54	55	55	55	50	46	43	41	40	40	42	44

The brand has been supported by two weeks of television advertising every March and September. From April 20X2 there has been heavy price-cutting by its competitors.

Required

(a) Calculate the following for 20X2.

    (i)   Cumulative monthly sales
    (ii)   Moving annual totals

(b) Plot a Z chart for this period.

(c) Explain what these data show.

Chapter 4 :
INDEX NUMBERS

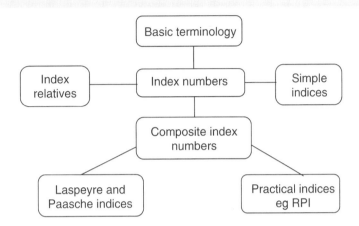

Introduction

A number of methods of data presentation looked at in Chapter 3 can be used to identify visually the trends in data over a period of time. It may also be useful, however, to identify trends using statistical rather than visual means. This is frequently achieved by constructing a set of index numbers.

Index numbers provide a standardised way of comparing the values, over time, of prices, wages, volume of output and so on. They are used extensively in business, government and commerce.

No doubt you will be aware of some index numbers – the RPI, the Financial Times All Share Index and so on. This chapter will explain to you how to construct indices and will look at associated issues such as their limitations.

Your objectives

After completing this chapter, you should:

(a)   understand the terminology associated with index numbers;

(b)   be able to construct simple indices, index relatives and composite index numbers;

(c)   know the difference between weighted means of relatives indices and weighted aggregate indices;

(d)   be able to construct Laspeyre and Paasche indices and know when each should be used;

(e)   be able to deal with the practical issues associated with index numbers;

(f)   have an awareness of the Retail Prices Index.

1 BASIC TERMINOLOGY

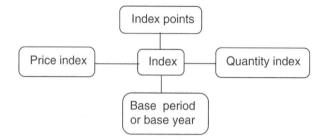

Definition

> An *index* is a measure, over time, of the average changes in the values (prices or quantities) of a group of items. An index comprises a series of index numbers.

1.1 Although it is possible to prepare an index for a single item, for example the price of an ounce of gold, such an index would probably be unnecessary. It is only when there is a group of items that a simple list of changes in their values over time becomes rather hard to interpret, and an index provides a useful single measure of comparison.

Price indices and quantity indices

Definitions

> A *price index* measures the change in the money value of a group of items over time.
>
> A *quantity index* (also called a volume index) measures the change in the non-monetary values of a group of items over time.

1.2 An index may be a price index or a quantity index. Perhaps the best known price index in the UK is the Retail Prices Index (RPI) which measures changes in the costs of items of expenditure of the average household. An example of a quantity index is a productivity index, which measures changes in the productivity of various departments or groups of workers.

Index points

1.3 The term 'points' refers to the difference between the index values in two years.

For example, suppose that the index of food prices in 20X1–20X6 was as follows.

20X1	180
20X2	200
20X3	230
20X4	250
20X5	300
20X6	336

The index has risen 156 points between 20X1 and 20X6. This is an increase of $(156/180) \times 100 = 86.7\%$.

Similarly, the index rose 36 points between 20X5 and 20X6, a rise of 12%.

The base period, or base year

1.4 Index numbers normally take the value for a base date, usually the starting point of the series though it could be part way through the series, as 100.

2 SIMPLE INDICES

2.1 When one commodity only is under consideration, we have the following formulae.

(a) Price index $= 100 \times \dfrac{P_1}{P_0}$

where P_1 is the price for the period under consideration and P_0 is the price for the base period.

(b) Quantity index $= 100 \times \dfrac{Q_1}{Q_0}$

where Q_1 is the quantity for the period under consideration and Q_0 is the quantity for the base period.

EXAMPLE: SINGLE-ITEM INDICES

If the price of a cup of coffee was 40p in 20X0, 50p in 20X1 and 76p in 20X2, then using 20X0 as a base year the price index numbers for 20X1 and 20X2 would be as follows:

$$20X1 \text{ price index} = 100 \times \frac{50}{40} = 125$$

$$20X2 \text{ price index} = 100 \times \frac{76}{40} = 190$$

If the number of cups of coffee sold in 20X0 was 500,000, in 20X1 700,000 and in 20X2 600,000, then using 20X0 as a base year, the quantity index numbers for 20X1 and 20X2 would be as follows

$$20X1 \text{ quantity index} = 100 \times \frac{700,000}{500,000} = 140$$

$$20X2 \text{ quantity index} = 100 \times \frac{600,000}{500,000} = 120$$

3 INDEX RELATIVES

Definition

An *index relative* (sometimes just called a *relative*) is the name given to an index number which measures the change in a single distinct commodity.

3.1 A price relative is calculated as $100 \times P_1/P_0$. We calculated price relatives for a cup of coffee in the example following paragraph 2.1.

3.2 A quantity relative is calculated as $100 \times Q_1/Q_0$. We calculated quantity relatives for cups of coffee in the example following paragraph 2.1.

Time series of relatives

3.3 Given the values of some commodity over time (a time series), there are two ways in which index relatives can be calculated.

3.4 In the *fixed base method*, a base year is selected (index 100), and all subsequent changes are measured against this base. Such an approach should only be used if the basic nature of the commodity is unchanged over time.

3.5 In the *chain base method*, changes are calculated with respect to the value of the commodity in the period immediately before. This approach can be used for any set of commodity values but must be used if the basic nature of the commodity is changing over time.

EXAMPLE: FIXED BASE AND CHAIN METHODS

The price of a commodity was £2.70 in 20X0, £3.11 in 20X1, £3.42 in 20X2 and £3.83 in 20X3. Construct both a chain base index and a fixed base index for the years 20X0 to 20X3 using 20X0 as the base year.

SOLUTION

Chain base index	20X0	100	
	20X1	115	$(100 \times 3.11/2.70)$
	20X2	110	$(100 \times 3.42/3.11)$
	20X3	112	$(100 \times 3.83/3.42)$
Fixed base index	20X0	100	
	20X1	115	
	20X2	127	$(100 \times 3.42/2.70)$
	20X3	142	$(100 \times 3.83/2.70)$

The chain base relatives show the rate of change in prices from year to year, whereas the fixed base relatives show changes relative to prices in the base year.

Changing the base of fixed base relatives

3.6 It is sometimes necessary to change the base of a time series of fixed base relatives, perhaps because the base time point is too far in the past. The following time series has a base date of 1970 which would probably be considered too out of date.

	1990	1991	1992	1993	1994	1995
Index (1970 = 100)	451	463	472	490	499	505

To change the base date (to rebase), divide each relative by the relative corresponding to the new base time point and multiply the result by 100.

Activity 1

Rebase the index in Paragraph 3.6 to 1993.

Comparing sets of fixed base relatives

3.7 You may be required to compare two sets of time series relatives. For example, an index of the annual number of advertisements placed by an organisation in the press and the index of the number of the organisation's product sold per annum might be compared. If the base years of the two indices differ, however, comparison is extremely difficult (as the illustration below shows).

	20W8	20W9	20X0	20X1	20X2	20X3	20X4
Number of advertisements placed (20X0 = 100)	90	96	100	115	128	140	160
Volumes of sales (20W0 = 100)	340	347	355	420	472	515	572

3.8 From the figures above it is impossible to determine whether sales are increasing at a greater rate than the number of advertisements placed, or vice versa. This difficulty can be overcome by rebasing one set of relatives so that the base dates are the same. For example, we could rebase the index of volume of sales to 20X0.

	20W8	20W9	20X0	20X1	20X2	20X3	20X4
Number of advertisements placed (20X0 = 100)	90	96	100	115	128	140	160
Volumes of sales (20X0 = 100)	96	98★	100	118	133★★	145	161

★ $100 \times 347/355$
★★ $100 \times 472/355$

3.9 The two sets of relatives are now much easier to compare. They show that volume of sales is increasing at a slightly faster rate, in general, than the number of advertisements placed.

Time series deflation

3.10 The real value of a commodity can only be measured in terms of some 'indicator' such as the rate of inflation (normally represented by the Retail Prices Index) or the Index of Output of Production Industries. For example the cost of a commodity may have been £10 in 20X0 and £11 in 20X1, representing an increase of 10%. However, if we are told the prices in general (as measured by the RPI) increased by 12% between 20X0 and 20X1, we can argue that the real cost of the commodity has decreased.

EXAMPLE: DEFLATION

Mack Johnson works for Pound of Flesh Ltd. Over the last five years he has received an annual salary increase of £500. Despite his employer assuring him that £500 is a reasonable annual salary increase, Mack is unhappy because, although he agrees £500 is a lot of money, he finds it difficult to maintain the standard of living he had when he first joined the company.

Consider the figures below.

	(a)	(b)	(c)	(d)
Year	Wages £	RPI	Real wages £	Real wages index
1	12,000	250	12,000	100.0
2	12,500	260	12,019	100.2
3	13,000	275	11,818	98.5
4	13,500	295	11,441	95.3
5	14,000	315	11,111	92.6

(a) This column shows Mack's wages over the five-year period.

(b) This column shows the current RPI.

(c) This column shows what Mack's wages are worth taking prices, as represented by the RPI, into account. The wages have been deflated relative to the new base period (year 1). Economists call these deflated wage figures real wages. The real wages for years 2 and 4, for example, are calculated as follows.

Year 2: £12,500 × 250/260 = £12,019
Year 4: £13,500 × 250/295 = £11,441

(d) This column is calculated by dividing the entries in column (c) by £12,000

$$\text{Real index} = \frac{\text{current value}}{\text{base value}} \times \frac{\text{base indicator}}{\text{current indicator}}$$

So, for example, the real wage index in year $4 = 100 \times \frac{13,500}{12,000} \times \frac{250}{295} = 95.3$

The real wages index shows that the real value of Mack's wages has fallen by 7.4% over the five-year period. In real terms he is now earning £11,111 compared to £12,000 in year 1. He is probably justified, therefore, in being unhappy.

Activity 2

The mean weekly take-home pay of the employees of Staples Ltd and a price index for the 11 years from 20X0 to 20Y0 are as follows.

Year	Weekly wage £	Price index (20X0 = 100)
20X0	150	100
20X1	161	103
20X2	168	106
20X3	179	108
20X4	185	109
20X5	191	112
20X6	197	114
20X7	203	116
20X8	207	118
20X9	213	121
20Y0	231	123

Required

Construct a time series of real wages for 20X0 to 20Y0 using a price index with 20X6 as the base year.

---

4 COMPOSITE INDEX NUMBERS

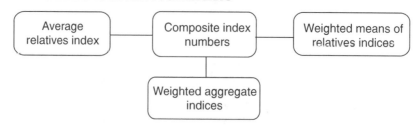

4.1 Most practical indices cover more than one item and are hence termed composite index numbers. The RPI, for example, considers components such as food, alcoholic drink, tobacco and housing. An index of motor car costs might consider components such as finance payments, service costs, repairs, insurance and so on.

4.2 Suppose that the cost of living index is calculated from only three commodities: bread, tea and caviare, and that the prices for 20X1 and 20X2 were as follows.

	20X1	*20X2*
Bread	20p a loaf	40p a loaf
Tea	25p a packet	30p a packet
Caviare	450p a jar	405p a jar

4.3 A simple index could be calculated by adding the prices for single items in 20X2 and dividing by the corresponding sum relating to 20X1 (if 20X1 is the base year). In general, if the sum of the prices in the base year is ΣP_0 and the sum of the prices in the new year is ΣP_1, the index is

$$100 \times \frac{\Sigma P_1}{\Sigma P_0}$$

The index, known as a *simple aggregate price index*, would therefore be calculated as follows.

	P_0 *20X1* £	P_1 *20X2* £
Bread	0.20	0.40
Tea	0.25	0.30
Caviare	4.50	4.05
	$\Sigma P_0 = 4.95$	$\Sigma P_1 = 4.75$

Year	$\Sigma P_1/\Sigma P_0$	*Simple aggregate price index*
20X1	4.95/4.95 = 1.00	100
20X2	4.75/4.95 = 0.96	96

4.4 This type of index has a number of disadvantages. It ignores the amounts of bread, tea and caviare consumed (and hence the importance of each item), and the units to which the prices refer. If, for example, we had been given the price of a cup of tea rather than a packet of tea, the index would have been different.

Average relatives indices

4.5 To overcome the problem of different units we consider the changes in prices as ratios rather than absolutes so that all price movements, whatever their absolute values, are treated as equally important.

4.6 Price changes are considered as ratios rather than absolutes by using the *average price relatives index* which is calculated as

$$100 \times \frac{1}{n} \times \Sigma(P_1/P_0)$$

where n is the number of goods. Here, the price relative P_1/P_0 (so called because it gives the new price level of each item relative to the base year price) for a particular commodity will have the same value whatever the unit for which the price is quoted.

4.7 Using the information in Paragraph 4.2, we can construct the average price relatives index as follows.

Commodity	P_0	P_1	P_1/P_0
	£	£	
Bread	0.20	0.40	2.00
Tea	0.25	0.30	1.20
Caviare	4.50	4.05	0.90
			4.10

Year	$\frac{1}{n}\Sigma(P_1/P_0)$	Average price relatives index
20X1	$1/3 \times 3.00 = 1.00$	100
20X2	$1/3 \times 4.10 = 1.37$	137

4.8   There has therefore been an average price increase of 37% between 20X1 and 20X2.

4.9   We could, of course, construct an average quantity relatives index if we had been given information on quantities purchased per time period.

4.10   However, no account has been taken of the relative importance of each item, in this index. Bread is probably more important than caviare. To overcome both the problem of quantities in different units and the need to attach importance to each item, we can use weightings which reflect the importance of each item. To decide the weightings of different items in an index, it is necessary to obtain information, perhaps by market research, about the relative importance of each item. Thus, in our example of a simple cost of living index, it would be necessary to find out how much the average person or household spends each week on each item to determine weightings.

4.11   There are two types of index which give different weights to different items, weighted means of relatives indices and weighted aggregate indices.

Weighted means of relatives indices

4.12   This method of weighting involves calculating index relatives for each of the components and using the weights given to obtain a weighted average of the relatives.

4.13   The general form of a weighted means of relatives index number is

$$\frac{\Sigma wI}{\Sigma w}$$

where   w is the weighting factor
and   I is the index relative.

4.14   Values (price × quantity) relating to some point in time are usually used as weights.

4.15   Note that the weights may be from a year other than the base year. This is the method used for the index of wholesale prices. We could, for example, produce a weighted means of relatives index using 20X4 as base year, 20X6 as the given year and 20X5 values as weights.

4.16   Weighted means of relatives are very important in practice, and the great majority of indices published in the UK are of this type.

EXAMPLE: WEIGHTED MEANS OF RELATIVES INDICES

Use both the information in Paragraph 4.2 and the following details about quantities purchased by each household in a week in 20X1 to determine a weighted means of price relatives index number for 20X2 using 20X1 as the base year.

	Quantity
Bread	6
Tea	2
Caviare	0.067

SOLUTION

Price relatives (I)	Bread	40/20 =	2.00
	Tea	30/25 =	1.20
	Caviare	405/450 =	0.90
Weightings (w)	Bread	$6 \times 0.20 =$	1.20
	Tea	$2 \times 0.25 =$	0.50
	Caviare	$0.067 \times 4.50 =$	0.30
	$\Sigma w =$		2.00
Index	Bread	$2 \times 1.2 =$	2.40
	Tea	$1.2 \times 0.5 =$	0.60
	Caviare	$0.9 \times 0.3 =$	0.27
	$\Sigma wI =$		3.27

$$\text{Index number} = 100 \times \frac{3.27}{2} = 163.5$$

Weighted aggregate indices

4.17 This method of weighting involves multiplying each component value by its corresponding weight and adding these products to form an aggregate. This is done for both the base period and the period in question. The aggregate for the period under consideration is then divided by the base period aggregate.

4.18 The general form of a weighted aggregate index is

$$\frac{\Sigma wv_n}{\Sigma wv_0}$$

where   w is the weighting factor
v_0 is the value of the commodity in the base period
v_n is the value of the commodity in the period in question

4.19 Price indices are usually weighted by quantities and quantity indices are usually weighted by prices.

> ### Activity 3
>
> What are the formulae for calculating price and quantity weighted aggregate indices if base year weights are used?

EXAMPLE: A PRICE INDEX

In the previous example of the cost of living index, the 20X2 index value could have been calculated as follows.

Item	Quantity	Price in 20X1			Price in 20X2	
	Q_0	P_0	P_0Q_0		P_1	P_1Q_0
Bread	6.000	20	120		40	240
Tea	2.000	25	50		30	60
Caviare	0.067	450	30		405	27
			200			327

$$\text{Index in 20X2} = 100 \times \frac{327}{200} = 163.5$$

EXAMPLE: A QUANTITY INDEX

The Falldown Construction Company uses four items of materials and components in a standard production job.

In 20X0 the quantities of each material or component used per job and their cost were as follows.

	Quantity Units	Price per unit £
Material A	20	2
Material B	5	10
Component C	40	3
Component D	15	6

In 20X2 the quantities of materials and components used per job were as follows.

	Quantity Units
Material A	15
Material B	6
Component C	36
Component D	25

Using 20X0 as a base year, calculate the quantity index value in 20X2 for the amount of materials used in a standard job.

SOLUTION

	Price in 20X0	Quantity used in 20X0		Quantity used in 20X2	
	P_0	Q_0	P_0Q_0	Q_1	P_0Q_1
Material A	£2	20	40	15	30
Material B	£10	5	50	6	60
Component C	£3	40	120	36	108
Component D	£6	15	90	25	150
			300		348

$$\text{Quantity index} = 100 \times \frac{348}{300} = 116$$

This would suggest that the company is using 16% more materials in 20X2 than in 20X0 on a standard job.

5   LASPEYRE AND PAASCHE INDICES

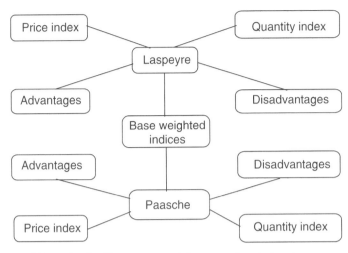

5.1   Laspeyre and Paasche indices are special cases of weighted aggregate indices.

Definition

> *Laspeyre indices* use weights from the base period and are therefore sometimes called *base weighted indices*.

Laspeyre price index

5.2   A Laspeyre price index uses quantities consumed in the base period as weights. In the notation already used it can be expressed as follows.

$$\text{Laspeyre price index} = 100 \times \frac{\Sigma Q_0 P_1}{\Sigma Q_0 P_0}$$

Laspeyre quantity index

5.3   A Laspeyre quantity index uses prices from the base period as weights and can be expressed as follows.

$$\text{Laspeyre quantity index} = 100 \times \frac{\Sigma Q_1 P_0}{\Sigma Q_0 P_0}$$

Definition

> *Paasche indices* use current time period weights. In other words the weights are changed every time period.

Paasche price index

5.4 A Paasche price index uses quantities consumed in the current period as weights and can be expressed as follows.

$$\text{Paasche price index} = 100 \times \frac{\Sigma Q_1 P_1}{\Sigma Q_1 P_0}$$

Paasche quantity index

5.5 A Paasche quantity index uses prices from the current period as weights and can be expressed as follows.

$$\text{Paasche quantity index} = 100 \times \frac{\Sigma Q_1 P_1}{\Sigma Q_0 P_1}$$

EXAMPLE: LASPEYRE AND PAASCHE PRICE INDICES

The wholesale price index in Ruritania is made up from the prices of five items. The price of each item, and the average quantities purchased by manufacturing and other companies each week were as follows, in 20X0 and 20X2.

Item	Quantity 20X0 '000 units	Price per unit 20X0 Roubles	Quantity 20X2 '000 units	Price per unit 20X2 Roubles
P	60	3	80	4
Q	30	6	40	5
R	40	5	20	8
S	100	2	150	2
T	20	7	10	10

Required

Calculate the price index in 20X2, if 20X0 is taken as the base year, using the following.

(a) A Laspeyre index
(b) A Paasche index

SOLUTION

Workings

Item	Q_0	P_0	Q_1	P_1	Laspeyre Q_0P_0	Q_0P_1	Paasche Q_1P_1	Q_1P_0
P	60	3	80	4	180	240	320	240
Q	30	6	40	5	180	150	200	240
R	40	5	20	8	200	320	160	100
S	100	2	150	2	200	200	300	300
T	20	7	10	10	140	200	100	70
					900	1,110	1,080	950

20X2 index numbers are as follows.

(a) Laspeyre index $= 100 \times \dfrac{1{,}110}{900} = 123.3$

(b) Paasche index $= 100 \times \dfrac{1{,}080}{950} = 113.7$

The Paasche index for 20X2 reflects the decline in consumption of the relatively expensive items R and T since 20X0. The Laspeyre index for 20X2 fails to reflect this change.

Activity 4

A baker has listed the ingredients he used and their prices, in 20X3 and 20X4, as follows.

	Kg used 20X3 '000s	Price per kg 20X3 £	Kg used 20X4 '000s	Price per kg 20X3 £
Milk	3	1.20	4	1.50
Eggs	6	0.95	5	0.98
Flour	1	1.40	2	1.30
Sugar	4	1.10	3	1.14

Required

Calculate the following quantity indices for 20X4 (with 20X3 as the base year).

(a)   A Laspeyre index
(b)   A Paasche index

Which to use – Paasche or Laspeyre ?

5.6   Patterns of consumption and prices both change and a decision therefore has to be made as to whether a Paasche or a Laspeyre index should be used.

5.7   The following points should be considered when deciding which type of index to use.

(a)   A Paasche index requires quantities to be ascertained each year. A Laspeyre index only requires them for the base year. Constructing a Paasche index may therefore cost more.

(b)   For the Paasche index the denominator has to be recalculated each year because the quantities/prices must be changed to current year consumption/price levels.

For the Laspeyre index, the denominator is fixed. The Laspeyre index can therefore be calculated as soon as current prices/quantities are known. The Paasche index, on the other hand, cannot be calculated until the end of a period, when information about current quantities/prices becomes available.

(c)   The denominator of a Laspeyre index is fixed and therefore the Laspeyre index numbers for several different years can be directly compared. With the Paasche index, on the other hand, comparisons can only be drawn directly between the current year and the base year (although indirect comparisons can be made).

(d)   The weights for a Laspeyre index become out of date, whereas those for the Paasche index are updated each year.

(e)   A Laspeyre price index implicitly assumes that, whatever the price changes, the quantities purchased will remain the same. In terms of economic theory, no substitution of cheaper alternative goods and services is allowed to take place. Even if goods become relatively more expensive, it assumes that the same quantities are bought. As a result, the index tends to overstate inflation.

(f) The effect of current year weighting when using the Paasche price index means that greater importance is placed on goods that are relatively cheaper now than they were in the base year. As a consequence, the Paasche price index tends to understate inflation.

In practice, it is common to use a Laspeyre index and revise the weights every few years. (Where appropriate, a new base year may be created when the weights are changed.)

6 PRACTICAL ISSUES

What items to include

6.1 The purpose to which the index is to be put must be carefully considered. Once this has been done, the items selected must be as representative as possible, taking into account this purpose. Care must be taken to ensure that the items are unambiguously defined and that their values are readily ascertainable.

6.2 For some indices, the choice of items might be relatively straightforward. For example, the FT Actuaries All-Share Index, compiled jointly by the *Financial Times*, the Institute of Actuaries and the Faculty of Actuaries, is made up of the share prices of approximately 800 companies quoted on the Stock Exchange. The weights are based on the market capitalisations of the companies (the number of shares in issue multiplied by their market value).

6.3 For other indices, the choice of items will be more difficult. The Retail Prices Index provides an excellent example of the problem. It would be impossible to include all items of domestic spending and a selective, representative basket of goods and services must be found, ranging from spending on mortgages and rents, to cars, public transport, food and drink, electricity, gas, telephone, clothing, leisure activities and so on.

Collecting the data

6.4 Data are required to determine the following.

(a) The values for each item
(b) The weight that will be attached to each item

Consider as an example a cost of living index. The prices of a particular commodity will vary from place to place, from shop to shop and from type to type. Also the price will vary during the period under consideration. The actual prices used must obviously be some sort of average. The way in which the average is to be obtained should be clearly defined at the outset.

6.5 When constructing a price index, it is common practice to use the quantities consumed as weights; similarly, when constructing a quantity index, the prices may be used as weights. Care must be taken in selecting the basis for the weighting. For example, in a cost of living index, it may be decided to use the consumption of a typical family as the weights, but it may prove difficult to define a typical family.

The choice of a base year

6.6 The choice of a base date, or base year is not significant, except that it should be representative. In the construction of a price index, the base year must not be one in which there were abnormally high or low prices for any items in the basket of goods making up the index. For example, a year in which there is a potato famine would be unsuitable as a base period for the Retail Prices Index.

The limitations and misinterpretation of index numbers

Limitations

6.7 Index numbers are usually only approximations of changes in price or quantity over time, and must be interpreted with care.

(a) As we have seen, weightings become out of date over time. Unless a Paasche index is used, the weightings will gradually cease to reflect current reality.

(b) New products or items may appear, and old ones may cease to be significant. Such changes can make an index out of date.

(c) The data used to calculate index numbers might be incomplete, out of date, or inaccurate. For example, the quantity indices of imports and exports are based on records supplied by traders which may be prone to error or even deliberate falsification.

(d) The base year of an index should be a normal year, but there is probably no such thing as a perfectly normal year. Some error in the index will be caused by atypical values in the base period.

(e) The 'basket of items' in an index is necessarily selective. For example, the Retail Prices Index (RPI) is constructed from a sample of households and from a basket of around 600 items.

(f) A national index may not be very relevant to an individual town or region. For example, if the national index of wages and salaries rises from 100 to 115, we cannot conclude that the wages and salaries of people in, say, Glasgow have gone up by 15%.

(g) An index may exclude important items: for example, the RPI excludes payments of income tax out of gross wages.

Misinterpretation

6.8 You must be careful not to misinterpret index numbers. Several possible mistakes will be explained, using the following example of a retail prices index.

20X0		*20X1*		*20X2*	
January	340.0	January	360.6	January	436.3
		February	362.5	February	437.1
		March	366.2	March	439.5
		April	370.0	April	442.1

(a) It would be wrong to say that prices rose by 2.6% between March and April 20X2. It is correct to say that prices rose 2.6 points, or

$$100\% \times \frac{2.6}{439.5} = 0.6\%$$

(b) It would be correct to say that the annual rate of price increases (the rate of inflation) fell between March and April 20X2. It would be a mistake, however, to suppose that a fall in the rate of inflation means that prices are falling, therefore the price index is falling.

The rate of price increases has slowed down, but the trend of prices is still upwards.

(i)   The annual rate of inflation from March 20X1 to March 20X2 is

$$100\% \times \left(\frac{439.5 - 366.2}{366.2} \right) = 20\%$$

(ii)   The annual rate of inflation from April 20X1 to April 20X2 is

$$100\% \times \left(\frac{442.1 - 370.0}{370.0} \right) = 19.5\%$$

Thus the annual rate of inflation has dropped from 20% to 19.5% between March and April 20X2, even though prices went up in the month between March and April 20X2 by 0.6%. (The price increase between March and April 20X1 was over 1%. This is included in the calculation of the rate of inflation between March 20X1 and March 20X2, but is excluded in the comparison between April 20X1 and April 20X2 where it has been replaced by the lower price increase, 0.6%, between March and April 20X2.)

7   THE RETAIL PRICES INDEX FOR THE UNITED KINGDOM (RPI)

7.1   We will conclude our study of index numbers by looking at the construction of the UK Retail Prices Index (RPI).

7.2   On one particular day of each month, data are collected about prices of the following groups of items.

Food
Alcohol
Tobacco
Housing
Fuel and light
Household goods
Clothing and footwear
Motoring expenditure
Leisure services
Household services
Leisure goods
Catering
Personal goods and services
Fares and other travel

7.3   Each group is sub-divided into sections: for example 'food' will be subdivided into bread, butter, potatoes and so on. These sections may in turn be subdivided into more specific items. The groups do not cover every item of expenditure (for example they exclude income tax, pension fund contributions and football pools).

7.4   The weightings given to each group, section and subsection are based on information provided by the *Family Expenditure Survey* which is based on a survey of over 10,000 households, spread evenly over the year.

Each member of the selected households (aged 16 or over) is asked to keep a detailed record of their expenditure over a period of 14 days, and to provide information about longer-term payments (such as insurance premiums). Information is also obtained about their income.

7.5   The weightings used in the construction of the RPI are revised every year, using information in the *Family Expenditure Survey* of the previous year. As well as annual changes to the weights, the items included in the index are changed to reflect changing spending habits. For example, CDs and CD players were added in 1987; in 1994 the shampoo and set was replaced by highlights; in 1996, Doc Marten style boots and charges for aerobics classes were added.

In the last chapter we saw how data can be presented in a variety of formats. In this chapter we have looked at the calculation of index numbers in order to analyse data more fully. In the next chapter we shall look at ways of obtaining further information from data by applying some sort of numerical analysis – we shall be looking at measures of centrality (averages) and measures of dispersion (or spread).

Chapter roundup

- An index is a measure, over time, of the average changes in the value (price or quantity) of a group of items relative to the situation at some period in the past.

- An index relative is an index number which measures the change in a single distinct commodity.

- Index relatives can be calculated using the fixed base method or the chain base method.

- In order to compare two time series of relatives, each series should have the same base period and hence one (or both) may need rebasing.

- The real value of a commodity can only be measured in terms of some 'indicator' (such as the RPI).

- Time series deflation is a technique used to obtain a set of index relatives that measure the changes in the real value of some commodity with respect to some given indicator.

- Composite indices cover more than one item.

- Weighting is used to reflect the importance of each item in the index.

- Weighted means of relatives indices are found by calculating indices and then applying weights.

- Weighted aggregate indices are found by applying weights and then calculating the index.

- There are two types of weighted aggregate index, the Laspeyre (which uses quantities/prices from the base period as the weights) and the Paasche (which uses quantities/prices from the current period as weights).

- Index numbers are a very useful way of summarising a large amount of data in a single series of numbers. You should remember, however, that any summary hides some detail and that index numbers should therefore be interpreted with caution.

Quick quiz

1   How are index relatives calculated using the chain base method?

2   How is a time series of relatives rebased?

3   Why must the real value of a commodity be measured in terms of some indicator?

4   What is the general form of

    (a)   a weighted means of relatives index?
    (b)   a weighted aggregate index?

5   What do Laspeyre indices use as weights?

6   What are the limitations of index numbers?

7   Give some examples of how index numbers might be misinterpreted.

Answers to activities

1

	1990	1991	1992	1993	1994	1995
Index (1993 = 100)	92*	94	96	100**	102***	103

   * $100 \times 451/490$
  ** $100 \times 490/490$
 *** $100 \times 499/490$

2   The index number for each year with 20X6 as the base year will be the original index number divided by 1.14, and the real wages for each year will be (100 × money wages)/index number for the year.

Year	Index	Real wage £
20X0	88	170
20X1	90	179
20X2	93	181
20X3	95	188
20X4	96	193
20X5	98	195
20X6	100	197
20X7	102	199
20X8	104	199
20X9	106	201
20Y0	108	214

3   Price index: $100 \times \dfrac{\Sigma Q_0 P_1}{\Sigma Q_0 P_0}$

    where P_0 represents the prices of items in the base year
              P_1 represents the prices of items in the new year
              Q_0 represents the quantities of the items consumed in the base year

    Quantity index: $100 \times \dfrac{\Sigma Q_1 P_0}{\Sigma Q_0 P_0}$

    where Q_0 represents the quantities consumed in the base year
              Q_1 represents the quantities consumed in the new year
              P_0 represents the prices in the base year

4   *Workings*

	Q_0	P_0	Q_1	P_1	Laspeyre		Paasche	
					$Q_0 P_0$	$Q_1 P_0$	$Q_1 P_1$	$Q_0 P_1$
Milk	3	1.20	4	1.50	3.60	4.80	6.00	4.50
Eggs	6	0.95	5	0.98	5.70	4.75	4.90	5.88
Flour	1	1.40	2	1.30	1.40	2.80	2.60	1.30
Sugar	4	1.10	3	1.14	4.40	3.30	3.42	4.56
					15.10	15.65	16.92	16.24

Quantity index numbers for 20X4 are as follows.

(a)   Laspeyre method $= \quad 100 \times \dfrac{15.65}{15.10} = 103.64$

(b)   Paasche method $= \quad 100 \times \dfrac{16.92}{16.24} = 104.19$

Assignment 4   **(45 minutes)**

The data below refer to Average Earnings Index numbers in the UK for different sectors of industry, 1988 = 100, and the Retail Prices Index, 1987 = 100.

Date	Whole economy	Production industries	Service industries	Retail Prices Index
1988	100.0	100.0	100.0	107.0
1989				
Feb	104.6	104.9	104.4	111.5
May	107.5	108.1	107.2	115.0
Aug	109.1	109.2	108.7	115.8
Nov	112.8	112.9	112.7	118.5
1990				
Feb	114.0	114.3	113.7	120.2
May	118.5	118.2	118.6	126.2
Aug	120.9	119.7	121.1	128.1
Nov	123.8	123.7	123.0	130.0
1991				
Feb	124.7	125.2	123.8	130.9
May	128.1	129.2	127.1	133.5
Aug	130.8	130.2	130.4	134.1
Nov	130.8	131.8	129.7	135.6

(Source: *Employment Gazette*, January 1992)

Required

(a)   Using 1988 = 100 as base throughout, deflate the Production Industries Index and comment briefly on the real (inflation-adjusted) change in its average earnings over the period 1989/91.

(b)   A retired person from the Service Industries had an index-linked pension of £5,000 a year, starting in May 1989 and updated each November in line with the average earnings index for that sector. Find the pension rates for November in each of the years 1989, 1990, 1991 and comment on their value in real terms.

Chapter 5 :
AVERAGES AND DISPERSION

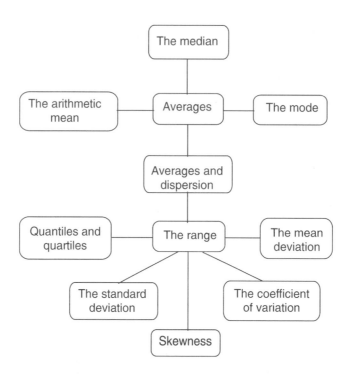

Introduction

In Chapter 3 we saw how data can be summarised and presented in tabular, chart and graphical formats. Such formats provide an overview of a situation and show the key features of the data. For example, a bar chart might show that very few people in Ruritania earn less than 100 Ruritanian dollars a month and that very few earn more than 700 Ruritanian dollars a month, the majority earning somewhere between the two extremes. Sometimes you might need more information than diagrammatic representations of data can provide, however. In such circumstances you may need to apply some sort of numerical analysis. A teacher in Ruritania, for example, might want some means of comparing her salary with those of other teachers.

There are two initial measures that we can take from a set of data to help in such a situation: a measure of centrality (an average) and a measure of dispersion (or spread).

An average is a representative figure that is used to give some impression of the size of all the items in the population. The average salary earned in Ruritania will therefore be representative of all salaries in Ruritania. You may have thought that an average is simply 'an average' but there are in fact three main types of average: the mean; the mode; the median.

In the first part of this chapter we will therefore be looking at each of these averages in turn, their calculation, advantages and disadvantages.

Averages are a method of determining the 'location' or central point of a distribution, but they give no information about the dispersion of values in the distribution. Although the mean, modal and median monthly salaries in North Ruritania might be identical to those in South Ruritania, monthly salaries in North Ruritania might vary between 100 and 1,000 Ruritanian dollars whereas those in South Ruritania might vary between 400 and 700 Ruritanian dollars. The spread or dispersion of the distribution of the salaries are therefore different and measures of dispersion, the topic of the second part of the chapter, would provide the teacher we mentioned above with additional means of comparing her salary with those other teachers.

Your objectives

After completing this chapter you should:

(a)   understand the difference between the arithmetic mean, mode and median of a set of data and be aware of their advantages and disadvantages;

(b)   be able to calculate the arithmetic mean, mode and median of both ungrouped and grouped data;

(c)   understand and be able to calculate the range, quartiles, mean deviation, standard deviation and coefficient of variation of a set of data;

(d)   be aware of the concept of the skewness of a distribution.

1   THE ARITHMETIC MEAN

Definition

> The *arithmetic mean* is calculated from the sum of values of items divided by the number of items. The arithmetic mean of a variable x is shown as $\bar{x}$ ('x bar').

1.1   The arithmetic mean is the best known type of average. For ungrouped data, it is calculated by the formula

$$\text{Arithmetic mean} = \frac{\text{Sum of values of items}}{\text{Number of items}}$$

For example, the mean wage of a work force of ten men is the amount each worker would receive if all their earnings were pooled and then shared out equally among them.

EXAMPLE: THE ARITHMETIC MEAN

The demand for a product on each of 20 days was as follows (in units).

3 12 7 17 3 14 9 6 11 10 1 4 19 7 15 6 9 12 12 8

The arithmetic mean of daily demand is

$$\frac{\text{Sum of demand}}{\text{Number of days}} = \frac{185}{20} = 9.25 \text{ units}$$

1.2   The arithmetic mean of a variable x is shown as $\bar{x}$ ('x bar').

Thus in the above example $\bar{x} = 9.25$ units.

1.3 In the above example, demand on any one day is never actually 9.25 units. The arithmetic mean is merely an average representation of demand on each of the 20 days.

Finding the arithmetic mean of data in a frequency distribution

1.4 It is more likely in an exam that you will be asked to calculate the arithmetic mean of a frequency distribution. In our previous example, the frequency distribution would be shown as follows.

Daily demand	Frequency	Demand ×frequency
x	f	fx
1	1	1
3	2	6
4	1	4
6	2	12
7	2	14
8	1	8
9	2	18
10	1	10
11	1	11
12	3	36
14	1	14
15	1	15
17	1	17
19	1	19
	20	185

$$\overline{x} = \frac{185}{20} = 9.25$$

The summation sign, sigma(Σ)

1.5 The statistical notation for the arithmetic mean of a set of data uses the symbol Σ (sigma). Σ means 'the sum of' and is used as shorthand to mean 'the sum of a set of values'.

Thus, in the previous example:

(a) Σf would mean the sum of all the frequencies, which is 20;

(b) Σfx would mean the sum of all the values of 'frequency multiplied by daily demand', that is, all 14 values of fx, so $\Sigma fx = 185$.

The symbolic formula for the arithmetic mean of a frequency distribution

1.6 Using the Σ sign, the formula for the arithmetic mean of a frequency distribution is

$$\overline{x} = \frac{\Sigma fx}{n} \text{ or } \frac{\Sigma fx}{\Sigma f}$$

where n is the number of values recorded, or the number of items measured.

Finding the arithmetic mean of grouped data in class intervals

1.7 You might also be asked to calculate (or at least approximate) the arithmetic mean of a frequency distribution, where the frequencies are shown in class intervals.

BPP PUBLISHING

1.8 Using the example in Paragraph 1.4, the frequency distribution might have been shown as follows.

Daily demand	Frequency
$> 0 \leq 5$	4
$> 5 \leq 10$	8
$>10 \leq 15$	6
$>15 \leq 20$	2
	20

1.9 There is, of course, an extra difficulty with finding the average now; as the data have been collected into classes, a certain amount of detail has been lost and the values of the variables to be used in the calculation of the mean are not clearly specified.

1.10 To calculate the arithmetic mean of grouped data we therefore need to decide on a value which best represents all of the values in a particular class interval.

The mid-point of each class interval is conventionally taken, on the assumption that the frequencies occur evenly over the class interval range. In the example above, the variable is discrete, so the first class includes 1, 2, 3, 4 and 5, giving a mid-point of 3. With a continuous variable (such as quantities of fuel consumed in litres), the mid-points would have been 2.5, 7.5 and so on. Once the value of x has been decided, the mean is calculated in exactly the same way as in Paragraph 1.6.

EXAMPLE: THE ARITHMETIC MEAN OF GROUPED DATA

Daily demand	Mid point x	Frequency f	fx
$>0 \leq 5$	3	4	12
$>5 \leq 10$	8	8	64
$>10 \leq 15$	13	6	78
$>15 \leq 20$	18	2	36
		$\Sigma f = 20$	$\Sigma fx = 190$

$$\text{Arithmetic mean } \overline{x} = \frac{\Sigma fx}{\Sigma f} = \frac{190}{20} = 9.5 \text{ units}$$

Because the assumption that frequencies occur evenly within each class interval is not quite correct in this example, our approximate mean of 9.5 is not exactly correct, and is in error by 0.25.

As the frequencies become larger, the size of this approximating error should become smaller.

Finding the arithmetic mean of combined data

1.11 Suppose that the mean age of a group of five people is 27 and the mean age of another group of eight people is 32. How would we find the mean age of the whole group of 13 people?

1.12 Remember that the arithmetic mean is calculated as

$$\frac{\text{Sum of values of items}}{\text{Number of items}}$$

The sum of the ages in the first group is $5 \times 27 \qquad = 135$

The sum of the ages in the second group is 8×32 = 256
The sum of all 13 ages is 135 + 256   = 391

Activity 1

The mean weight of 10 units at 5 kg, 10 units at 7 kg and 20 units at X kg is 8 kg. What is the value of X?

The mean age is therefore $\dfrac{391}{13} = 30.07$ years.

The advantages and disadvantages of the arithmetic mean

1.13   The advantages of the arithmetic mean are as follows.

(a)   It is easy to calculate.

(b)   It is widely understood.

(c)   The value of every item is included in the computation of the mean and so it can be determined with arithmetical precision and is representative of the whole set of data.

(d)   It is supported by mathematical theory and is suited to further statistical analysis.

1.14   The disadvantages of the arithmetic mean are as follows.

(a)   Its value may not correspond to any actual value. For example, the 'average' family might have 2.3 children, but no family can have exactly 2.3 children.

(b)   An arithmetic mean might be distorted by extremely high or low values. For example, the mean of 3, 4, 4 and 6 is 4.25, but the mean of 3, 4, 4, 6 and 15 is 6.4. The high value, 15, distorts the average and in some circumstances the mean would be a misleading and inappropriate figure. (Note that extreme values are not uncommon in economic data.)

Activity 2

For the week ended 15 November, the wages earned by the 69 operators employed in the machine shop of Mermaid Ltd were as follows.

Wages	Number of Operatives
≤ £60	3
>£60 ≤ £70	11
>£70 ≤ £80	16
>£80 ≤ £90	15
>£90 ≤ £100	10
>£100 ≤ £110	8
>£110	6
	69

Required

Calculate the arithmetic mean wage of the machine operators of Mermaid Ltd for the week ended 15 November.

2   THE MODE

2.1   The second type of average is the mode or modal value.

Definition

The *mode* is an average which indicates the most frequently occurring value.

EXAMPLE: THE MODE

The daily demand for stock in a ten-day period is as follows.

Demand Units	Number of days
6	3
7	6
8	$\frac{1}{10}$

The mode is 7 units, because it is the value which occurs most frequently.

Finding the mode of a grouped frequency distribution

2.2   The mode of a grouped frequency distribution can be calculated from a histogram.

EXAMPLE: FINDING THE MODE FROM A HISTOGRAM

Consider the following grouped frequency distribution.

Value At least	Value Less than	Frequency
0	10	0
10	20	50
20	30	150
30	40	100

The modal class (the one with the highest frequency) is 'at least 20, less than 30'. But how can we find a single value to represent the mode?

What we need to do is draw a histogram of the frequency distribution.

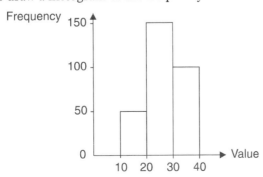

The modal class is always the class with the tallest bar, which may not be the class with the highest frequency if the classes do not all have the same width.

We can estimate the mode graphically as follows.

(a) Join with a straight line the top left-hand corner of the bar for the modal class and the top left-hand corner of the next bar to the right.

(b) Join with a straight line the top right-hand corner of the bar for the modal class and the top right-hand corner of the next bar to the left.

Where these two lines intersect, we find the estimated modal value. In this example it is approximately 27.

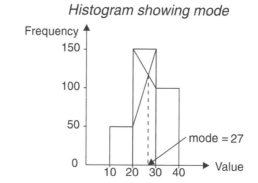

Histogram showing mode

2.3 We are assuming that the frequencies occur evenly within each class interval but this may not always be correct. It is unlikely that the 150 values in the modal class occur evenly. Hence the mode in a grouped frequency distribution is only an estimate.

The advantages and disadvantages of the mode

2.4 The mode is a more appropriate average to use than the mean in situations where it is useful to know the most common value. For example, if a manufacturer wishes to start production in a new industry, it might be helpful to him to know what sort of product made by that industry is most in demand with customers.

2.5 The advantages of the mode are as follows.

(a) It is easy to find.

(b) It is not influenced by a few extreme values.

(c) It can be used for data which are not even numerical (unlike the mean and median).

(d) It can be the value of an actual item in the distribution.

2.6 The mode does have a number of disadvantages.

(a) It may be unrepresentative; it takes no account of a high proportion of the data, only representing the most common value.

(b) It does not take every value into account

(c) There can be two or more modes within a set of data.

(d) If the modal class is only very slightly bigger than another class, just a few more items in this other class could mean a substantially different result, suggesting some instability in the measure.

3 THE MEDIAN

3.1 The third type of average is the median.

Definition

> The *median* is the value of the middle member of a distribution once all of the items have been arranged in order of magnitude.

3.2 The median of a set of ungrouped data is found by arranging the items in ascending or descending order of value, and selecting the item in the middle of the range. A list of items in order of value is called an array.

EXAMPLE: THE MEDIAN

The median of the following nine values:

8	6	9	12	15	6	3	20	11

is found by taking the middle item (the fifth one) in the array:

3	6	6	8	9	11	12	15	20

The median is 9.

The middle item of an odd number of items is calculated as the $\dfrac{(n+1)^{\text{th}}}{2}$ item.

Consider the following array.

1	2	2	2	3	5	6	7	8	11

The median is 4 because, with an even number of items, we have to take the arithmetic mean of the two middle ones (in this example, (3 + 5)/2 = 4). When there are many items, however, it is not worth doing this.

Activity 3

The following times taken to produce a batch of 100 units of Product X have been noted.

21 min 17 min 24 min 11 min 37 min 27 min
20 min 15 min 17 min 23 min 29 min 30 min
24 min 18 min 17 min 21 min 24 min 20 min

What is the median time?

Finding the median of an ungrouped frequency distribution

3.3   The median of an ungrouped frequency distribution is found in a similar way. Consider the following distribution.

Value x	Frequency f	Cumulative frequency
8	3	3
12	7	10
16	12	22
17	8	30
19	5	35
	35	

The median would be the $(35 + 1)/2 = 18$th item. The 18th item has a value of 16, as we can see from the cumulative frequencies in the right hand column of the above table.

Finding the median of a grouped frequency distribution

3.4   We can establish the median of a grouped frequency distribution from an ogive.

EXAMPLE: THE MEDIAN FROM AN OGIVE

Construct an ogive of the following frequency distribution and hence establish the median.

Class	Frequency	Cumulative frequency
£		
≥ 340 < 370	17	17
≥ 370 < 400	9	26
≥ 400 < 430	9	35
≥ 430 < 460	3	38
≥ 460 < 490	2	40
	40	

SOLUTION

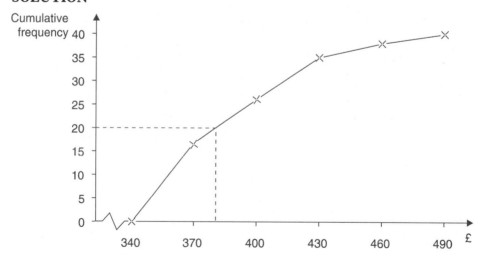

The median is at the $\frac{1}{2} \times 40 = 20$th item. Reading off from the horizontal axis on the ogive, the value of the median is approximately £380.

Note that because we are assuming that the values are spread evenly within each class, the median calculated is only approximate.

The advantages and disadvantages of the median

3.5   The median is only of interest where there is a range of values and the middle item is of some significance. Perhaps the most suitable application of the median is in comparing changes in a 'middle of the road' value over time.

3.6   The median is easy to understand and (like the mode) is unaffected by extremely high or low values. It can be the value of an actual item in the distribution. On the other hand, it fails to reflect the full range of values, it is unsuitable for further statistical analysis and arranging the data in order of size can be tedious.

4   THE RANGE

Definition

> The *range* is the difference between the highest observation and the lowest observation.

4.1   The main properties of the range as a measure of dispersion are as follows.

   (a)   It is easy to find and to understand.
   (b)   It is easily affected by one or two extreme values.
   (c)   It gives no indication of spread between the extremes.
   (d)   It is not suitable for further statistical analysis.

Activity 4

Calculate the mean and the range of each of the following sets of data.

(a) x_1 =   4   8   7   3   5   16   24   5

(b) x_2 =   10   7   9   11   11   8   9   7

What do your calculations show about the dispersion of the data sets?

5 QUARTILES AND QUANTILES

Quartiles

5.1 Quartiles are one means of identifying the range within which most of the values in the population occur. The lower quartile is the value below which 25% of the population fall and the upper quartile is the value above which 25% of the population fall. If there were 11 data items the lower quartile would be the third item and the upper quartile the ninth item. It follows that 50% of the total population fall between the lower and the upper quartiles. The quartiles and the median divide the population into four groups of equal size.

Deciles and percentiles

5.2 In a similar way, a population could be divided into ten equal groups, and this time the value of each dividing point is referred to as a *decile*.

When a population is divided into 100 parts, the value of each dividing point is referred to as a *percentile*. For example, in a population of 200 values, the percentiles would be the second, fourth, sixth, eighth and so on, up to the 198th item, in rising order of values.

Quantiles

Definition

> Quartiles, deciles and percentiles, and any other similar dividing points for analysing a frequency distribution, are referred to collectively as *quantiles*.

5.3 The purpose of quantiles is to analyse the dispersion of data values.

All quantiles can be found easily from an ogive.

The inter-quartile range

5.4 The lower and upper quartiles can be used to calculate a measure of dispersion called the inter-quartile range.

Definition

> The *inter-quartile range* is the difference between the values of the upper and lower quartiles and hence shows the range of values of the middle half of the population.

The smaller the inter-quartile range, the less dispersed the population. Because values at the ends of the distribution are not taken into account, the inter-quartile range is not affected by extreme values.

5.5 For example, if the lower and upper quartiles of a frequency distribution were 6 and 11, the inter-quartile range would be 11 − 6 = 5. This shows that the range of values of the middle half of the population is 5 units.

EXAMPLE: QUARTILES

The hours of overtime worked in a particular quarter by the 60 employees of ABC Ltd are shown below. The company has decided to give a bonus of £15 to the 10% of the workforce who worked the most overtime, a bonus of £5 to the 20% of the workforce who worked the least overtime and a £10 bonus to all other employees.

	Hours	
More than	*Not more than*	*Frequency*
0	10	3
10	20	6
20	30	11
30	40	15
40	50	12
50	60	7
60	70	6
		60

Required

Calculate the range of overtime hours worked by those employees receiving a £10 bonus.

SOLUTION

Hours	*Cumulative frequency*
$> 0 \le 10$	3
$>10 \le 20$	9
$>20 \le 30$	20
$>30 \le 40$	35
$>40 \le 50$	47
$>50 \le 60$	54
$>60 \le 70$	60

The 9th decile is at $60 - (10\% \text{ of } 60) = 54$

The 2nd decile is at 20% of 60 $= 12$

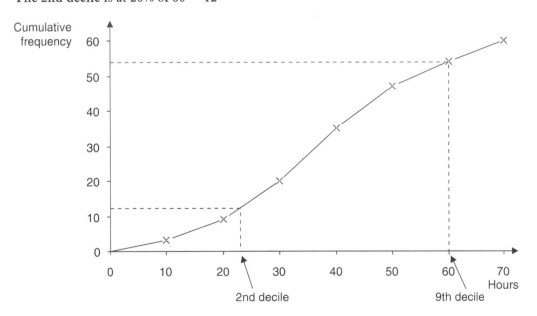

From the ogive the range of hours is approximately 23 to 60.

Activity 5

Find the values of the upper and lower quartiles of the frequency distribution detailed in the example following Paragraph 3.4 of this chapter.

6 THE MEAN DEVIATION

6.1 Because it only uses the middle 50% of the population, the inter-quartile range is a useful measure of dispersion if there are extreme values in the distribution. If there are no extreme values which could potentially distort a measure of dispersion, however, it seems unreasonable to exclude 50% of the data. The mean deviation, which we will look at in this section, and the standard deviation (the topic of Section 7) are therefore often more useful measures.

Definition

The *mean deviation* is a measure of the average amount by which the values in a distribution differ from the arithmetic mean.

6.2 Mean deviation $= \dfrac{\sum f|x - \bar{x}|}{n}$

6.3 (a) $|x - \bar{x}|$ is the difference between each value (x) in the distribution and the arithmetic mean $\bar{x}$ of the distribution. When calculating the mean deviation for grouped data the deviations should be measured to the midpoint of each class: that is, x is the midpoint of the class interval. The vertical bars mean that all differences are taken as positive since the total of all of the differences, if this is not done, will always equal zero. Thus if x = 3 and $\bar{x}$ = 5, then $x - \bar{x} = -2$ but $|x - \bar{x}| = 2$.

(b) $f|x - \bar{x}|$ is the value in (a) above, multiplied by the frequency for the class.

(c) $\sum f|x - \bar{x}|$ is the sum of the results of all the calculations in (b) above.

(d) n (which equals $\sum f$) is the number of items in the distribution.

EXAMPLE: THE MEAN DEVIATION

Calculate the mean deviation of the frequency distribution in the example following paragraph 5.5.

SOLUTION

Midpoint x	f	fx	$\|x - \bar{x}\|$	$f\|x - \bar{x}\|$
5	3	15	32	96
15	6	90	22	132
25	11	275	12	132
35	15	525	2	30
45	12	540	8	96
55	7	385	18	126
65	6	390	28	168
	$\Sigma f = 60$	$\Sigma fx = 2,220$		780

$$\bar{x} = \frac{\Sigma fx}{\Sigma f} = \frac{2,220}{60} = 37$$

$$\text{Mean deviation} = \frac{780}{60} = 13 \text{ hours}$$

Thus the mean is 37 hours and the mean deviation is 13 hours.

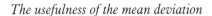

Activity 6

Calculate the mean deviation of the following frequency distribution.

Value	Frequency of occurrence
5	4
15	6
25	8
35	20
45	6
55	6
	50

The usefulness of the mean deviation

6.4 The mean deviation is a measure of dispersion which shows by how much, on average, each item in the distribution differs in value from the arithmetic mean of the distribution.

Unlike quartiles, it uses all values in the distribution to measure the dispersion, but it is not greatly affected by a few extreme values because an average is taken.

The mean deviation is not, however, suitable for further statistical analysis.

7 THE STANDARD DEVIATION

Definitions

> The *variance* is the average of the squared mean deviation for each value in a distribution.
>
> The *standard deviation* is the square root of the variance.

7.1 Instead of taking the absolute value of the difference between the value and the mean to avoid the total of the differences summing to zero as we did with the mean deviation, we can square the differences. If we do this, we get the most important measure of dispersion in statistics, the standard deviation. It is denoted by σ, the lower case Greek letter sigma.

7.2 Difference between value and mean $\qquad x - \overline{x}$

Square of the difference $\qquad (x - \overline{x})^2$

Sum of the squares of the difference $\qquad \Sigma(x - \overline{x})^2$

Average of the sum (= variance = σ^2) $\qquad \dfrac{\Sigma(x - \overline{x})^2}{n}$

7.3 The units of the variance are the square of those in the original data because we squared the differences. We therefore need to take the square root to get back to the units of the original data.

Square root of the variance = standard deviation = $\sqrt{\dfrac{\Sigma(x - \overline{x})^2}{n}}$

The same process can be applied to determine the standard deviation of data in a frequency distribution.

Square of the difference between value and mean $\qquad (x - \overline{x})^2$

Sum of the squares of the difference $\qquad \Sigma f(x - \overline{x})^2$

Average of the sum (= variance) $\qquad \dfrac{\Sigma f(x - \overline{x})^2}{\Sigma f}$

Square root = standard deviation = $\sqrt{\dfrac{\Sigma f(x - \overline{x})^2}{\Sigma f}}$

This formula can prove time consuming to use. An alternative formula for the standard deviation is shown as follows.

Standard deviation = $\sqrt{\dfrac{\Sigma fx^2}{\Sigma f} - \overline{x}^2}$

Note that these formulae are appropriate if all the details are known of the whole population.

EXAMPLE: THE VARIANCE AND THE STANDARD DEVIATION

Calculate the variance and the standard deviation of the frequency distribution in the example following paragraph 5.5.

SOLUTION

Using the alternative formula for the standard deviation, the calculation is as follows.

Midpoint			
x	*f*	*x²*	*fx²*
5	3	25	75
15	6	225	1,350
25	11	625	6,875
35	15	1,225	18,375
45	12	2,025	24,300
55	7	3,025	21,175
65	6	4,225	25,350
	60		97,500

Mean = (from the example following paragraph 6.3) = 37

$$\text{Variance} = \frac{\Sigma fx^2}{\Sigma f} - \bar{x}^2 = \frac{97,500}{60} - (37)^2 = 256 \text{ hours}$$

Standard deviation = $\sqrt{256}$ = 16 hours

Activity 7

Calculate the variance and the standard deviation of the frequency distribution in Activity 6.

The main properties of the standard deviation

7.4 The standard deviation's main properties are as follows.

(a) It is based on all the values in the distribution and so is more comprehensive than dispersion measures based on quantiles, such as the quartile deviation.

(b) It is suitable for further statistical analysis.

(c) It is more difficult to understand than some other measures of dispersion.

The importance of the standard deviation lies in its suitability for further statistical analysis.

8   THE COEFFICIENT OF VARIATION

Definition

> The *coefficient of variation* compares the dispersion of two distributions.

8.1   It is sometimes useful to be able to compare the spreads of two distributions.

This comparison can be done using the coefficient of variation.

$$\text{Coefficient of variation} = \frac{\text{Standard deviation}}{\text{mean}}$$

The coefficient of variation is sometimes known as the coefficient of relative dispersion.

8.2   The bigger the coefficient of variation, the wider the dispersion. For example, suppose that two sets of data, A and B, have the following means and standard deviations.

	A	B
Mean	120	125
Standard deviation	50	51
Coefficient of variation	0.417	0.408

Although B has a higher standard deviation in absolute terms (51 compared to 50) its relative dispersion is a bit less than A's since the coefficient of variation is a bit smaller.

Activity 8

Calculate the coefficient of variation of the distribution in Activities 6 and 7.

9   SKEWNESS

Definition

> *Skewness* is the asymmetry of a frequency distribution curve.

9.1   As well as being able to calculate the average and spread of a frequency distribution, you should be aware of the skewness of a distribution. A frequency distribution must be either symmetrical or asymmetrical; in other words, skewed.

9.2   A symmetrical frequency distribution is one which can be divided into two halves which are mirror images of each other. The arithmetic mean, the median and the mode will all have the same value, M.

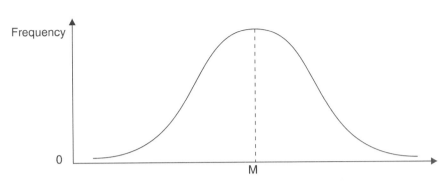

Figure 5.1 Symmetrical frequency distribution

9.3 A positively skewed distribution's graph will lean towards the left hand side, with a tail stretching out to the right. The mean, the median and the mode will have different values.

In a positively skewed distribution, the mode will have a lower value than the median and the mean will have a higher value than the median. The value of the mean is, in fact, higher than a great deal of the distribution.

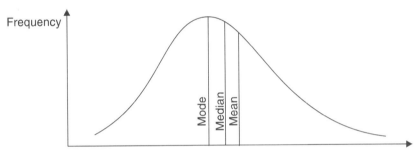

Figure 5.2 Positively skewed distribution graph

9.4 A negatively skewed distribution's graph will lean towards the right-hand side, with a tail stretching out to the left. Once again, the mean, median and mode will have different values.

In a negatively skewed distribution, the mode will have a higher value than the median and the mean will have a lower value than the median. The value of the mean is lower than a great deal of the distribution.

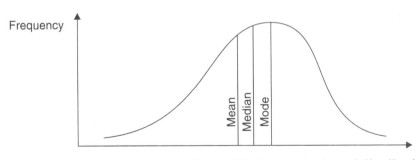

Figure 5.3 Negatively skewed distribution graph

It is a criticism of the mean as an average that for very skewed distributions its value may not be representative of the majority of the items in the distribution since it is affected by extreme values.

NOTES

This chapter has looked at one-variable measures of averages and dispersion from a set of data. The next chapter concentrates on the two-variable equivalents of the contents of this chapter: correlation and regression. Two-variable data are the heights and weights of pupils in a class, for example. The topic of correlation and regression is mainly concerned with identifying how related one variable is to another.

Chapter roundup

- This chapter has looked at the three main types of average and at measures of dispersion.

- The arithmetic mean is the best known type of average and is widely understood. It is used for further statistical analysis.

- The mode is the most frequently occurring value.

- The median is the value of the middle member of an array.

- The arithmetic mean, mode and median of a grouped frequency distribution can only be estimated approximately

- You should now be able to calculate any of the three averages for a basic set of values, an ungrouped frequency distribution and a grouped frequency distribution.

- Measures of dispersion give some idea of the spread of variables about the average.

- The range is the difference between the highest and lowest observations.

- The quartiles and the median divide the population into four groups of equal size.

- Quartiles, deciles and percentiles are referred to collectively as quantiles.

- The inter-quartile range is the difference between the upper and lower quartiles.

- The mean deviation is a measure of the average amount by which the values in a distribution differ from the arithmetic mean.

- The standard deviation, which is the square root of the variance, is the most important measure of dispersion used in statistics. Make sure you understand how to calculate the standard deviation of a set of data.

- The spreads of two distributions can be compared using the coefficient of variation.

- Skewness is the asymmetry of a frequency distribution curve.

Quick quiz

1 State a formula for the arithmetic mean of a frequency distribution.

2 Define the mode.

3 Explain how to estimate the mode from a histogram of a distribution.

4 Define the median.

5 How is the median of a grouped frequency distribution estimated?

6 What are quantiles?

7 When calculating the mean deviation for grouped data, to where should the deviations be measured?

PUBLISHING

8   Why are the differences between the value and the mean squared in the formula for the standard deviation?

9   Give a formula for the variance of data in a frequency distribution.

10   Define the coefficient of variation of a distribution.

11   Distinguish between positive skewness and negative skewness.

Answers to activities

1    $\text{Mean} = \dfrac{\text{Sum of values of items}}{\text{Number of items}}$

Sum of first 10 units = $5 \times 10 = 50$ kg

Sum of second 10 units = $7 \times 10 = 70$ kg

Sum of third 20 units = $20 \times X = 20X$

Sum of all 40 units = $50 + 70 + 20X = 120 + 20X$

$\therefore \text{Arithmetic mean} = 8 = \dfrac{120 + 20X}{40}$

$\therefore$

$$8 \times 40 = 120 + 20X$$

$$320 - 120 = 20X$$

$$10 = X$$

2   The mid-point of the range 'under £60' is assumed to be £55 and that of the range over £110 to be £115, since all other class intervals are £10. This is obviously an approximation which might result in a loss of accuracy; nevertheless, there is no better alternative assumption to use. Because wages can vary in steps of only 1p, they are virtually a continuous variable and hence the mid-points of the classes are halfway between their end points.

Mid-point of class	Frequency	
x	*f*	*fx*
£		
55	3	165
65	11	715
75	16	1,200
85	15	1,275
95	10	950
105	8	840
115	6	690
	69	5,835

$\text{Arithmetic mean} = \dfrac{£5,835}{69} = £84.57$

3   The times can be arranged as follows.

11	15	17	17	17	18	20	20	21
21	23	24	24	24	27	29	30	37

The median = 21 mins. (We could have found the average of the 10th and 11th items if we had wanted to.)

NOTES

4   (a) $\bar{x}_1 = \dfrac{72}{8} = 9$

The figures have a mean of 9 and a range of $24 - 3 = 21$.

(b) $\bar{x}_2 = \dfrac{72}{8} = 9$

The figures have a mean of 9 and a range of $11 - 7 = 4$.

The set of data x_1 is more widely dispersed than the set of data x_2.

5

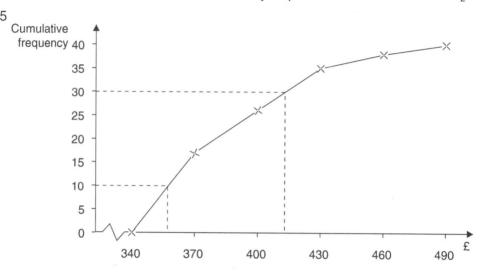

The upper quartile is the $^3/_4 \times 40 = $ 30th value.

The lower quartile is the $^1/_4 \times 40 = $ 10th value.

Reading off from the ogive these values are at approximately £358 and £412 respectively.

6

x	f	fx	$\lvert x - \bar{x} \rvert$	$f\lvert x - \bar{x} \rvert$
5	4	20	27.2	108.8
15	6	90	17.2	103.2
25	8	200	7.2	57.6
35	20	700	2.8	56.0
45	6	270	12.8	76.8
55	6	330	22.8	136.8
	$\overline{50}$	$\overline{1,610}$		$\overline{539.2}$

Arithmetic mean $\bar{x} = \dfrac{1,610}{50} = 32.2$

Mean deviation $= \dfrac{539.2}{50} = 10.784$, say 10.8.

7

x	f	x^2	fx^2
5	4	25	100
15	6	225	1,350
25	8	625	5,000
35	20	1,225	24,500
45	6	2,025	12,150
55	6	3,025	18,150
	$\overline{50}$		$\overline{61,250}$

$\bar{x} = 32.2$ (from Activity 6)

Variance $= \dfrac{61{,}250}{50} - (32.2)^2 = 188.16$

Standard deviation $= \sqrt{188.16} = 13.72$

8   Coefficient of variation $= \dfrac{\text{Standard deviation}}{\text{mean}} = \dfrac{13.72}{32.2} = 0.426$

Assignment 5   **(45 minutes)**

A firm is comparing the age structure of its workforce in the current year with that of five years ago, as shown in the table below.

	5 years ago	*Current year*
Age group (years)	*Number in group*	*Number in group*
25 < 30	2	5
30 < 35	6	10
35 < 40	8	13
40 < 45	13	28
45 < 50	15	21
50 < 55	35	12
55 < 60	12	8
60 < 65	9	3

The mean age and standard deviation of ages five years ago were as follows.

Mean age   49.05 years
Standard deviation   8.45 years

Required

(a)   Calculate the mean age and the associated standard deviation for the current year.

(b)   Compare the results in (a) with the calculations for five years ago, saying why you think the means and standard deviations may have changed.

   Note. You are not expected to conduct statistical tests.

(c)   Draw a bar chart that will illustrate the changes in the age structure of the workforce over the five-year period.

Chapter 6 :
CORRELATION AND REGRESSION

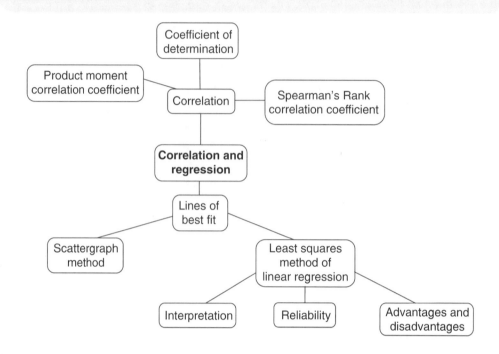

Introduction

We are now going to turn our attention to the statistical analysis of two-variable data (sales over time, advertising expenditure and sales revenue, output and costs and so on). Measures of correlation and regression can be thought of as the two-variable equivalents of the one-variable measures of location and dispersion: regression locates two-variable data in terms of a mathematical relationship which can be graphed as a curve or a line and correlation describes the nature of the spread of the items about the curve or line. The overall basic aim of correlation and regression is to ascertain the extent to which one variable is related to another.

Your objectives

After completing this chapter you should:

    (a)   understand the concept of correlation;

    (b)   be aware of the difference between partial and perfect correlation and positive and negative correlation;

    (c)   be able to calculate and interpret the correlation coefficient;

    (d)   be able to calculate and interpret the coefficient of determination;

    (e)   be able to calculate and interpret Spearman's rank correlation coefficient and know when to use it;

    (f)   be able to construct a scattergraph and insert a line of best fit;

    (g)   be able to estimate a line of best fit using linear regression analysis;

(h)   understand the meaning of 'least squares';

(i)   be able to interpret regression coefficients;

(j)   be aware of the degree of reliance that can be placed on estimates.

1   CORRELATION

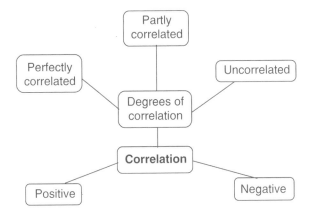

Definition

Correlation means an inter-relationship or correspondence.

1.1   When the value of one variable is related to the value of another, they are said to be correlated.

1.2   Examples of variables which might be correlated are as follows.

    (a)   A person's height and weight
    (b)   The distance of a journey and the time it takes to make it

1.3   One way of showing the correlation between two related variables is on a scattergraph or scatter diagram, plotting a number of pairs of data on the graph.

1.4   For example, a scattergraph showing monthly selling costs against the volume of sales for a 12-month period might be as follows.

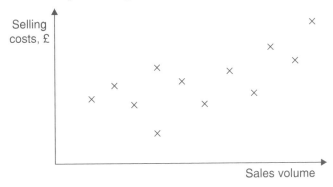

Figure 6.1 A scattergraph

This scattergraph suggests that there is some correlation between selling costs and sales volume, so that as sales volume rises, selling costs tend to rise as well.

Degrees of correlation

1.5   Two variables can be one of the following.

    (a)   Perfectly correlated

    (b)   Partly correlated

    (c)   Uncorrelated

These differing degrees of correlation can be illustrated by scatter diagrams.

1.6   *Perfect correlation*

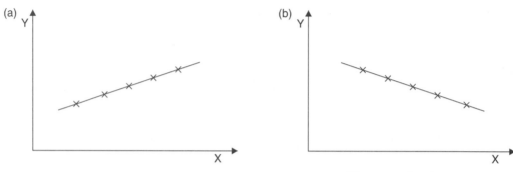

Figure 6.2 Perfect correlation

All the pairs of values lie on a straight line. An exact linear relationship exists between the two variables.

1.7   *Partial correlation*

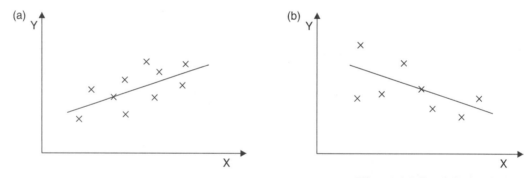

Figure 6.3 Partial correlation

In (a), although there is no exact relationship, low values of X tend to be associated with low values of Y, and high values of X with high values of Y.

In (b), again there is no exact relationship, but low values of X tend to be associated with high values of Y and vice versa.

1.8 *No correlation*

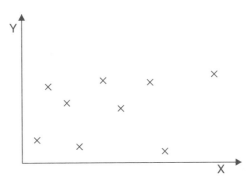

Figure 6.4 No correlation

The values of these two variables are not correlated with each other.

Positive and negative correlation

1.9   Correlation, whether perfect or partial, can be positive or negative.

Definitions

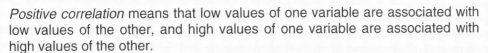

Positive correlation means that low values of one variable are associated with low values of the other, and high values of one variable are associated with high values of the other.

Negative correlation means that low values of one variable are associated with high values of the other, and high values of one variable with low values of the other.

Activity 1

Which of the diagrams in Paragraphs 1.6 and 1.7 demonstrate negative correlation?

2   THE PRODUCT MOMENT CORRELATION COEFFICIENT AND THE COEFFICIENT OF DETERMINATION

The correlation coefficient

2.1   The degree of correlation between two variables can be measured, and we can decide, using actual results in the form of pairs of data, whether two variables are perfectly or partially correlated, and if they are partially correlated, whether there is a high or low degree of partial correlation.

2.2   This degree of correlation is measured by the product moment correlation coefficient (the coefficient of correlation), r (also called the Pearsonian correlation coefficient).

Definition

> The *coefficient of correlation/product moment correlation coefficient/ Pearsonian correlation coefficient* measures the degree of correlation between two variables.

There are several formulae for the correlation coefficient, although each formula will give the same value. These include the following.

2.3 Correlation coefficient, $r = \dfrac{n\Sigma xy - \Sigma x\Sigma y}{\sqrt{[n\Sigma x^2 - (\Sigma x)^2][n\Sigma y^2 - (\Sigma y)^2]}}$

where x and y represent pairs of data for two variables x and y, and n is the number of pairs of data used in the analysis.

This is the formula which will be used in subsequent examples.

2.4 r must always fall between –1 and +1. If you get a value outside this range you have made a mistake.

$r = +1$ means that the variables are *perfectly positively correlated*
$r = -1$ means that the variables are *perfectly negatively correlated*
$r = 0$ means that the variables are *uncorrelated*

EXAMPLE: THE CORRELATION COEFFICENT

The cost of output at a factory is thought to depend on the number of units produced. Data have been collected for the number of units produced each month in the last six months, and the associated costs, as follows.

Month	Output '000s of units x	Cost £'000 y
1	2	9
2	3	11
3	1	7
4	4	13
5	3	11
6	5	15

Required

Assess whether there is there any correlation between output and cost.

SOLUTION

$r = \dfrac{n\Sigma xy - \Sigma x\Sigma y}{\sqrt{[n\Sigma x^2 - (\Sigma x)^2][n\Sigma y^2 - (\Sigma y)^2]}}$

We need to find the values for the following.

(a) Σxy Multiply each value of x by its corresponding y value, so that there are six values for xy. Add up the six values to get the total.

(b) Σx Add up the six values of x to get a total. $(\Sigma x)^2$ will be the square of this total.

(c) Σy Add up the six values of y to get a total. $(\Sigma y)^2$ will be the square of this total.

(d) Σx^2 Find the square of each value of x, so that there are six values for x^2. Add up these values to get a total.

(e) Σy^2 Find the square of each value of y, so that there are six values for y^2. Add up these values to get a total.

Workings

x	y	xy	x^2	y^2
2	9	18	4	81
3	11	33	9	121
1	7	7	1	49
4	13	52	16	169
3	11	33	9	121
5	15	75	25	225
Σx = 18	Σy = 66	Σxy = 218	Σx^2 = 64	Σy^2 = 766

$(\Sigma x)^2 = 18^2 = 324$ $(\Sigma y)^2 = 66^2 = 4{,}356$

n   = 6

$$r = \frac{(6 \times 218) - (18 \times 66)}{\sqrt{(6 \times 64 - 324) \times (6 \times 766 - 4{,}356)}}$$

$$= \frac{1{,}308 - 1{,}188}{\sqrt{(384 - 324) \times (4{,}596 - 4{,}356)}}$$

$$= \frac{120}{\sqrt{60 \times 240}} = \frac{120}{\sqrt{14{,}400}} = \frac{120}{120} = 1$$

There is perfect positive correlation between the volume of output at the factory and costs.

Correlation in a time series

2.5 Correlation exists in a time series if there is a relationship between the period of time and the recorded value for that period of time. The correlation coefficient is calculated with time as the x variable although it is convenient to use simplified values for x instead of year numbers.

For example, instead of having a series of years 1987 to 1991, we could have values for x from 0 (1987) to 4 (1991).

Note that whatever starting value you use for x (be it 0, 1, 2, ..., 721, ..., 953), the value of r will always be the same.

Activity 2

Sales of product A between 20X7 and 20Y1 were as follows.

Year	Units sold ('000s)
20X7	20
20X8	18
20X9	15
20Y0	14
20Y1	11

Required

Determine whether there is a trend in sales. In other words, decide whether there is any correlation between the year and the number of units sold.

The coefficient of determination, r^2

2.6 Unless the correlation coefficient r is exactly or very nearly +1, −1 or 0, its meaning or significance is a little unclear. For example, if the correlation coefficient for two variables is +0.8, this would tell us that the variables are positively correlated, but the correlation is not perfect. It would not really tell us much else. A more meaningful analysis is available from the square of the correlation coefficient, r^2, which is called the coefficient of determination.

Definition

The *coefficient of determination*, r^2 (alternatively R^2), measures the proportion of the total variation in the value of one variable that can be explained by variations in the value of the other variable.

2.7 In the activity above, r = −0.992, therefore r^2 = 0.984. This means that over 98% of variations in sales can be explained by the passage of time, leaving 0.016 (less than 2%) of variations to be explained by other factors.

2.8 Similarly, if the correlation coefficient between a company's output volume and maintenance costs was 0.9, r^2 would be 0.81, meaning that 81% of variations in maintenance costs could be explained by variations in output volume, leaving only 19% of variations to be explained by other factors (such as the age of the equipment).

2.9 Note, however, that if r^2 = 0.81, we would say that 81% of the variations in y can be explained by variations in x. We do not necessarily conclude that 81% of variations in y are caused by the variations in x. We must beware of reading too much significance into our statistical analysis.

Non-linear relationships

2.10 The formulae used above for r and r^2 only work for linear or near linear relationships. All the points on a scatter diagram might lie on a smooth curve as follows.

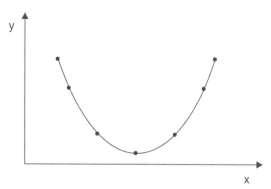

Figure 6.5 Non-linear relationship

If the formula for r were used in a situation such as this, a low value of r would be obtained, suggesting that very little correlation exists, whereas in fact the two sets of variables are perfectly correlated by a non-linear relationship. There are methods of testing correlations of this type, but they are outside the scope of this Course Book.

Correlation and causation

2.11 If two variables are well correlated, either positively or negatively, this may be due to pure chance or there may be a reason for it. The larger the number of pairs of data collected, the less likely it is that the correlation is due to chance, though that possibility should never be ignored entirely.

2.12 If there is a reason, it may not be causal. For example, monthly net income is well correlated with monthly credit to a person's bank account, for the logical (rather than causal) reason that for most people the one equals the other.

2.13 Even if there is a causal explanation for a correlation, it does not follow that variations in the value of one variable cause variations in the value of the other. For example, sales of ice cream and of sunglasses are well correlated, not because of a direct causal link but because the weather influences both variables.

2.14 Having said this, it is of course possible that where two variables are correlated, there is a direct causal link to be found.

3 SPEARMAN'S RANK CORRELATION COEFFICIENT

3.1 In the examples considered above, the data were given in terms of the values of the relevant variables, such as the number of units. Sometimes however, they are given in terms of order or rank rather than actual values. When this occurs, a correlation coefficient known as *Spearman's rank correlation coefficient*, *R*, should be calculated using the following formula.

Spearman's rank correlation coefficient, $R = 1 - \left[\dfrac{6\Sigma d^2}{n(n^2 - 1)} \right]$

where n = number of pairs of data
d = the difference between the rankings in each set of data.

Definition

Spearman's rank correlation coefficient, R, is used to measure the correlation between the order or rank of two variables.

The coefficient of rank correlation can be interpreted in exactly the same way as the ordinary correlation coefficient. Its value can range from –1 to +1.

EXAMPLE: THE RANK CORRELATION COEFFICIENT

The examination placings of seven students were as follows.

Student	Statistics placing	Economics placing
A	2	1
B	1	3
C	4	7
D	6	5
E	5	6
F	3	2
G	7	4

Required

Judge whether the placings of the students in statistics correlate with their placings in economics.

SOLUTION

Correlation must be measured by Spearman's coefficient because we are given the placings of students, and not their actual marks.

$$R = 1 - \left[\frac{6\Sigma d^2}{n(n^2 - 1)} \right]$$

where d is the difference between the rank in statistics and the rank in economics for each student.

Student	Rank statistics	Rank economics	d	d²
A	2	1	1	1
B	1	3	2	4
C	4	7	3	9
D	6	5	1	1
E	5	6	1	1
F	3	2	1	1
G	7	4	3	9
				$\Sigma d^2 = 26$

$$R = 1 - \frac{6 \times 26}{7 \times (49 - 1)} = 1 - \frac{156}{336} = 0.536$$

The correlation is positive, 0.536, but the correlation is not strong.

Tied ranks

3.2 If in a problem some of the items tie for a particular ranking, these must be given an average place before the coefficient of rank correlation is calculated. Here is an example.

Position of students in examination   *Express as*

A	1 =	} average of 1 and 2	1.5
B	1 =		1.5
C	3		3
D	4		4
E	5 =	} average of 5, 6 and 7	6
F	5 =		6
G	5 =		6
H	8		8

Activity 3

Five artists were placed in order of merit by two different judges as follows.

Artist	Judge P Rank	Judge Q Rank
A	1	4 =
B	2 =	1
C	4	3
D	5	2
E	2 =	4 =

Required

Assess how the two sets of rankings are correlated.

---

4 LINES OF BEST FIT

4.1 The correlation coefficient measures the degree of correlation between two variables, but it does not tell us how to predict values for one variable (y) given values for the other variable (x). To do that, we need to find a line which is a good fit for the points on a scattergraph, and then use that line to find the value of y corresponding to each given value of x.

4.2 We will be looking at two ways of doing this, the scattergraph method and linear regression using the least squares method.

5 THE SCATTERGRAPH METHOD

Definition

The *scattergraph method* is to plot pairs of data for two related variables on a graph, to produce a scattergraph, and then to *use judgement* to draw what seems to be a line of best fit through the data.

5.1 For example, suppose we have the following pairs of data about sales revenue and advertising expenditure.

Period	Advertising expenditure £	Sales revenue £
1	17,000	180,000
2	33,000	270,000
3	34,000	320,000
4	42,000	350,000
5	19,000	240,000
6	41,000	300,000
7	26,000	320,000
8	27,000	230,000

These pairs of data would be plotted on a scattergraph (the horizontal axis representing the independent variable and the vertical axis the dependent) and a line of best fit might be judged as the one shown below. It was drawn to pass through the middle of the data points, thereby having as many data points below the line as above it.

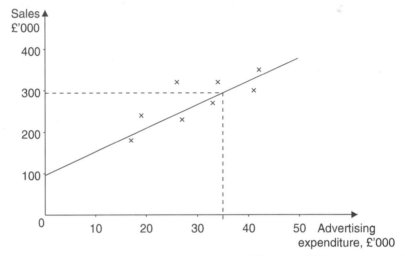

Figure 6.6 The scattergraph method

5.2 Suppose the company to which these data relate wants a forecast sales figure, given a marketing decision to spend £35,000 on advertising. An estimate of sales can be read directly from the scattergraph as shown (£290,000).

6   LINEAR REGRESSION USING THE LEAST SQUARES METHOD

Definition

The *least squares method of linear regression analysis* provides a technique for estimating the equation of a line of best fit.

6.1 The equation of a straight line has the form y = a + bx

where   x and y are related variables
         x is the independent variable
         y is the dependent variable
         a is the intercept of the line on the vertical axis
    and   b is the gradient of the line.

6.2 The least squares method provides estimates for the values of a and b using the following formulae.

$$b = \frac{n\Sigma xy - \Sigma x\Sigma y}{n\Sigma x^2 - (\Sigma x)^2}$$

$$a = \frac{\Sigma y}{n} - \frac{b\Sigma x}{n}$$

where n is the number of pairs of data.

6.3 There are some points to note about these formulae.

(a) The line of best fit that is derived represents the *regression of y upon x*.

A different line of best fit could be obtained by interchanging x and y in the formulae. This would then represent the *regression of x upon y* (x = a + by) and it would have a slightly different slope. For examination purposes, always use the regression of y upon x, where x is the independent variable, and y is the dependent variable whose value we wish to forecast for given values of x. In a time series, x will represent time.

(b) Since $a = \frac{\Sigma y}{n} - \frac{b\Sigma x}{n}$, it follows that the line of best fit must *always* pass

through the point $\frac{\Sigma y}{n}, \frac{\Sigma x}{n}$.

(c) If you look at the formula for b and compare it with the formula we gave for the correlation coefficient (Paragraph 2.3) you should see some similarities between the two formulae.

EXAMPLE: THE LEAST SQUARES METHOD

You are given the following data for output at a factory and costs of production over the past five months.

Month	Output x '000 units	Costs y £'000
1	20	82
2	16	70
3	24	90
4	22	85
5	18	73

There is a high degree of correlation between output and costs, and so it is decided to calculate fixed costs and the variable cost per unit of output using the least squares method.

Required

(a) Calculate an equation to determine the expected level of costs, for any given volume of output.

(b) Prepare a budget for total costs if output is 22,000 units.

(c) Confirm that the degree of correlation between output and costs is high by calculating the correlation coefficient.

SOLUTION

(a)   *Workings*

x	y	xy	x^2	y^2
20	82	1,640	400	6,724
16	70	1,120	256	4,900
24	90	2,160	576	8,100
22	85	1,870	484	7,225
18	73	1,314	324	5,329
$\Sigma x = 100$	$\Sigma y = 400$	$\Sigma xy = 8,104$	$\Sigma x^2 = 2,040$	$\Sigma y^2 = 32,278$

n   = 5 (There are five pairs of data for x and y values)

$$b = \frac{n\Sigma xy - \Sigma x \Sigma y}{n\Sigma x^2 - (\Sigma x)^2}$$

$$= \frac{(5 \times 8,104) - (100 \times 400)}{(5 \times 2,040) - 100^2}$$

$$= \frac{40,520 - 40,000}{10,200 - 10,000} = \frac{520}{200}$$

$$= 2.6$$

$$a = \frac{\Sigma y}{n} - \frac{b \Sigma x}{n}$$

$$= \frac{400}{5} - 2.6 \times \left(\frac{100}{5}\right)$$

$$= 28$$

$$y = 28 + 2.6x$$

where   y = total cost, in thousands of pounds
        x = output, in thousands of units.

(b)   If the output is 22,000 units, we would expect costs to be

$28 + 2.6 \times 22 = 85.2 = £85,200.$

(c) $$r = \frac{520}{\sqrt{200 \times (5 \times 32,278 - 400^2)}}$$

$$= \frac{520}{\sqrt{200 \times 1,390}} = \frac{520}{527.3} = +0.99$$

Activity 4

The expense claims and recorded car mileages on company business, relating to a particular day, of a sample of salesmen of a company are as follows.

Salesman	Mileage	Expenses £
A	100	60
B	80	48
C	20	20
D	120	55
E	70	38
F	50	38
G	80	44
H	40	30
I	50	40
J	60	50

Required

(a) Plot the data on a scatter diagram.

(b) Determine, by the method of least squares, a linear model to predict expenses, mileage having been given.

(c) Plot the model on your scatter diagram.

(d) Three further salesmen submit expense claims with mileages as follows.

Salesman	Mileage	Expenses £
K	110	64
L	30	48
M	160	80

Discuss in each case whether or not the claim is reasonable.

Regression lines and time series

6.4 The same technique can be applied to calculate a regression line (a trend line) for a time series. This is particularly useful for purposes of forecasting. As with correlation, years can be numbered from 0 upwards.

Activity 5

Sales of product B over the seven year period from 20X1 to 20X7 were as follows.

Year	Sales of B '000 units
20X1	22
20X2	25
20X3	24
20X4	26
20X5	29
20X6	28
20X7	30

There is high correlation between time and the volume of sales.

Required

Calculate the trend line of sales, and forecast sales in 20X8 and 20X9.

The meaning of 'least squares'

6.5   The term 'squares' in 'least squares regression analysis' refers to the squares of the differences between actual values of the dependent variable (y) and predicted values given by the regression line of best fit. These differences are referred to as *residuals* or *residual errors*. 'Least squares' means that the line of best fit that is calculated is the one that minimises the sum of the squares of all the residuals. The differences are measured vertically on a graph, not at an angle to take the shortest route to the regression line.

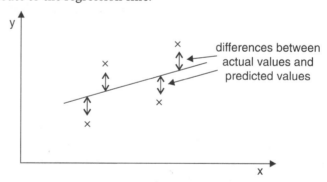

Figure 6.7 Graph showing 'least squares' method

7   INTERPRETATION OF THE REGRESSION COEFFICIENTS

7.1   We said earlier that the least squares method of linear regression analysis provides estimates for a and b and, given values for x and y, you should now be able to determine a and b yourself.

7.2   a and b are known as the coefficients of the regression line y = a + bx but what do they actually mean?

7.3   We explained in Paragraph 6.1 that a is the intercept of the line of best fit on the vertical axis. The scatter diagram from Activity 4 has been reproduced after Paragraph 7.6 but the regression line has been extended so that it meets the y axis. The intercept of this line on the y axis would appear to be approximately 18 or 19;

the value of a was calculated as 18.18 using linear regression analysis. This means that when mileage is zero, expenses are £18.00. In other words, there are other costs, unrelated to the distance travelled, of £18 per day. These might include subsistence costs.

7.4 b is the gradient or slope of the line of best fit. The slope of a line is dependent upon the change in y for an increase in x. In diagram (a) below, an increase in the value of x from 5 to 6 produces an increase in y of 10 from 10 to 20. In diagram b, a similar increase in x produces an increase of 5 in y.

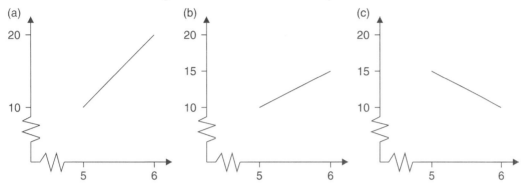

Figure 6.8 Graphs showing different gradients

The gradient of the line in a $= \dfrac{\text{change in y}}{\text{increase in x}} = \dfrac{20-10}{6-5} = \dfrac{10}{1} = 10$

The gradient of the line in b $= \dfrac{\text{change in y}}{\text{increase in x}} = \dfrac{15-10}{6-5} = 5$

The gradient of the line in c $= \dfrac{\text{change in y}}{\text{increase in x}} = \dfrac{10-15}{6-5} = -5$

In (a) and (b), y *increases* as x *increases* and the gradient is *positive*. In (c), however, y *decreases* as x *increases* and hence the gradient is *negative*.

7.5 In numerical terms the gradient gives the rate of change in y for an increase in x.

7.6 In the scatter diagram below the gradient $= \dfrac{\text{change in y}}{\text{increase in x}} = \dfrac{61-18}{120} = 0.36$

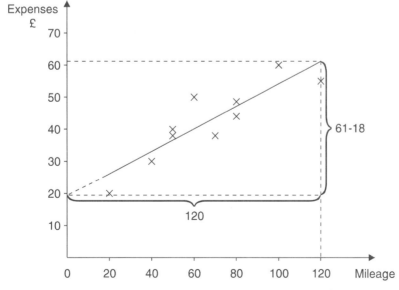

Figure 6.9 Scatter diagram of expenses and mileage

This means that an increase of one mile travelled produces an increase in costs of £0.36. The coefficient 0.36 therefore indicates that there is a variable motoring cost of 36p per mile on average.

Activity 6

Interpret the coefficients of the regression line determined in the example following Paragraph 6.3.

---

8 RELIABILITY OF ESTIMATES

8.1 The coefficient of determination (r^2) which is computed by squaring the correlation coefficient provides an estimate of the variation in y which is due to the regression (ie changes in the other variable). In Activity 5, $r = 0.94$ (working shown below) and so $r^2 = 0.884$. This tells us that 88.4% of the variation in sales can be explained by the variation in time. This would suggest that a fairly large degree of reliance can be placed on the estimate for 20X8 and 20X9.

We do not necessarily conclude that 88.4% of variations in y are caused by variations in time. It might be that high sales happened to coincide with a general economic boom, which was the real cause of increase.

$$r = \frac{(7 \times 587) - (21 \times 184)}{\sqrt{[(7 \times 91) - (21 \times 21)] \times [(7 \times 4,886) - (184 \times 184)]}}$$

$$= \frac{4,109 - 3,864}{\sqrt{(637 - 441) \times (34,202 - 33,856)}}$$

$$= \frac{245}{\sqrt{196 \times 346}} = \frac{245}{260.4}$$

$$= 0.94$$

8.2 If there is a perfect linear relationship between x and y ($r = \pm 1$) then we can predict y from any given value of x with great confidence.

8.3 If correlation is high (for example $r = 0.9$) the actual values will all lie quite close to the regression line and so predictions should not be far out. If correlation is below about 0.7, predictions will only give a very rough guide as to the likely value of y.

8.4 As with any analytical process, the amount of data available is very important. Even if correlation is high, if we have fewer than about 10 pairs of values, we must regard any estimate as being somewhat unreliable.

8.5 When calculating a line of best fit, there will be a range of values for x. In the least squares method example following paragraph 6.3 the line $y = 28 + 2.6x$ was predicted from data with output values ranging from $x = 16$ to $x = 24$. Depending on the degree of correlation between x and y, we might safely use the estimated line of best fit to predict values for y, provided that the value of x remains within the range 16 to 24. We would be on less safe ground if we used the formula to predict a value for y when $x = 10$, or 30, or any other value outside the range 16 – 24, because we would have to assume that the trend line applies outside the range of x values used to establish the line in the first place.

(a) Interpolation means using a line of best fit to predict a value within the two extreme points of the observed range.

(b)   Extrapolation means using a line of best fit to predict a value outside the two extreme points.

9   THE ADVANTAGES AND DISADVANTAGES OF REGRESSION ANALYSIS

9.1   The advantages of the least squares method of regression analysis are as follows.

(a)   It can be used to estimate a line of best fit using all the data available. It is likely to provide a more reliable estimate than any other technique of producing a straight line of best fit (for example, estimating by eye).

(b)   The reliability of the estimated line can be evaluated by calculating the correlation coefficient r.

9.2   The disadvantages of the method are as follows.

(a)   It assumes a linear relationship between the two variables, whereas a non-linear relationship may exist.

(b)   It assumes that what has happened in the past will provide a reliable guide to the future. For example, if a line is calculated for total costs of production, based on historical data, the estimate could be used to budget for future costs. However, if there has been cost inflation, a productivity agreement with the workforce, a move to new premises, the dismissal of large numbers of office staff and the introduction of new equipment, future costs of production might bear no relation to costs in the past.

(c)   The technique assumes that the value of one variable, y, can be predicted or estimated from the value of one other variable, x. In reality, the value of y might depend on several other variables, not just on x.

In this chapter we have looked at how the degree of correlation between two variables can be assessed. In the next chapter we shall be looking at how to use data that has been analysed over time to make forecasts about future values.

Chapter roundup

- When the value of one variable is related to the value of another, they are said to be correlated.

- Two variables might be perfectly correlated, partly correlated or uncorrelated. Correlation can be positive or negative.

- The degree of correlation between two variables is measured by the product moment correlation coefficient, r. The nearer r is to +1 or −1, the stronger the relationship.

- The coefficient of determination, r^2, measures the proportion of the total variation in the value of one variable that can be explained by the variation in the value of the other variable.

- Spearman's rank correlation coefficient is used when data is given in terms of order or rank rather than actual values.

- The scattergraph method involves the use of judgement to draw what seems to be a line of best fit through plotted data.

- Linear regression analysis (the least squares method) is one technique for estimating a line of best fit. Ensure that you know how to use the formulae to calculate a and b in y = a + bx.

- Correlation and regression analysis do not indicate cause and effect. Even if r = 1, the correlation could still be spurious, both variables being influenced by a third.

Quick quiz

1   Give some examples of variables which might be correlated.

2   Distinguish between positive and negative correlation.

3   What range of values can the product moment correlation coefficient take?

4   How should the coefficient of determination be interpreted?

5   When should Spearman's rank correlation coefficient be used?

6   What is the scattergraph method for finding a line of best fit?

7   When using the least squares method of linear regression, does it matter which variable is chosen as x?

8   What is a residual?

9   What are the advantages and disadvantages of the least squares method of linear regression?

Answers to activities

1   Diagrams in Paragraphs 1.6 (b) and 1.7 (b)

2   *Workings*

Let 20X7 to 20Y1 be years 0 to 4.

x	y	xy	x^2	y^2
0	20	0	0	400
1	18	18	1	324
2	15	30	4	225
3	14	42	9	196
4	11	44	16	121
$\Sigma x = 10$	$\Sigma y = 78$	$\Sigma xy = 134$	$\Sigma x^2 = 30$	$\Sigma y^2 = 1{,}266$

$(\Sigma x)^2 = 100$ $(\Sigma y)^2 = 6{,}084$

n   = 5

$$r = \frac{(5 \times 134) - (10 \times 78)}{\sqrt{(5 \times 30 - 100) \times (5 \times 1{,}266 - 6{,}084)}}$$

$$= \frac{670 - 780}{\sqrt{(150 - 100) \times (6{,}330 - 6{,}084)}} = \frac{-110}{\sqrt{50 \times 246}}$$

$$= \frac{-110}{\sqrt{12{,}300}} = \frac{-110}{110.90537} = -0.992$$

There is partial negative correlation between the year of sale and units sold. The value of r is close to −1, therefore a high degree of correlation exists, although it is not quite perfect correlation. This means that there is a clear downward trend in sales.

3

	Judge P Rank	Judge Q Rank	d	d^2
A	1.0	4.5	3.5	12.25
B	2.5	1.0	1.5	2.25
C	4.0	3.0	1.0	1.00
D	5.0	2.0	3.0	9.00
E	2.5	4.5	2.0	4.00
				28.50

$$R = 1 - \frac{6 \times 28.5}{5 \times (25 - 1)} = -0.425$$

There is a slight negative correlation between the rankings.

4 (a)

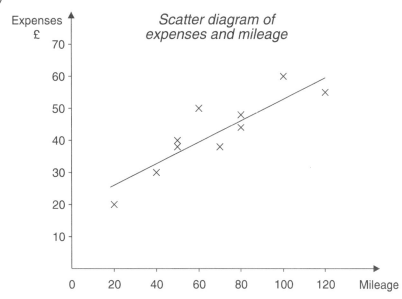

Scatter diagram of expenses and mileage

(b) The independent variable, x, is the mileage. The dependent variable, y, is the expenses in pounds.

x	y	x^2	xy
100	60	10,000	6,000
80	48	6,400	3,840
20	20	400	400
120	55	14,400	6,600
70	38	4,900	2,660
50	38	2,500	1,900
80	44	6,400	3,520
40	30	1,600	1,200
50	40	2,500	2,000
60	50	3,600	3,000
670	423	52,700	31,120

$$b = \frac{(10 \times 31{,}120) - (670 \times 423)}{10 \times 52{,}700 - 670^2}$$

$$= \frac{311{,}200 - 283{,}410}{527{,}000 - 448{,}900}$$

$$= \frac{27{,}790}{78{,}100}$$

$$= 0.36$$

$$a \quad = \frac{423}{10} - 0.36 \times \frac{670}{10} = 18.18$$

The linear model is y = 18.18 + 0.36x.

(c) The line may be plotted using two points as follows.

x = 20, y = 25.38
x = 120, y = 61.38

The line is plotted on the graph above.

(d) For mileage of 110 miles, the model would predict expenses of 18.18 + (0.36 × 110) = £57.78, so K's claim of £64 is not unreasonably high.

For mileage of 30 miles, the model would predict expenses of 18.18 + (0.36 × 30) = £28.98, so L's claim of £48 is very high and should be investigated.

The model is based on data for mileages from 20 to 120 miles. It should not be used to extrapolate to 160 miles, but if it were to be so used it would predict expenses of 18.18 + (0.36 × 160) = £75.78. On this basis, M's claim for £80 is not unreasonable.

5   *Workings*

Year	x	y	xy	x^2
20X1	0	22	0	0
20X2	1	25	25	1
20X3	2	24	48	4
20X4	3	26	78	9
20X5	4	29	116	16
20X6	5	28	140	25
20X7	6	30	180	36
	$\Sigma x = 21$	$\Sigma y = 184$	$\Sigma xy = 587$	$\Sigma x^2 = 91$

n = 7

Where y = a + bx

$$b \quad = \frac{(7 \times 587) - (21 \times 184)}{(7 \times 91) - (21^2)}$$

$$= \frac{245}{196}$$

$$= 1.25$$

$$a = \frac{184}{7} - \frac{1.25 \times 21}{7}$$

$$= 22.5357, \text{ say } 22.5$$

$$y = 22.5 + 1.25x \text{ where } x = 0 \text{ in 20X1, } x = 1 \text{ in 20X2 and so on.}$$

Using this trend line, predicted sales in 20X8 (year 7) would be $22.5 + 1.25 \times 7 = 31.25 = 31,250$ units.

Similarly, for 20X9 (year 8) predicted sales would be $22.5 + 1.25 \times 8 = 32.50 = 32,500$ units.

6 The coefficient a = 28 indicates that when there is no output costs of £28,000 will still be incurred. In other words, fixed costs are £28,000.

The coefficient b = 2.6 indicates as output levels increase by one unit, costs increase by £2.60. The variable cost per unit is therefore £2.60.

Assignment 6 (5 minutes)

A company has a fleet of vehicles and is trying to predict the annual maintenance costs per vehicle. The following data have been supplied for a sample of vehicles.

Vehicle number	Age in years (x)	Maintenance cost per annum £ x 10) (y)
1	2	60
2	8	132
3	6	100
4	8	120
5	10	150
6	4	84
7	4	90
8	2	68
9	6	104
10	10	140

Required

(a) Using the least squares technique, calculate the values of a and b in the equation y = a + bx, to allow managers to predict the likely maintenance cost, knowing the age of the vehicle.

(b) Prepare a table of maintenance costs covering vehicles from 1 to 10 years of age, based on your calculations in (a).

(c) Estimate the maintenance costs of a 12-year-old vehicle and comment on the validity of making such an estimate.

Chapter 7 :
TIME SERIES ANALYSIS

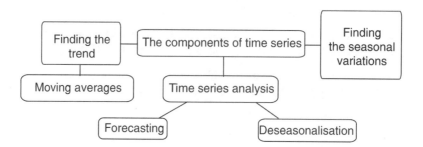

Introduction

In Chapter 6 we looked at how the relationship between two variables, and the strength of that relationship, can be assessed. This chapter looks at how the relationship between a variable (such as turnover, customer levels, output) and time can be analysed so as to forecast future values for the variable.

Your objectives

After completing this chapter you should:

(a)   know what a time series is;

(b)   know what a historigram is;

(c)   be able to describe the components of a time series;

(d)   be able to find the trend using moving averages;

(e)   be able to find seasonal variations using both the additive and multiplicative models;

(f)   be able to forecast by extrapolating a trend and adjusting for seasonal variations;

(g)   understand the concept of residuals;

(h)   be aware of the concept of deseasonalisation.

1 THE COMPONENTS OF TIME SERIES

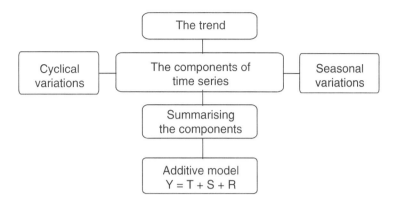

Definition

> A *time series* is a series of figures or values recorded over time.

1.1 The following are examples of time series.

(a) Output at a factory each day for the last month

(b) Monthly sales over the last two years

(c) Total annual costs for the last 10 years

(d) The Retail Prices Index each month for the last 10 years

(e) The number of people employed by a company each year for the last 20 years

Definition

> A graph of a time series is called a *historigram*. (Note the 'ri'; this is not the same as a histogram.)

1.2 Consider the following time series.

Year	Sales £'000
20X0	20
20X1	21
20X2	24
20X3	23
20X4	27
20X5	30
20X6	28

The historigram is as follows.

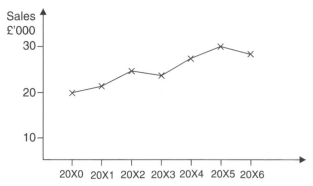

Figure 7.1 An historigram

The horizontal axis is always chosen to represent time, and the vertical axis represents the values of the data recorded.

1.3   There are several features of a time series which it may be necessary to identify.

(a)   A trend

(b)   Seasonal variations or fluctuations

(c)   Cycles, or cyclical variations

(d)   Non-recurring, random variations. These may be caused by unforeseen circumstances, such as a change in the government of the country, a war, the collapse of a company, technological change or a fire.

The trend

Definition

> The *trend* is the underlying long-term movement over time in the values of the data recorded.

1.4   In the following examples of time series, there are three types of trend.

	Output per labour hour Units	Cost per unit £	Number of employees
20X4	30	1.00	100
20X5	24	1.08	103
20X6	26	1.20	96
20X7	22	1.15	102
20X8	21	1.18	103
20X9	17	1.25	98
	(A)	(B)	(C)

(a)   In time series (A) there is a downward trend in the output per labour hour. Output per labour hour did not fall every year, because it went up between 20X5 and 20X6, but the long-term movement is clearly a downward one.

(b)   In time series (B) there is an upward trend in the cost per unit. Although unit costs went down in 20X7 from a higher level in 20X6, the basic movement over time is one of rising costs.

(c)   In time series (C) there is no clear movement up or down, and the number of employees remained fairly constant around 100. The trend is therefore a static, or level one.

Seasonal variations

Definition

> *Seasonal variations* are short-term fluctuations in recorded values, due to different circumstances which affect results at different times of the year, on different days of the week, at different times of day, or whatever.

1.5   Here are some examples.

(a)   Sales of ice cream will be higher in summer than in winter, and sales of overcoats will be higher in autumn than in spring.

(b)   Shops might expect higher sales shortly before Christmas, or in their winter and summer sales.

(c)   Sales might be higher on Friday and Saturday than on Monday.

(d)   The telephone network may be heavily used at certain times of the day (such as mid-morning and mid-afternoon) and much less used at other times (such as in the middle of the night).

1.6   'Seasonal' is a term which may appear to refer to the seasons of the year, but its meaning in time series analysis is somewhat broader, as the examples given above show.

EXAMPLE: A TREND PLUS SEASONAL VARIATIONS

The number of customers served by a company of travel agents over the past four years is shown in the following historigram.

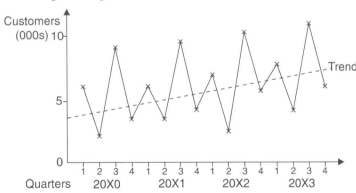

In this example, there would appear to be large seasonal fluctuations in demand, but there is also a basic upward trend.

Activity 1

What seasonal variations would you expect to see in sales of video recorders?

Cyclical variations

1.7 Cyclical variations are medium-term changes in results caused by circumstances which repeat in cycles. In business, cyclical variations are commonly associat ed with economic cycles, successive booms and slumps in the economy. Economic cycles may last a few years. Cyclical variations are longer term than seasonal variations.

Summarising the components

1.8 In practice a time series could incorporate all four features and, to make reasonably accurate forecasts, the four features often have to be isolated. We can begin the process of isolating each feature by summarising the components of a time series by the following equation

$$Y = T + S + C + R$$

where Y = the actual time series
T = the trend series
S = the seasonal component
C = the cyclical component
R = the residual component

Though you should be aware of the cyclical component, it is unlikely that you will be expected to carry out any calculation connected with isolating it. The mathematical model which we will use, the additive model, therefore excludes any reference to C and is

$$Y = T + S + R$$

We will begin by isolating the trend.

2 FINDING THE TREND

2.1 There are three principal methods of finding a trend.

(a) *Inspection.* As we saw in Chapter 6, the trend line can be drawn by eye on a graph in such a way that it appears to lie evenly between the recorded points, that is, a line of best fit is drawn by eye. It should be drawn to pass through the middle of the recorded points, thereby having as many data points below it as above it. The line on the historigram in the example following Paragraph 1.6 is an example.

(b) *Regression analysis by the least squares method.* This method, which we looked at in Chapter 6, makes the assumption that the trend line, whether up or down, is a straight line. Periods of time (such as quarters for which sales figures are given) are numbered, commonly from 0, and the regression line of the data on those period numbers is found. That line is then taken to be the trend.

(c)   *Moving averages.* This method attempts to remove seasonal (or cyclical) variations by a process of averaging and is looked at in detail in the next section.

3   MOVING AVERAGES

Finding the trend by moving averages

Definition

> *Moving averages* are consecutive averages of the results of a fixed number of periods.

3.1   Since a moving average is an average of several time periods, it is related to the mid-point of the overall period.

3.2   Moving averages could cover the sales of a shop over periods of seven days (Monday to the next Sunday for example) or a business's costs over periods of four quarters, or whatever else was appropriate to the circumstances.

EXAMPLE: MOVING AVERAGES

Year	Sales
	Units
20X0	390
20X1	380
20X2	460
20X3	450
20X4	470
20X5	440
20X6	500

Required

Take a moving average of the annual sales over a period of three years.

SOLUTION

(a)   Average sales in the three year period 20X0 – 20X2 were

$$\left(\frac{390+380+460}{3}\right) = \frac{1,230}{3} = 410$$

This average relates to the middle year of the period, 20X1.

(b)   Similarly, average sales in the three year period 20X1 – 20X3 were

$$\left(\frac{380+460+450}{3}\right) = \frac{1,290}{3} = 430$$

This average relates to the middle year of the period, 20X2.

NOTES

Core Unit 5: Quantitative Techniques for Business

(c) The average sales can also be found for the periods 20X2 – 20X4, 20X3 - 20X5 and 20X4 - 20X6, to give the following.

Year	Sales	Moving total of 3 years' sales	Moving average of 3 years' sales (÷3)
20X0	390		
20X1	380	1,230	410
20X2	460	1,290	430
20X3	450	1,380	460
20X4	470	1,360	453
20X5	440	1,410	470
20X6	500		

Note the following points.

(i) The moving average series has five figures relating to the years from 20X1 to 20X5. The original series had seven figures for the years from 20X0 to 20X6.

(ii) There is an upward trend in sales, which is more noticeable from the series of moving averages than from the original series of actual sales each year.

3.3 The above example averaged over a three-year period. Over what period should a moving average be taken? The answer to this question is that the moving average which is most appropriate will depend on the circumstances and the nature of the time series. Note the following points.

(a) A moving average which takes an average of the results in many time periods will represent results over a longer term than a moving average of two or three periods.

(b) On the other hand, with a moving average of results in many time periods, the last figure in the series will be out of date by several periods. In our example, the most recent average related to 20X5. With a moving average of five years' results, the final figure in the series would relate to 20X4.

(c) When there is a known cycle over which seasonal variations occur, such as all the days in the week or all the seasons in the year, the most suitable moving average would be one which covers one full cycle.

Activity 2

Using the following data, what is the three-month moving average for April?

Month	No of new houses finished
January	500
February	450
March	700
April	900
May	1,250
June	1,000

PUBLISHING

Moving averages of an even number of results

3.4 In the previous example, moving averages were taken of the results in an odd number of time periods, and the average then related to the mid-point of the overall period.

3.5 If a moving average were taken of results in an even number of time periods, the basic technique would be the same, but the mid-point of the overall period would not relate to a single period. For example, suppose an average were taken of the following four results.

Spring	120	
Summer	90	average 115
Autumn	180	
Winter	70	

The average would relate to the mid-point of the period, between summer and autumn.

3.6 The trend line average figures need to relate to a particular time period; otherwise, seasonal variations cannot be calculated. To overcome this difficulty, we take a moving average of the moving average. An example will illustrate this technique.

EXAMPLE: MOVING AVERAGES OVER AN EVEN NUMBER OF PERIODS

Calculate a moving average trend line of the following results.

Year	Quarter	Volume of sales '000 units
20X5	1	600
	2	840
	3	420
	4	720
20X6	1	640
	2	860
	3	420
	4	740
20X7	1	670
	2	900
	3	430
	4	760

SOLUTION

A moving average of four will be used, since the volume of sales would appear to depend on the season of the year, and each year has four quarterly results.

The moving average of four does not relate to any specific period of time; therefore we will take a moving total of pairs of four-quarter totals and divide that moving total by 8 (ie the number of data items which contributed to the total).

Year	Quarter	Actual volume of sales '000 units (A)	Moving total of 4 quarters' sales '000 units (B)	Moving average of 4 quarters' sales '000 units (B ÷ 4)	Mid-point of 2 moving averages Trend line '000 units (C)
19X5	1	600			
	2	840			
	3	420	2,580	5,200	650.00
	4	720	2,620	5,260	657.50
19X6	1	640	2,640	5,280	660.00
	2	860	2,640	5,300	662.50
	3	420	2,660	5,350	668.75
	4	740	2,690	5,420	677.50
19X7	1	670	2,730	5,470	683.75
	2	900	2,740	5,500	687.50
	3	430	2,760		
	4	760			

The final moving averages are related to specific quarters (from the third quarter of 20X5 to the second quarter of 20X7).

4 FINDING THE SEASONAL VARIATIONS

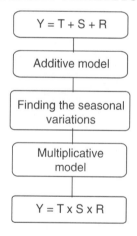

4.1 Once a trend has been established, by whatever method, we can find the seasonal variations.

4.2 The additive model for time series analysis is $Y = T + S + R$. We can therefore write $Y - T = S + R$. In other words, if we deduct the trend series from the actual series, we will be left with the seasonal and residual components of the time series. If we assume that the residual component is relatively small, and hence negligible, the seasonal component can be found as $S = Y - T$, the de-trended series.

4.3 We will use an example to illustrate the process.

EXAMPLE: THE TREND AND SEASONAL VARIATIONS

Output at a factory appears to vary with the day of the week. Output over the last three weeks has been as follows.

	Week 1	*Week 2*	*Week 3*
	'000 units	'000 units	'000 units
Monday	80	82	84
Tuesday	104	110	116
Wednesday	94	97	100
Thursday	120	125	130
Friday	62	64	66

Required

Find the seasonal variation for each of the 15 days, and the average seasonal variation for each day of the week using the moving averages method.

SOLUTION

Actual results fluctuate up and down according to the day of the week and so a moving average of five will be used. The difference between the actual result on any one day (Y) and the trend figure for that day (T) will be the seasonal variation (S) for the day.

The seasonal variations for the 15 days are as follows.

		Actual (Y)	*Moving total of five days' output*	*Trend* (T)	*Seasonal variation* (Y–T)
Week 1	Monday	80			
	Tuesday	104			
	Wednesday	94	460	92.0	+2.0
	Thursday	120	462	92.4	+27.6
	Friday	62	468	93.6	–31.6
Week 2	Monday	82	471	94.2	–12.2
	Tuesday	110	476	95.2	+14.8
	Wednesday	97	478	95.6	+1.4
	Thursday	125	480	96.0	+29.0
	Friday	64	486	97.2	–33.2
Week 3	Monday	84	489	97.8	–13.8
	Tuesday	116	494	98.8	+17.2
	Wednesday	100	496	99.2	+0.8
	Thursday	130			
	Friday	66			

	Monday	*Tuesday*	*Wednesday*	*Thursday*	*Friday*
Week 1			+2.0	+27.6	–31.6
Week 2	–12.2	+14.8	+1.4	+29.0	–33.2
Week 3	–13.8	+17.2	+0.8		
Average	–13.0	+16.0	+1.4	+28.3	–32.4

You will notice that the variation between the actual results on any one particular day and the trend line average is not the same from week to week. This is because Y – T contains not only seasonal variations but random variations (residuals). In calculating the averages of the deviations, Y – T, for each day of the week, the residual components are expected to cancel out, or at least to be reduced to a negligible level.

Our estimate of the 'seasonal' or daily variation is almost complete, but there is one more important step to take. Variations around the basic trend line should cancel each other out, and add up to 0. In practice this is rarely the case because of random variation. The average seasonal estimates must therefore be corrected so that they add up to zero.

	Mon	Tues	Wed	Thurs	Fri	Total
Estimated average daily variation	–13.00	+16.00	+1.40	+28.30	–32.40	0.30
Adjustment to reduce ~ total variation to 0	–0.06	–0.06	–0.06	–0.06	–0.06	–0.30
Final estimate of average daily variation	–13.06	+15.94	+1.34	+28.24	–32.46	0.00

These might be rounded up or down as follows.

Monday –13; Tuesday +16; Wednesday +1; Thursday +28; Friday –32; Total 0

Activity 3

Calculate a four-quarter moving average trend centred on actual quarters and then find seasonal variations from the following.

Sales in £000

	Spring	Summer	Autumn	Winter
20X7	200	120	160	280
20X8	220	140	140	300
20X9	200	120	180	320

Seasonal variations using the multiplicative model

4.4 The method of estimating the seasonal variations in the above example was to use the differences between the trend and actual data. This is called the *additive model*.

Definition

> The *additive model* for time series analysis assumes that the components of the series are independent of each other, an increasing trend not affecting the seasonal variations, for example.

4.5 The alternative is to use the *multiplicative model*. Sometimes this method is called the *proportional model*.

Definition

> The *multiplicative* or *proportional model* for time series analysis expresses each actual figure as a proportion of the trend.

The model summarises a time series as $Y = T \times S \times R$. Note that the trend component will be the same whichever model is used but the values of the seasonal and residual components will vary according to the model being applied.

4.6 The example following paragraph 4.3 on seasonal variations can be reworked on this alternative basis. The trend is calculated in exactly the same way as before but we need a different approach for the seasonal variations.

The multiplicative model is $Y = T \times S \times R$ and, just as we calculated $S = Y - T$ for the additive model (Paragraph 4.2) we can calculate $Y/T = S$ for the multiplicative model.

		Actual (Y)	Trend (T)	Seasonal percentage (Y/T)
Week 1	Monday	80		
	Tuesday	104		
	Wednesday	94	92.0	1.022
	Thursday	120	92.4	1.299
	Friday	62	93.6	0.662
Week 2	Monday	82	94.2	0.870
	Tuesday	110	95.2	1.155
	Wednesday	97	95.6	1.015
	Thursday	125	96.0	1.302
	Friday	64	97.2	0.658
Week 3	Monday	84	97.8	0.859
	Tuesday	116	98.8	1.174
	Wednesday	100	99.2	1.008
	Thursday	130		
	Friday	66		

The summary of the seasonal variations expressed in proportional terms is as follows.

	Monday %	Tuesday %	Wednesday %	Thursday %	Friday %
Week 1			1.022	1.299	0.662
Week 2	0.870	1.155	1.015	1.302	0.658
Week 3	0.859	1.174	1.008		
Total	1.729	2.329	3.045	2.601	1.320
Average	0.8645	1.1645	1.0150	1.3005	0.6600

Instead of summing to zero, as with the absolute approach, these should sum (in this case) to 5 (an average of 1).

They actually sum to 5.0045 so 0.0009 has to be deducted from each one. This is too small to make a difference to the figures above, so we should deduct 0.002 and 0.0025 from each of two seasonal variations. We could arbitrarily decrease Monday's variation to 0.8625 and Tuesday's to 1.162.

Activity 4

A company's quarterly sales figures have been analysed into a trend and seasonal variations using moving averages. Here is an extract from the analysis.

Year	Quarter	Actual	Trend
		£'000	£'000
20X1	1	350	366
	2	380	370
	3	400	380
	4	360	394
20X2	1	410	406
	2	430	414
	3	450	418
	4	370	423

Required

Find the average seasonal variation for each quarter, using the multiplicative model.

---

5 FORECASTING

5.1 Forecasting is an essential, but difficult task of management. Many forecasts are made by guessing, but they are unlikely to be reliable.

5.2 There are several mathematical techniques of forecasting which could be used. These techniques will not necessarily provide accurate forecasts but, on the whole, they are likely to provide more reliable estimates than guesswork. Techniques cannot eliminate uncertainty about the future, but they can help to ensure that managers take account of all currently-known facts in the preparation of their forecasts.

5.3 The technique which will be discussed here is that of extrapolating a trend and then adjusting for seasonal variations.

5.4 Forecasts of future values should be made as follows.

(a) Calculate a trend line using moving averages or regression analysis. You may be asked to plot the trend line on a scatter diagram. It should be drawn as a straight line using the first and last available trend line figures.)

(b) Use the trend line to forecast future trend line values. (You can insert the appropriate value for x (= time) into a regression equation or calculate an average seasonal increase (or decrease) as the following example shows.)

(c) Adjust these values by the average seasonal variation applicable to the future period, to determine the forecast for that period. With the additive model, add (or subtract for negative variations) the variation. With the multiplicative model, multiply the trend value by the variation proportion.

5.5 Extending a trend line outside the range of known data, in this case forecasting the future from a trend line based on historical data, is known as extrapolation.

EXAMPLE: FORECASTING

Sales of product X each quarter for the last three years have been as follows (in thousands of units). Trend values, found by a moving averages method, are shown in brackets.

Year	1st quarter	2nd quarter	3rd quarter	4th quarter
1	18	30	20 (18.75)	6 (19.375)
2	20 (20)	33 (20.5)	22 (21)	8 (21.5)
3	22 (22.125)	35 (22.75)	25	10

Average seasonal variations for quarters 1 to 4 are –0.1, +12.4, +1.1 and –13.4 respectively.

Required

Use the trend line and estimates of seasonal variations to forecast sales in each quarter of year 4.

SOLUTION

The trend line indicates an increase of about 0.6 per quarter. This can be confirmed by calculating the average quarterly increase in trend line values between the third quarter of year 1 (18.75) and the second quarter of year 2 (22.75). The average rise is

$$\frac{22.75 - 18.75}{7} = \frac{4}{7} = 0.57, \text{ say } 0.6$$

Taking 0.6 as the quarterly increase in the trend, the forecast of sales for year 4, before seasonal adjustments (the trend line forecast) would be as follows.

Year	Quarter			Trend line
3	*2nd	(actual trend)	22.75, say	22.8
	3rd			23.4
	4th			24.0
4	1st			24.6
	2nd			25.2
	3rd			25.8
	4th			26.4

* last known trend line value.

Seasonal variations should now be incorporated to obtain the final forecast.

	Quarter	Trend line forecast '000 units	Average seasonal variation '000 units	Forecast of actual sales '000 units
Year 4	1st	24.6	–0.1	24.5
	2nd	25.2	+12.4	37.6
	3rd	25.8	+1.1	26.9
	4th	26.4	–13.4	13.0

If we had been using the multiplicative model, with an average variation for (for example) quarter 3 of 1.057, our prediction for the third quarter of year 4 would have been 25.8 × 1.057 = 27.3.

5.6 Note that the multiplicative model is better than the additive model for forecasting when the trend is increasing or decreasing over time. In such circumstances, seasonal variations are likely to be increasing or decreasing too. The additive model simply adds absolute and unchanging seasonal variations to the trend figures whereas the multiplicative model, by multiplying increasing or decreasing trend values by a constant seasonal variation factor, takes account of changing seasonal variations.

5.7 All forecasts are, however, subject to error, but the likely errors vary from case to case.

(a) The further into the future the forecast is for, the more unreliable it is likely to be.

(b) The less data available on which to base the forecast, the less reliable the forecast.

(c) The pattern of trend and seasonal variations cannot be guaranteed to continue in the future.

(d) There is always the danger of random variations upsetting the pattern of trend and seasonal variation.

Activity 5

The percentage of employees absent from work was recorded over a four-week period as follows.

Week	Mon	Tues	Weds	Thurs	Fri
1	8.4	5.1	5.7	4.8	6.3
2	8.1	5.5	6.0	4.6	6.5
3	8.4	5.6	6.2	5.0	6.8
4	8.6	5.6	6.3	4.9	6.9

Required

(a) Draw a graph of the time series of absenteeism.

(b) By means of a moving average and the additive model, find the trend and the seasonal adjustments.

(c) Plot the trend line by eye and use it as a basis to forecast daily absenteeism for week 5.

(d) Personnel have suggested that the absenteeism figure for Friday of week 8 could be as high as 8%. Discuss whether or not you would support this.

Residuals

Definition

A *residual* is the difference between the results which would have been predicted (for a past period for which we already have data) by the trend line adjusted for the average seasonal variation and the actual results.

5.8 The residual is therefore the difference which is not explained by the trend line and the average seasonal variation. The residual gives some indication of how much actual results were affected by other factors. Large residuals suggest that any forecast is likely to be unreliable. It is a good idea to calculate the residual series (Y – T – S) in order to assess the adequacy of predictions. This will also test whether the assumption (made in Paragraph 4.2) is reasonable.

5.9 In the example following Paragraph 5.5, the 'prediction' for the third quarter of year 1 would have been 18.75 + 1.1 = 19.85. As the actual value was 20, the residual was only 20 – 19.85 = 0.15. The residual for the fourth quarter of year 2 was 8 – (21.5 – 13.4) = 8 – 8.1 = –0.1. An analysis of all the residuals associated with a particular time series will indicate whether the predictions based on the time series are reliable.

6 DESEASONALISATION

6.1 Economic statistics, such as unemployment figures, are often 'seasonally adjusted' or 'deseasonalised' so as to ensure that the overall trend (rising, falling or stationary) is clear. All this means is that seasonal variations (S) (derived from previous data) have been taken out, to leave a figure (Y – S) which might be taken as indicating the trend.

Definition

> *Deseasonalisation* is the process of removing seasonal variations from data to leave a figure indicating the trend.

EXAMPLE: DESEASONALISATION

Actual sales figures for four quarters, together with appropriate seasonal adjustment factors derived from previous data, are as follows.

			Seasonal adjustments	
			---	---
		Actual	*Additive*	*Multiplicative*
Quarter		*sales*	*model*	*model*
		£'000	£'000	
1		150	+3	1.02
2		160	+4	1.05
3		164	–2	0.98
4		170	–5	0.95

Required

Deseasonalise these data.

SOLUTION

We are reversing the normal process of applying seasonal variations to trend figures, so with the additive model we subtract positive seasonal variations (and add negative ones), and with the multiplicative model we divide by the seasonal variation factors (expressed as proportions).

Quarter	Actual sales £'000	Deseasonalised sales	
		Additive model £'000	Multiplicative model £'000
1	150	147	147
2	160	156	152
3	164	166	167
4	170	175	179

The topic of the next chapter in this Course Book is that of Linear Programming. Sometimes we are faced with a situation where we have limited resources and in such a situation we might wish to know how we can best use our resources in order to achieve maximum profit or revenue or in order to minimise our costs. Linear programming is a technique which does exactly that.

Chapter roundup

- A time series is a series of figures or values recorded over time.

- A time series has four features: a trend, seasonal variations, cyclical variations and random variations (residuals).

- A time series can be summarised by the additive model (Y = T + S + R) or the multiplicative (or proportional) model (Y = T × S × R).

- The most commonly used method in practice for finding the trend is the moving averages method. Once the trend has been established, the seasonal component can be calculated as Y – T (if the additive model is being used) or Y/T (if the multiplicative model is being used).

- A process of averaging and adjusting the individual seasonal components is necessary to remove the effect of any residuals and to arrive at seasonal components for each season of the year, day of the week as necessary.

- By extrapolating the trend line and adjusting the resulting figures for the seasonal component of the time series, forecasts can be obtained.

- Calculating the residuals of the time series assesses the adequacy and reliability of the predictions made using the trend and seasonal components.

- Deseasonalised data (Y – S) are often used by economic commentators.

Quick quiz

1   What is the definition of a time series?

2   What are the four components that combine to form a time series?

3   How can trend lines be found?

4   How are trend values calculated when moving averages of an even number of results are taken?

5   Why are average seasonal variations adjusted to sum to zero?

6   Distinguish between the additive model and the multiplicative model of time series.

7   In what circumstances should the proportional model rather than the additive model be used?

8   Describe how the additive model may be used in forecasting.

9   What is extrapolation?

10 What is the term for the difference which is not explained by the trend line and the average seasonal variation?

Answers to activities

1   Sales of video recorders might peak at Christmas and also before major sporting events such as Wimbledon.

2   $\dfrac{700 + 900 + 1{,}250}{3} = 950$

3

		Sales (Y)	4-quarter total	8-quarter total	Moving average (T)	Seasonal variation (Y-T)
20X7	Spring	200				
	Summer	120				
			760			
	Autumn	160		1,540	192.5	−32.5
			780			
	Winter	280		1,580	197.5	+82.5
			800			
20X8	Spring	220		1,580	197.5	+22.5
			780			
	Summer	140		1,580	197.5	−57.5
			800			
	Autumn	140		1,580	197.5	−57.5
			780			
	Winter	300		1,540	192.5	+107.5
			760			
20X9	Spring	200		1,560	195.0	+5.0
			800			
	Summer	120		1,620	202.5	−82.5
			820			
	Autumn	180				
	Winter	320				

We can now average the seasonal variations.

	Spring	Summer	Autumn	Winter	Total
20X7			−32.5	+82.5	
20X8	+22.5	−57.5	−57.5	+107.5	
20X9	+5.0	−82.5			
	+27.5	−140.0	−90.0	+190.0	
Average variation (in £'000)	+13.75	−70.00	−45.00	+95.00	−6.25
Adjustment so sum is zero	+1.5625	+1.5625	+1.5625	+1.5625	+6.25
Adjusted average variations	+15.3125	−68.4375	−3.4375	+96.5625	0

These might be rounded up or down to:

Spring £15,000, Summer −£68,000, Autumn −£43,000, Winter £96,000

BPP
PUBLISHING

4

Quarter	1	2	3	4
	%	%	%	%
Variation,20X1	0.956	1.027	1.053	0.914
Variation,20X2	1.010	1.039	1.077	0.875
Average variation	0.983	1.033	1.065	0.895
Adjustment	0.006	0.006	0.006	0.006
Adjusted average variation	0.989	1.039	1.071	0.901

5   (a)

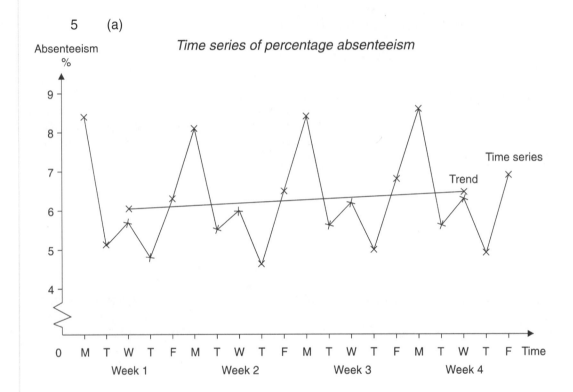

Time series of percentage absenteeism

(b)

Week	Day	Data %	Five-day total %	Five-day average (trend) %	Seasonal variation %
1	M	8.4			
	T	5.1			
	W	5.7	30.3	6.06	− 0.36
	T	4.8	30.0	6.00	− 1.20
	F	6.3	30.4	6.08	+ 0.22
2	M	8.1	30.7	6.14	+ 1.96
	T	5.5	30.5	6.10	− 0.60
	W	6.0	30.7	6.14	− 0.14
	T	4.6	31.0	6.20	− 1.60
	F	6.5	31.1	6.22	+ 0.28
3	M	8.4	31.3	6.26	+ 2.14
	T	5.6	31.7	6.34	− 0.74
	W	6.2	32.0	6.40	− 0.20
	T	5.0	32.2	6.44	− 1.44
	F	6.8	32.2	6.44	+ 0.36
4	M	8.6	32.3	6.46	+ 2.14
	T	5.6	32.2	6.44	− 0.84
	W	6.3	32.3	6.46	− 0.16
	T	4.9			
	F	6.9			

Week	M %	T %	W %	T %	F %	Total
1			− 0.36	− 1.20	+ 0.22	
2	+ 1.96	− 0.60	− 0.14	− 1.60	+ 0.28	
3	+ 2.14	− 0.74	− 0.20	− 1.44	+ 0.36	
4	+ 2.14	− 0.84	− 0.16			
	6.24	− 2.18	− 0.86	− 4.24	0.86	
Average	+ 2.08	− 0.73	− 0.22	− 1.41	+ 0.29	+ 0.01
Adjustment					− 0.01	− 0.01
Adjusted average	+ 2.08	− 0.73	− 0.22	− 1.41	+ 0.28	0.00

The seasonal adjustments are as shown in the last line of the above table.

(c) The trend line has been plotted on the graph above, using the figures for Wednesday of week 1 (6.06%) and Wednesday of week 4 (6.46%).

The trend rose by 0.4% over this period, an average daily rise of 0.4/15 = 0.027%. This average will be used to derive the trend for week 5.

NOTES

Week 5 predictions

Day	Trend	Seasonal variation	Prediction	Rounded prediction
	%	%	%	%
Monday	6.541*	+ 2.08	8.621	8.6
Tuesday	6.568	− 0.73	5.838	5.8
Wednesday	6.595	− 0.22	6.375	6.4
Thursday	6.622	− 1.41	5.212	5.2
Friday	6.649	+ 0.28	6.929	6.9

* $6.46 + (3 \times 0.027)$

(d) A forecast for Friday of week 8, based on the above computations, would be $6.46 + (22 \times 0.027) + 0.28 = 7.334\%$, which is significantly below the personnel department's forecast. It is probable that the personnel department have estimated a more steeply rising trend. However, no forecast so far into the future and based on only four weeks data is likely to be reliable. The estimate of 8% cannot be supported.

Assignment 7   **(45 minutes)**

The sales of Yelesol ice cream for the last twelve quarters have been as follows.

			Sales Thousand units	Moving annual total Thousand units
20X1		Q4	14	
20X2		Q1	16	
				100
		Q2	30	
				104
		Q3	40	
				104
		Q4	18	
				108
20X3		Q1	16	
				112
		Q2	34	
				108
		Q3	44	
				108
		Q4	14	
				112
20X4		Q1	16	
				120
		Q2	38	
		Q3	52	
		Q4		

Required

(a) Calculate a centred moving average.
(b) Plot a graph of the data and the centred moving average.
(c) Find the average quarterly seasonal variations.
(d) Calculate sales forecasts for the next two quarters.

Chapter 8:
LINEAR PROGRAMMING

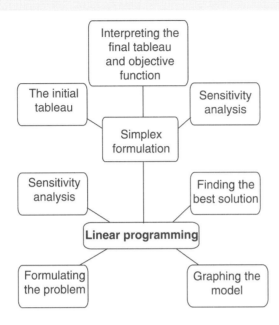

Introduction

In this chapter we will be looking at a technique which can be used to allocate resources (which might be materials, labour, money and so on) in order to achieve the best possible results. The name 'linear programming' sounds rather formidable and the technique *can* get quite complicated. But don't worry. You are only expected to be able to analyse *fully* the simplest examples, using a graphical technique (ie draw lines!). The more complex approach, the Simplex method, is usually carried out on a computer and we will only be considering the construction of what is called the initial tableau and the interpretation of the final tableau.

Your objectives

After completing this chapter you should:

(a)   understand the circumstances in which linear programming can be used;

(b)   be able to set up a linear programming model;

(c)   be able to graph the model;

(d)   be able to find the feasible solutions to the problem and the best solution;

(e)   be able to apply sensitivity analysis;

(f)   understand and be able to calculate dual/shadow prices;

(g)   be aware of the circumstances in which the Simplex method of linear programming should be used;

(h)   be able to set up and interpret an initial tableau;

(i)   be able to interpret the final tableau and objective function.

EXAMPLE: WHEN LINEAR PROGRAMMING CAN HELP

Suppose that Jack Russell is the production manager of Barkers Ltd, a small company which manufactures dog kennels. The company produces a number of different types of kennel but has a flexible workforce that can be switched easily from one production line to another. Much of the machinery is used in the production of more than one type of kennel, as are many of the raw materials, wood, paint, fleece and fur (for lining the kennels), plastic (for water and food bowls inside the kennels) and so on. Profit earned depends on the type of kennel sold. Pooch's Parlour (a model for small breeds such as poodles) does not generate as much profit as the Penthouse (centrally heated, and suitable for the most pampered of pets). The time taken to produce a kennel and the potential market also depend on the type of kennel in question.

Jack Russell's problem is to decide how the company should divide up its production among the various types of kennel it manufactures in order to obtain the maximum possible profit, taking the factors mentioned above into account. In other words, he cannot simply produce as many as possible of each model of kennel because there will be limitations or constraints within which the production must operate. Such constraints could be limited quantities of raw materials available, a fixed number of man-hours per week for each type of worker, limited machine hours and so on. Moreover, since the profits generated by each model of kennel vary, it may be better not to produce any of a less profitable line, but to concentrate all resources on producing the more profitable ones. On the other hand limitations in market demand could mean that all those kennels produced may not be sold.

You can see from this brief outline of the problem that the chances of Jack Russell arriving at the 'best solution' (the one giving maximum possible profits) by simply thinking about it are minimal. What Jack needs is a systematic way of tackling the problem which guarantees that he will end up with the most profitable solution and ensures that the company operates within the constraints of staff hours, machine hours, quantities of raw materials and so on. Linear programming is that 'systematic way of tackling the problem'.

Definition

> *Linear programming* is a technique for solving problems of profit maximisation (or cost minimisation) and resource allocation. The word programming is simply used to denote a series of events. The various aspects of the problem are expressed as linear equations.

1 FORMULATING THE PROBLEM

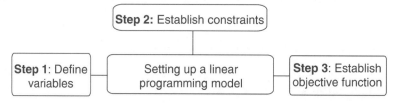

1.1 In common with many quantitative methods, we need a rather simple example to illustrate the basic linear programming techniques. Let us imagine that Barkers Ltd makes just two models, the Super and the Deluxe, and that monthly machine capacity is restricted to 400 hours. The Super requires 5 hours of machine time per unit and the Deluxe 1.5 hours. Government restrictions mean that the maximum number of kennels that can be sold each month is 150, that number being made up of any combination of the Super and the Deluxe.

1.2 Let us now work through the steps involved in setting up a linear programming model.

Setting up a linear programming model

Step 1: define variables

1.3 What are the quantities that the company can vary? Obviously not the number of machine hours or the maximum sales, which are fixed by external circumstances beyond the company's control. The only things which it can determine are the number of each type of kennel to manufacture. It is these numbers which Jack Russell has to determine in such a way as to get the maximum possible profit. Our variables will therefore be as follows.

Let x = the number of units of the Super kennel manufactured.

Let y = the number of units of the Deluxe kennel manufactured.

Step 2: establish constraints

1.4 Having defined these two variables we can now translate the two constraints into inequalities involving the variables.

1.5 Let us first consider the machine hours constraint. Each Super requires 5 hours of machine time. Producing five Supers therefore requires $5 \times 5 = 25$ hours of machine time and, more generally producing x Supers will require 5x hours. Likewise producing y Deluxes will require 1.5y hours. The total machine hours needed to make x Supers and y Deluxes is 5x + 1.5y. We know that this cannot be greater than 400 hours so we arrive at the following inequality.

$$5x + 1.5y \leq 400$$

1.6 We can obtain the other inequality more easily. The total number of Supers and Deluxes made each month is x + y but this has to be less than 150 due to government restrictions. The sales order constraint is therefore as follows.

$$x + y \leq 150$$

1.7 The variables in linear programming models should usually be non-negative in value. In this example, for instance, you cannot make a negative number of kennels and so we need the following constraints.

$$x \geq 0; y \geq 0$$

Do not forget these non-negativity constraints when formulating a linear programming model.

Step 3: establish objective function

Definition

An *objective function* is the mathematical expression of the aim of a linear programming exercise.

1.8 We have yet to introduce the question of profits. Let us assume that the profit on each type of kennel is as follows.

	£
Super	100
Deluxe	200

1.9 The objective of Barkers Ltd is to maximise profit and so the objective function to be maximised is as follows.

Profit (P) = 100x + 200y

Note that another organisation might have, for example, the minimisation of costs or the maximisation of contribution as its objective.

1.10 The problem has now been reduced to the following four inequalities and one equation.

$$5x + 1.5y \le 400$$
$$x + y \le 150$$
$$x \ge 0$$
$$y \ge 0$$
$$P = 100x + 200y$$

1.11 Have you noticed that the inequalities are all linear expressions? If plotted on a graph, they would all give straight lines. This explains why the technique is called linear programming and also gives a hint as to how we should proceed with trying to find the solution to Jack's problem.

1.12 Before we progress to the next step, let us look at an example.

EXAMPLE: FORMULATING A PROBLEM

Maxim Wise Ltd makes three products, A, B and C. Each product is made by the same grades of labour, and the time required to make one unit of each product is as follows.

	A	B	C
Skilled labour	3 hours	4 hours	1 hour
Unskilled labour	2.5 hours	2 hours	6 hours

The variable costs per unit of A, B and C are £28, £30 and £26 respectively. The products sell for £40, £40 and £34 respectively.

In March 20X3 the company expects to have only 600 hours of skilled labour and 2,000 hours of unskilled labour available. There is a minimum requirement for 40 units of B and 120 units of C in the month.

Monthly fixed costs are £1,500.

Required

Formulate a linear programming problem.

SOLUTION

The variables are the products A, B and C. We want to decide how many of each to produce in the month.

Let the number of units of product A made be a.
Let the number of units of product B made be b.
Let the number of units of product C made be c.

The objective is to maximise the monthly profit. Since fixed costs are a constant value of £1,500, which will be incurred regardless of which production plan is selected, these are irrelevant to the objective function, which can be stated as 'to maximise profit by maximising contribution'. The contribution per unit is £12 for A, £10 for B and £8 for C.

The objective is therefore to maximise $12a + 10b + 8c$ (contribution).

There are constraints relating to the availability of skilled labour and unskilled labour, and the minimum requirements for B and C. In addition, there are the constraints that A, B and C cannot have negative values, but since B and C must exceed 40 and 120 respectively, the non-negativity constraints are redundant for these two variables.

The programme may therefore be formulated as follows.

Objective: maximise $12a + 10b + 8c$ (contribution)

subject to the constraints:

$$
\begin{aligned}
3a + 4b + c &\leq 600 &&\text{(skilled labour)} \\
2.5a + 2b + 6c &\leq 2{,}000 &&\text{(unskilled labour)} \\
b &\geq 40 &&\text{(requirement for B)} \\
c &\geq 120 &&\text{(requirement for C)} \\
a &\geq 0
\end{aligned}
$$

2 GRAPHING THE MODEL

2.1 We have looked at how to formulate a problem and in this section we will look at solving a problem using (as hinted in Paragraph 1.11) graphs.

2.2 A graphical solution is only possible when there are two variables in the problem. One variable is represented by the x axis and one by the y axis of the graph. Since non-negative values are not usually allowed, the graph shows only zero and positive values of x and y.

2.3 A linear equation with one or two variables is shown as a straight line on a graph. Thus $y = 6$ would be shown as follows.

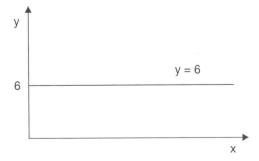

Figure 8.1 Linear equation where $y = 6$

If the problem included a constraint that y could not exceed 6, the *inequality* $y \leq 6$ would be represented by the shaded area of the graph below.

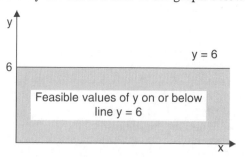

Figure 8.2 Constraint $y \leq 6$

2.4 The equation $4x + 3y = 24$ is also a straight line on a graph. To draw any straight line, we need only to plot two points and join them up. The easiest points to plot are the following.

(a) $x = 0$ (in this example, if $x = 0$, $3y = 24$, $y = 8$)
(b) $y = 0$ (in this example, if $y = 0$, $4x = 24$, $x = 6$)

By plotting the points, $(0, 8)$ and $(6, 0)$ on a graph, and joining them up, we have the line for $4x + 3y = 24$.

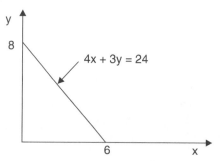

Figure 8.3 Linear equation where $4x + 3y = 24$

2.5 If we had a constraint $4x + 3y \leq 24$, any combined value of x and y within the shaded area below (on or below the line) would satisfy the constraint.

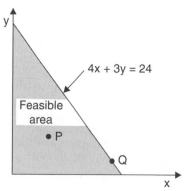

Figure 8.4 Constraint $4x + 3y \leq 24$

For example, at point P ($x = 2$, $y = 2$), $4x + 3y = 14$ which is less than 24; and at point Q ($x = 5.5$, $y = 2/3$), $4x + 3y = 24$. Both P and Q lie within the *feasible area* (the area where the inequality is satisfied, also called the feasible region). A *feasible area* enclosed on all sides may also be called a *feasible polygon*.

Definition

> The area on a graph of a linear programming problem within which all of the inequalities are satisfied is known as a *feasible area*.

2.6   The inequalities $y \geq 6$, $x \geq 6$ and $4x + 3y \geq 24$, would be shown graphically as follows.

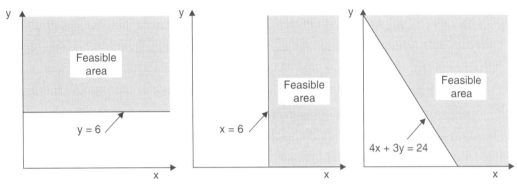

Figure 8.5 Graphical representations of inequalities

2.7   When there are several constraints, the feasible area of combinations of values of x and y must be an area where all the inequalities are satisfied.

Thus, if $y \leq 6$ *and* $4x + 3y \leq 24$ the feasible area would be the shaded area in Figure 11.6.

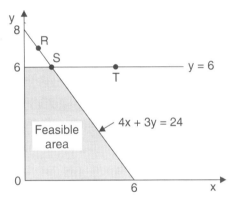

Figure 8.6 Graph showing more than one constraint (1)

(a)   Point R (x = 0.75, y = 7) is not in the feasible area because although it satisfies the inequality $4x + 3y \leq 24$, it does not satisfy $y \leq 6$.

(b)   Point T (x = 5, y = 6) is not in the feasible area, because although it satisfies the inequality $y \leq 6$, it does not satisfy $4x + 3y \leq 24$.

(c)   Point S (x = 1.5, y = 6) satisfies both inequalities and lies just on the boundary of the feasible area since y = 6 exactly, and $4x + 3y = 24$. Point S is thus at the intersection of the two equation lines.

2.8   Similarly, if $y \geq 6$ and $4x + 3y \geq 24$ but $x \leq 6$, the feasible area would be the shaded area in the graph below.

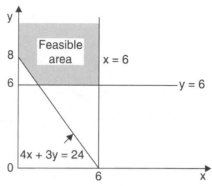

Figure 8.7 Graph showing more than one constraint (2)

Activity 1

Draw the feasible region which arises from the constraints facing Barkers.

Activity 2

Draw the feasible area for the following inequalities.

$$2x + 3y \leq 12$$
$$y \geq 2x$$
$$x, y \geq 0$$

---

3 FINDING THE BEST SOLUTION

3.1 Having found the feasible region (which includes all the possible solutions to the problem) we need to find which of these possible solutions is 'best' in the sense that it yields the maximum possible profit. We could do this by finding out what profit each of the possible solutions would give, and then choosing as our 'best' combination the one for which the profit is greatest.

3.2 Consider, however, the feasible region of the problem faced by Barkers Ltd (see the solution to Activity 1). Even in such a simple problem as this, there are a great many possible solution points within the feasible area. Even to write them all down would be a time-consuming process and also an unnecessary one, as we shall see.

3.3 Let us look again at the graph of Barker's problem.

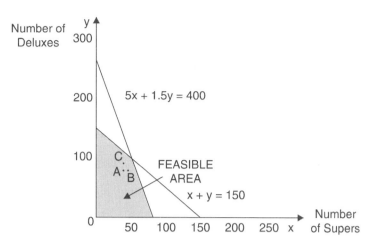

Figure 8.8 Barker's problem

Consider, for example, the point A at which 40 Supers and 80 Deluxes are being manufactured. This will yield a profit of $((40 \times 100) + (80 \times 200)) = £20,000$. We would clearly get more profit at point B, where the same number of Deluxes are being manufactured but where the number of Supers being manufactured has increased by five, or from point C where the same number of Supers but 10 more Deluxes are manufactured. This argument suggests that the 'best' solution is going to be a point on the edge of the feasible area rather than in the middle of it.

3.4   This still leaves us with quite a few points to look at but there is a way we can narrow down the candidates for the best solution still further. Suppose that Barkers wish to make a profit of £10,000. The company could sell the following combinations of Supers and Deluxes.

(a)   100 Super, no Deluxe

(b)   No Super, 50 Deluxe

(c)   A proportionate mix of Super and Deluxe, such as 80 Super and 10 Deluxe or 50 Super and 25 Deluxe

3.5   The possible combinations of Supers and Deluxes required to earn a profit of £10,000 could be shown by the straight line $100x + 200y = 10,000$.

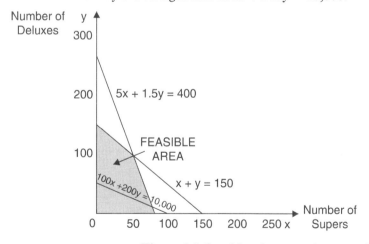

Figure 8.9 Combinations earning a profit of £10,000

3.6   For a total profit of £15,000, a similar line $100x + 200y = 15,000$ could be drawn to show the various combinations of Supers and Deluxes which would achieve the total of £15,000.

Similarly a line 100x + 200y = 8,000 would show the various combinations of Supers and Deluxes which would earn a total profit of £8,000.

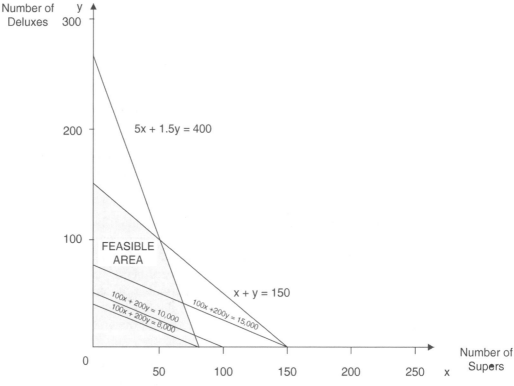

Figure 8.10 Combinations earning various profits

3.7 These profit lines are all parallel. (They are called *iso-profit lines*, 'iso' meaning equal.) A similar line drawn for any other total profit would also be parallel to the three lines shown here. This means that if we wish to know the slope or gradient of the profit line, for any value of total profit, we can simply draw one line for any convenient value of profit, and we will know that all the other lines will be parallel to the one drawn: they will have the same slope.

3.8 Bigger profits are shown by lines further from the origin (100x + 200y = 15,000), smaller profits by lines closer to the origin (100x + 200y = 8,000). As Barkers try to increase possible profit we need to slide the profit line outwards from the origin, while always keeping it parallel to the other profit lines.

3.9 As we do this there will come a point at which, if we were to move the profit line out any further, it would cease to lie in the feasible region and therefore larger profits could not be achieved in practice because of the constraints. In our example concerning Barkers this will happen, as you should test for yourself, where the profit line is just passing through the intersection of x + y = 150 with the y axis (at (0, 150)). The point (0, 150) will therefore give us the best production combination of the Super and the Deluxe, that is, to produce 150 Deluxe models and no Super models.

EXAMPLE: A MAXIMISATION PROBLEM

Brunel Ltd manufactures plastic-covered steel fencing in two qualities, standard and heavy gauge. Both products pass through the same processes, involving steel-forming and plastic bonding.

Standard gauge fencing sells at £18 a roll and heavy gauge fencing at £24 a roll. Variable costs per roll are £16 and £21 respectively. There is an unlimited market for the standard gauge, but demand for the heavy gauge is limited to 1,300 rolls a year. Factory operations are limited to 2,400 hours a year in each of the two production processes.

	Processing hours per roll	
Gauge	*Steel-forming*	*Plastic-bonding*
Standard	0.6	0.4
Heavy	0.8	1.2

Required

Determine the production mix which will maximise total contribution. Calculate the total contribution.

SOLUTION

Let S be the number of standard gauge rolls per year.
Let H be the number of heavy gauge rolls per year.

The objective is to maximise $2S + 3H$ (contribution) subject to the following constraints.

$$
\begin{aligned}
0.6S + 0.8H &\leq 2,400 && \text{(steel-forming hours)} \\
0.4S + 1.2H &\leq 2,400 && \text{(plastic-bonding hours)} \\
H &\leq 1,300 && \text{(sales demand)} \\
S, H &\geq 0
\end{aligned}
$$

Note that the constraints are *inequalities*, and are not equations. There is no requirement to use up the total hours available in each process, nor to satisfy all the demand for heavy gauge rolls.

If we take the production constraint of 2,400 hours in the steel-forming process

$$0.6S + 0.8H \leq 2,400$$

it means that since there are only 2,400 hours available in the process, output must be limited to a maximum of:

(a) $\dfrac{2,400}{0.6} = 4,000$ rolls of standard gauge;

(b) $\dfrac{2,400}{0.8} = 3,000$ rolls of heavy gauge; or

(c) a proportionate combination of each.

This maximum output represents the boundary line of the constraint, where the inequality becomes the equation

$$0.6S + 0.8H = 2,400$$

The line for this equation may be drawn on a graph by joining up two points on the line (such as $S = 0$, $H = 3,000$; $H = 0$, $S = 4,000$).

The other constraints may be drawn in a similar way with lines for the following equations.

$$
\begin{aligned}
0.4S + 1.2H &= 2,400 && \text{(plastic-bonding)} \\
H &= 1,300 && \text{(sales demand)}
\end{aligned}
$$

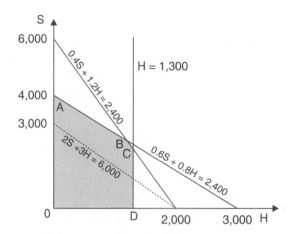

To satisfy all the constraints simultaneously, the values of S and H must lie on or below each constraint line. The outer limits of the feasible polygon are the lines, but all combined values of S and H within the shaded area are feasible solutions.

The next step is to find the optimal solution, which maximises the objective function. Since the objective is to maximise contribution, the solution to the problem must involve relatively high values (within the feasible polygon) for S, or H or a combination of both.

If, as is likely, there is only one combination of S and H which provides the optimal solution, this combination will be one of the outer corners of the feasible polygon. There are four such corners, A, B, C and D. However, it is possible that any combination of values for S and H on the boundary line between two of these corners might provide solutions with the same total contribution.

To solve the problem we establish the slope of the iso-contribution lines, by drawing a line for any one level of contribution. In our solution, a line $2S + 3H = 6,000$ has been drawn. (6,000 was chosen as a convenient multiple of 2 and 3.) This line has no significance except to indicate the slope, or gradient, of every iso-contribution line for $2S + 3H$.

Using a ruler, we can draw an iso-contribution line which is as far to the right as possible (that is, away from the origin) but which still touches the feasible polygon.

This occurs at corner B where the constraint line $0.4S + 1.2H = 2,400$ crosses with the constraint line $0.6S + 0.8H = 2,400$. At this point, there are simultaneous equations, from which the exact values of S and H may be calculated.

$$
\begin{aligned}
0.4S + 1.2H &= 2,400 &\quad (1) \\
0.6S + 0.8H &= 2,400 &\quad (2) \\
1.2S + 3.6H &= 7,200 &\quad (3)\,((1) \times 3) \\
1.2S + 1.6H &= 4,800 &\quad (4)\,((2) \times 2) \\
2H &= 2,400 &\quad (5)\,((3) - (4)) \\
H &= 1,200 &\quad (6)
\end{aligned}
$$

Substituting 1,200 for H in either equation, we can calculate that $S = 2,400$.

The contribution is maximised where $H = 1,200$ and $S = 2,400$.

	Units	Contribution per unit £	Total contribution £
Standard gauge	2,400	2	4,800
Heavy gauge	1,200	3	3,600
			8,400

Activity 3

The Dervish Chemical Company operates a small plant. Operating the plant requires two raw materials, A and B, which cost £5 and £8 per litre respectively. The maximum available supply per week is 2,700 litres of A and 2,000 litres of B.

The plant can operate using either of two processes, which have differing contributions and raw materials requirements, as follows.

Process	Raw materials consumed (litres per processing hour)		Contribution per hour
	A	B	£
1	20	10	70
2	30	20	60

The plant can run for 120 hours a week in total, but for safety reasons, process 2 cannot be operated for more than 80 hours a week.

Required

Formulate a linear programming model, and then solve it, to determine how many hours process 1 should be operated each week and how many hours process 2 should be operated each week.

Minimisation problems in linear programming

3.10 Although decision problems with limiting factors usually involve the maximisation of contribution, there may be a requirement to minimise costs. A graphical solution, involving two variables, is very similar to that for a maximisation problem, with the exception that instead of finding a contribution line touching the feasible area as far away from the origin as possible, we look for a total cost line touching the feasible area as close to the origin as possible.

EXAMPLE: A MINIMISATION PROBLEM

Bilton Sandys Ltd has undertaken a contract to supply a customer with at least 260 units in total of two products, X and Y, during the next month. At least 50% of the total output must be units of X. The products are each made by two grades of labour, as follows.

	X Hours	Y Hours
Grade A labour	4	6
Grade B labour	4	2
Total	8	8

Although additional labour can be made available at short notice, the company wishes to make use of 1,200 hours of Grade A labour and 800 hours of Grade B labour which has already been assigned to working on the contract next month. The total variable cost per unit is £120 for X and £100 for Y.

Bilton Sandys Ltd wishes to minimise expenditure on the contract next month.

Required

Calculate how much of X and Y should be supplied in order to meet the terms of the contract.

SOLUTION

Let the number of units of X supplied be x, and the number of units of Y supplied be y.

The objective is to minimise $120x + 100y$ (costs), subject to the following constraints.

$$
\begin{aligned}
x + y &\geq 260 && \text{(supply total)} \\
x &\geq 0.5(x + y) && \text{(proportion of x in total)} \\
4x + 6y &\geq 1,200 && \text{(Grade A labour)} \\
4x + 2y &\geq 800 && \text{(Grade B labour)} \\
x, y &\geq 0
\end{aligned}
$$

The constraint $x \geq 0.5(x + y)$ needs simplifying further.

$$
\begin{aligned}
x &\geq 0.5(x + y) \\
2x &\geq x + y \\
x &\geq y
\end{aligned}
$$

In a graphical solution, the line will be $x = y$. Check this carefully in the following diagram.

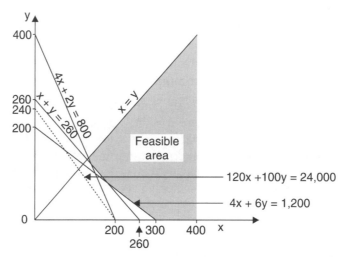

The cost line $120x + 100y = 24,000$ has been drawn to show the slope of every cost line $120x + 100y$. Costs are minimised where a cost line touches the feasible area as close as possible to the origin of the graph. This occurs where the constraint line $4x + 2y = 800$ crosses the constraint line $x + y = 260$. This point is found as follows.

$$
\begin{aligned}
x + y &= 260 && (1) \\
4x + 2y &= 800 && (2) \\
2x + y &= 400 && (3)\ ((2) \div 2) \\
x &= 140 && (4)\ ((3) - (1)) \\
y &= 120 && (5)
\end{aligned}
$$

Costs will be minimised by supplying the following.

	Unit cost £	Total cost £
140 units of X	120	16,800
120 units of Y	100	12,000
		28,800

The proportion of units of X in the total would exceed 50%, and demand for Grade A labour would exceed the 1,200 hours minimum. The minimum amount of Grade B labour would be used.

3.11 Another format of the cost minimisation problem incorporates quality requirements. An example will serve to illustrate this type of problem.

EXAMPLE: QUALITY REQUIREMENTS

J Farms Ltd can buy two types of fertiliser which contain the following percentages of chemicals.

	Nitrates	*Phosphates*	*Potash*
Type X	18	5	2
Type Y	3	2	5

For a certain crop the following minimum quantities (kg) are required.

Nitrates 100   Phosphates 50   Potash 40

Type X costs £10 per kg and Type Y costs £5 per kg. J Farms Ltd currently buys 1,000 kg of each type and wishes to minimise its expenditure on fertilisers.

Required

Recommend the quantity of each type of fertiliser which should be bought and the cost of these amounts.

SOLUTION

Define variables

Let the company buy x kg of Type X fertiliser.
Let the company buy y kg of Type Y fertiliser.

Establish constraints

$$
\begin{aligned}
0.18x + 0.03y &\geq 100 &&\text{(nitrates)} \\
0.05x + 0.02y &\geq 50 &&\text{(phosphates)} \\
0.02x + 0.05y &\geq 40 &&\text{(potash)} \\
x, y &\geq 0 &&\text{(non-negativity)}
\end{aligned}
$$

Establish objective function

The objective is to minimise the expenditure on fertilisers.

Minimise $10x + 5y$

Graph the model (see following page)

Determine optimal solution

If we move a ruler up the graph parallel to the objective function, the first point reached in the feasible region is point A. We find the co-ordinates of this point by solving the simultaneous equations below.

$$
\begin{aligned}
0.05x + 0.02y &= 50 &&(1) \\
0.02x + 0.05y &= 40 &&(2) \\
0.05x + 0.125y &= 100 &&(3)\,((2) \times 2.5) \\
0.105y &= 50 &&(4)\,((3) - (1)) \\
y &= 476.2
\end{aligned}
$$

NOTES

$$0.05x + (0.02 \times 476.2) = 50 \qquad (5) \text{ (Substitute in (1))}$$
$$0.05x + 9.52 \; = 50$$
$$0.05x \; = 40.48$$
$$x \; = 809.6$$

So the company should buy 809.6 kg of Type X fertiliser and 476.2 kg of Type Y fertiliser

The total cost is $(10 \times 809.6) + (5 \times 476.2) = £10,477$.

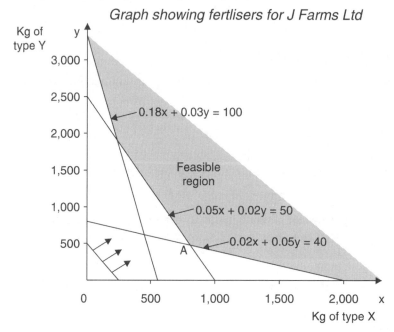

The use of simultaneous equations

3.12 You might think that a lot of time could be saved if we started by solving the simultaneous equations in a linear programming problem and did not bother to draw the graph. Certainly, this procedure may give the right answer, but in general (unless the example is very straightforward) it is *not* recommended until you have shown graphically which constraints are effective in determining the optimal solution. (In particular, if a question requires 'the graphical method', you *must* draw a graph.) To illustrate this point, consider the graph below.

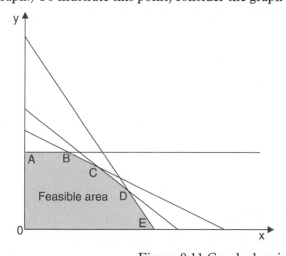

Figure 8.11 Graph showing feasible solutions

No figures have been given on the graph but the feasible area is OABCDE. When solving this problem, we would know that the optimum solution would be at one of the corners of the feasible area. We need to work out the profit at each of the corners of the feasible area and pick the one where the profit is greatest.

Once the optimum point has been determined graphically, simultaneous equations can be applied to find the exact values of x and y at this point.

Activity 4

Given the following constraints and objective function, determine the optimal production level of product X and product Y.

Constraints

$$Y \leq -\tfrac{x}{2} + 5 \qquad (1)$$
$$Y \leq 2X \qquad (2)$$
$$X \geq 0 \qquad (3)$$
$$Y \geq 0 \qquad (4)$$

Objective function

Profit = 3X + 4Y

---

4 SENSITIVITY ANALYSIS

Definition

Sensitivity analysis involves changing significant variables in order to determine the effect of these changes on the planned outcome.

4.1 In setting up the linear programming model we had to assume that we had adequate information about the amounts of the various resources by which production is constrained and about the profits which would be generated by the sale of the products. In practice, of course, these can be quite difficult to estimate, particularly when planning production not just for a week or two in advance, but for a whole year ahead. We may expect to be able to use a certain machine for 400 hours a month, only to find that, due to breakdowns, the figure is closer to 350 hours. We may hope to sell the Super at a price which will give us a profit of £100 per kennel, and then discover that a competitor has put a cheap new alternative on the market and we must cut our profit margins if we are to maintain our market share.

4.2 These circumstances could result in an optimal solution, worked out for a set of assumptions that are no longer valid, no longer being the optimal solution.

4.3 To examine this topic further a new example will be introduced.

NOTES

EXAMPLE: SENSITIVITY ANALYSIS

Dual Ltd makes two products, X and Y, which have the following selling prices and costs.

	X		Y	
	£	£	£	£
Unit selling price		14		15
Costs				
Materials (at £1 per kg)	3		2	
Labour (at £3 per hr)	6		9	
		9		11
Unit profit		5		4

What production plan would maximise profit in the next period, given that the supply of materials will be restricted to 600 kg, only 450 labour hours will be available, and a minimum demand for 150 units of product X must be met?

How would changes in the selling prices affect the solution?

SOLUTION

The problem could be solved graphically, as follows.

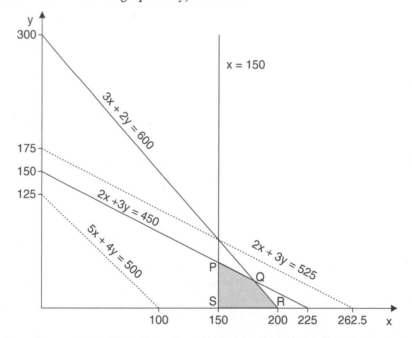

The feasible polygon is PQRS, and profit would be maximised at point Q, where

    $3x + 2y = 600$
    $2x + 3y = 450$

Therefore x = 180, y = 30, and total profit is £1,020.

The optimum will shift to point R (x = 200, y = 0) if X becomes sufficiently more profitable. It will shift when the iso-profit line becomes steeper than the line $3x + 2y = 600$. That line's gradient is –1.5, and the iso-profit line's gradient is

$$\frac{-\,\text{unit profit from X}}{\text{unit profit from Y}}$$

Thus the optimum will shift to R if the unit profit from Y remains at £4 but the unit profit from X increases to more than £6, corresponding to an increase in the unit selling price of more than £1 to more than £15.

> **Activity 5**
>
> In the above example, if the unit profit from X remains at £5, what would the unit profit from Y have to increase to in order to shift the optimum to point P? What unit selling price of Y does this new profit correspond to?

4.4 The point of sensitivity analysis is that it indicates the risk of our selecting the wrong solution. If small changes in prices would lead to a different optimum applying, there is a high risk of our selecting the wrong solution. If, on the other hand, large changes in prices would leave the optimum unchanged, errors in predicting prices are unlikely to lead to our selecting the wrong solution.

Dual prices

Definition

> The *dual price* (also called the *shadow price*) of a resource which is fully used at the optimum is the amount by which:
>
> (a) total profit would fall if the company were deprived of one unit of the resource;
>
> (b) total profit would rise if the company were able to obtain one extra unit of the scarce resource, *provided that* the resource remains an effective constraint on production and *provided also* that the extra unit of the resource can be obtained at its normal unit cost. The dual price is therefore the maximum amount which should be paid *in excess of the normal rate* for each extra unit of the resource.

4.5 The dual price is calculated on the assumption that there is a change in the availability of one resource, but with the availability of other resources being held constant.

4.6 In the above example (Dual Ltd), both materials and labour hours are used up fully in the planned production mix. Let us therefore calculate the effect on total profit if the company were deprived of one unit of materials, so that only 599 kg were available (but labour hours available remain at 450).

The new optimal production mix would be at the intersection point of the two constraint lines:

$$3x + 2y = 599$$
$$2x + 3y = 450$$

Solving the simultaneous equations, x = 179.4 units and y = 30.4 units:

Product	Units	Profit
		£
X	179.4 (× £5)	897.00
Y	30.4 (× £4)	121.60
		1,018.60
Profit in original problem		1,020.00
Reduction in profit from loss of 1 kg of materials		1.40

The dual price of materials is therefore £1.40 per kg.

4.7 Suppose that materials available are 600 kg, but that the labour supply is reduced by 20 hours to 430 hours. The optimal production mix occurs at the intersection of the two constraints:

$$2x + 3y = 430;$$
$$3x + 2y = 600.$$

Solving the simultaneous equations, $x = 188$ units and $y = 18$ units.

Product	Units	Profit
		£
X	188 (× £5)	940
Y	18 (× £4)	72
		1,012
Profit in original problem		1,020
Reduction in profit from loss of 20 labour hours		8

The dual price of labour is therefore 8/20 = £0.40 an hour.

4.8 The dual price of a resource also shows by how much profit would increase if an additional unit of the resource were made available. In our example, if the materials available were 600 kg but the labour supply were raised to 451 hours, the optimum production mix would be 179.6 units of X and 30.6 units of Y.

Product	Units	Profit
		£
X	179.6 (× £5)	898.00
Y	30.6 (× £4)	122.40
		1,020.40
Profit in original problem		1,020.00
Increase in profit from one extra unit of labour		0.40

Once again, the dual price of labour is £0.40 an hour.

4.9 The increase in contribution of £0.40 per extra labour hour is calculated on the assumption that the extra labour hour would be paid for at the normal variable cost, which is £3 an hour in the problem.

(a) The management of the company should be prepared to pay up to £0.40 extra per extra hour of labour in order to obtain more labour hours (perhaps through overtime working: the maximum value of overtime premium would then be £0.40 per hour). We assume that the existing 450 hours of labour are still paid only £3 an hour.

(b) This value of labour only applies as long as labour remains fully used. If more and more labour hours are made available, there will eventually be so much labour that it is no longer a scarce resource. In our problem, this will occur when the third constraint, $x \geq 150$, prevents a further reduction in the output of X in order to increase output of Y.

4.10 We can calculate how many hours must be available before labour ceases to be fully used. This will happen when the new labour constraint passes through the intersection of x = 150 and y = 75 (the intersection of 3x + 2y = 600 and x = 150), when it no longer forms a boundary to the feasible area. The labour constraint 2x + 3y would therefore be

2x + 3y = ?

If x = 150 and y = 75, 2x + 3y = (2 × 150) + (3 × 75) = 525

This is shown as the upper right dotted line on the graph on Page 271.

The dual price of labour is £0.40 per hour in the initial problem, but only up to a maximum supply of 525 labour hours (75 hours more than the original 450 hours). Extra labour above 525 hours would not have any use, and the two limiting factors would now be materials and the minimum demand for x. Beyond 525 hours, labour would have a dual price of zero. Once the labour constraint ceases to matter in this way, it becomes an *ineffective, non-binding* or *non-critical* constraint.

Any resource which is not fully used has a dual price of zero: losing one unit will not matter, and there is no point in paying over the normal rate for extra units.

Activity 6

A linear programming problem is as follows.

Maximise profit, 4x + 2y, subject to the following constraints.

3x + 6y ≤ 12,000 (hours of labour)
5x + 2y ≤ 10,000 (hours of machine time)
    x,y ≥ 0

The optimum is at the intersection of the labour constraint and the machine time constraint. What is the dual price per hour of machine time?

5 SIMPLEX FORMULATION

5.1 The linear programming problems in the previous sections included only two decision variables. In practice, few problems will be this simple. We therefore need to look at another technique.

Definition

The *simplex method* is a method of solving linear programming problems with two or more decision variables. It is a repetitive step by step process (and therefore an ideal computer application) that tests a number of feasible solutions in turn. If the manual process is used this is done in the form of a tableau (or table or matrix) of figures.

5.2 The formulation of the linear programming problem is identical whether it is the Simplex method or the graphical approach which is being used. It is in the solution of the problem that the difference lies.

5.3   Rather than explaining in words what is involved, the Simplex method is best illustrated by an example.

EXAMPLE: SIMPLEX METHOD

Shore Toffer Lott Ltd produces and sells two products, X and Y. Products X and Y require the following resources.

	Materials Units	*Labour* Hours	*Machine time* Hours	*Contribution per unit* £
X, per unit	5	1	3	20
Y, per unit	2	3	2	16
Total available, each week	3,000 units	1,750 hours	2,100 hours	

Although we have just two decision variables, we can still use the Simplex method to solve the problem. We begin by formulating the problem in the usual way.

Define variables	Let x = the number of units of X that should be produced and sold
	Let y = the number of units of Y that should be produced and sold
Establish constraints	Materials $5x + 2y \leq 3,000$ Labour $x + 3y \leq 1,750$ Machine time $3x + 2y \leq 2,100$ Non-negativity $x \geq 0, \quad y \geq 0$
Establish objective function	Maximise contribution (C) = $20x + 16y$

5.4   Now we change our approach and introduce the Simplex method.

Slack variables

5.5   Using the Simplex technique, we begin by turning each constraint (ignoring the non-negativity constraints now) into an equation. This is done by introducing slack variables.

Definition

> A *slack variable* represents the amount of a constraining resource or item that is unused.

Let   a   be the quantity of unused materials
      b   be the number of unused labour hours
      c   be the number of unused machine hours

5.6   We can now express the original constraints as equations.

$$5x + 2y + a = 3,000$$
$$x + 3y + b = 1,750$$
$$3x + 2y + c = 2,100$$

5.7 The slack variables a, b and c will be equal to 0 in the final solution only if the combined production of X and Y uses up all the available materials (a), labour hours (b) and machine hours (c).

5.8 If there are n constraints, there will be n variables with a value greater than 0 in any feasible solution. In this example, there are five variables (x, y, a, b and c) in the problem and three equations. In any feasible solution that is tested, three variables will therefore have a non-negative value (since there are three equations) which means that two variables will have a value of zero.

5.9 It is also usual to express the objective function as an equation with the right hand side equal to zero. In order to keep the problem consistent, the slack (or surplus) variables are inserted into the objective function equation, but as the quantities they represent should have no effect on the objective function they are given zero coefficients. In our example, the objective function will be expressed as follows.

Maximise contribution (C) given by $C - 20x - 16y + 0a + 0b + 0c = 0$.

6 THE INITIAL TABLEAU

6.1 The first feasible solution that we test has a zero value for all of the decision variables and a non-negative value for all the slack variables. Obviously this will not be the optimal solution but it gives us a starting point from which we can develop other feasible solutions.

6.2 Simplex tableaux can be drawn in several different ways but the general rules of construction are as follows.

   (a)   There should be a column for each variable (decision and slack). In our example there should be five columns.

   (b)   There should also be a solution column (on the right).

   (c)   It helps to add a further column the left, to indicate the variable in the solution (the non-negative value variables) to which the corresponding value in the solution column relates. In our example there will be three non-negative value variables.

   (d)   There is a row for each equation in the problem. Our example will therefore have three rows (for the three constraints).

   (e)   There is also a solution row.

6.3 The initial tableau for the Shore Toffer Lott Ltd problem is therefore as follows.

Variable in solution	x	y	a	b	c	Solution
a	5	2	1	0	0	3,000
b	1	3	0	1	0	1,750
c	3	2	0	0	1	2,100
Solution	−20	−16	0	0	0	0

6.4   Let us look at how this tableau was put together.

(a)   The figures in each row correspond with the coefficients of the variables in each of the revised constraints. The bottom row or solution row holds the coefficients of the revised objective function. For example the materials constraint $5x + 2y + a = 3,000$ gives us the first row, 5 (number of xs), 2 (number of ys), 1 (number of as) then zeros in the b and c columns (since these do not feature in the constraint equation) and finally 3,000 in the solution column.

(b)   The variables in the solution are a, b and c (as indicated by the left hand column).

(i)   The value of each variable is shown in the solution column.
(ii)   The column values for each *variable in the solution* are as follows.

(1)   1 in the variable's own solution row
(2)   0 in every other row, including the solution row.

(c)   The contribution per unit obtainable from x and y are given in the solution row. These are called the *shadow prices* or *dual values* of the products X and Y. The minus signs are of no particular significance. An optimal solution has been reached when all the elements of the solution row have become positive.

Interpretation of the tableau

6.5   Interpreting the tableau, we can see that the solution is testing $a = 3,000$, $b = 1,750$ and $c = 2,100$, contribution $= 0$.

6.6   The shadow prices in the initial solution (tableau) indicate the following.

(a)   The profit would be increased by £20 for every extra unit x produced (because the shadow price of x is £20 per unit).

(b)   Similarly, the profit would be increased by £16 for every extra unit of y produced (because its shadow price is £16).

6.7   Since the solution is not optimal, the contribution may be improved by introducing either x or y into the solution.

Activity 7

D Electronics produces three models of satellite dishes – Alpha, Beta and Gamma – which have contributions per unit of £400, £200 and £100 respectively.

There is a two-stage production process and the number of hours per unit for each process are as follows.

	Alpha	*Beta*	*Gamma*
Process 1	2	3	2.5
Process 2	3	2	2.0

There is an upper limit on process hours of 1,920 per period for Process 1 and 2,200 for Process 2.

The Alpha dish was designed for a low-power satellite which is now fading and the sales manager thinks that sales will be no more than 200 per period.

Fixed costs are £40,000 per period.

Required

(a) Formulate these data into a linear programming model using the following notation.

x_1: number of Alphas
x_2: number of Betas
x_3: number of Gammas

(b) Formulate (but do not attempt to solve) the initial Simplex tableau using

x_4 as slack for Process 1
x_5 as slack for Process 2
x_6 as slack for any sales limit

7   INTERPRETING THE FINAL TABLEAU AND OBJECTIVE FUNCTION

7.1   The following tableau is the final solution to the Short Toffer Lott Ltd problem.

Variable in solution	x	y	a	b	c	*Solution*
x	1	0	0	−0.2857	0.4286	400
a	0	0	1	0.5714	−1.8571	100
y	0	1	0	0.4286	−0.1429	450
Solution	0	0	0	1.1428	6.2858	15,200

7.2   The solution in this tableau is the optimal one because the shadow prices on the bottom row are all positive. The optimal solution is to make and sell 400 units of X and 450 units of Y, to earn a contribution of £15,200. The solution will leave 100 units of materials unused, but will use up all available labour and machine time.

The values in the solution row indicate the shadow price (or dual value) of the variables.

The shadow price of labour time (b) is £1.1428 per hour (bottom of column (b)), which indicates the amount by which contribution would increase/decrease if more/less labour time could be made available at its normal variable cost.

The shadow price of machine time (c) is £6.2858 per hour (bottom of column (c)), which indicates the amount by which contribution would increase/decrease if more/less machine time could be made available, at its normal variable cost.

The shadow price of materials is nil (bottom of column (a)) because there are 100 units of unused materials in the solution and therefore the materials constraint is not critical. Note, however, that if either x or y had a shadow price, this would indicate the amount by which the overall contribution would decrease if one more unit of x or y were produced.

7.3   You will usually be asked to interpret the final objective function rather than the final tableau.

7.4   The final objective function of our example is

CONTRIBUTION = 15,200 − 1.1428 (slack labour time) − 6.2858 (slack machine time)

Activity 8

When solved by the Simplex method, the final objective function of the problem set out in Activity 7 is:

CONTRIBUTION = 181,333.3 − 66.67 (Gammas) − 66.67 (slack process 1) − 266.7 (slack sales limit)

Discuss the information contained in this equation.

---

8   SENSITIVITY ANALYSIS

8.1   We looked at sensitivity analysis in Section 4. You might be required to carry out some sensitivity analysis on the solution to a problem solved by the Simplex method. You might have to work out how the value of the objective function might change if there were either more or less of a scarce resource. Alternatively you might have to test whether it would be worthwhile to obtain more of a scarce resource by paying a premium for the additional resources, for example by paying an overtime premium for extra labour hours, or by paying a supplier a higher price for extra raw materials.

8.2   Let us go back to our original example and the objective function of the optimal solution:

CONTRIBUTION = 15,200 − 1.1428 (slack labour time) − 6.2858 (slack machine time)

The effect of having more or less of a scarce resource

8.3   The objective function gives us information about the effect on contribution if additional labour hours or machine time becomes available. For example, if three additional labour hours became available, contribution would increase by 3 × £1.1428 = £3.4284. Note, however, that if extra materials become available contribution would be unaffected because materials availability is not a critical constraint.

8.4 There must be a limit to the number of extra labour hours that would earn an extra £1.1428 towards contribution. As we saw earlier in the chapter, there will be a point when there is so much labour available that it is no longer a scarce resource. You can use the same process as before to determine this point.

Activity 9

Draw a graph of the linear programming problem facing Short Toffer Lott Ltd and determine the number of additional labour hours (over and above the original 1,750 hours) over which the shadow price of £1.1428 per hour is valid.

Obtaining extra resources at a premium on cost

8.5 The shadow price, or dual price, of a scarce resource indicates the amount by which the value of the objective function would change if more or less units of the scarce resource were available at their *normal variable cost per unit*. It follows that if more units of a scarce resource were available at a premium over their normal variable cost, we can decide whether it would be worthwhile paying the premium in order to obtain the extra units.

8.6 Returning for the last time to the example of Shore Toffer Lott Ltd, we are given the following information.

(a) The normal variable cost of labour hours is £4 per hour, but extra labour hours could be worked as overtime, when the rate of pay would be time-and-a-half.

(b) The normal variable cost of machine time is £1.50 per hour, but some extra machine time could be made available by renting another machine for 40 hours per week, at a rental cost of £160. Variable running costs of this machine would be £1.50 per hour.

8.7 We know that the shadow price of labour hours is £1.1428 and of machine hours, £6.2858. We can therefore deduce the following.

(a) Paying an overtime premium of £2 per hour for labour would not be worthwhile, because the extra contribution of £1.1428 per hour would be more than offset by the cost of the premium, leaving the company worse off by £0.8572 per hour worked in overtime.

(b) Renting the extra machine would be worthwhile, but only by £91.43 (which is perhaps too small an amount to bother with).

	£
Extra contribution from 40 hours of machine time (× £6.2858)	251.43
Rental cost	160.00
Net increase in profit	91.43

Note that the variable running costs do not enter into this calculation since they are identical to the normal variable costs of machine time. We are concerned here only with the *additional* costs.

NOTES

Activity 10

A company manufactures three products, tanks, trays and tubs, each of which passes through three processes, X, Y and Z.

Process	Process hours per unit			Total process hours available
	Tanks	Trays	Tubs	
X	5	2	4	12,000
Y	4	5	6	24,000
Z	3	5	4	18,000

The contribution to profit of each product is £2 for each tank, £3 per tray and £4 per tub.

Required

(a) Formulate these data into a linear programming model using the following notation.

    Let a be the number of units of tanks produced
        b be the number of units of trays produced
        c be the number of units of tubs produced

(b) Formulate the initial Simplex tableau using the slack variables x, y and z to represent the number of unused hours in processes X, Y and Z respectively.

(c) When the problem is solved by the Simplex method, the final objective function is found to be:

CONTRIBUTION = 14,000 – 2.33 (tanks) – 0.667 (slack Process X) – 0.333 (Slack Process Z)

(i) Discuss the information contained in this equation.

(ii) What would happen to budgeted contribution if an order were received for 300 units of tanks which the company felt that it had to accept, because of the importance of the customer?

In this chapter we have been studying the ways in which you can arrive at the optimal solution when you are faced with a number of constraints. The next chapter looks at a method of mapping out the activities of a project and shows how each of the activities is related to the others. This 'mapping' out of activities is known as network analysis.

Chapter roundup

- Linear programming, at least at this fairly simple level, is a technique that can be carried out in a fairly 'handle-turning' manner once you have got the basic ideas sorted out. The steps in that technique are as follows.

    Define variables
    Establish constraints (including non-negativity)
    Construct objective function
    Draw a graph of the constraints
    Establish the feasible region
    Add an iso-profit/contribution line
    Determine optimal solution

The apparent simplicity of the technique should not, however, allow you to disregard the following practical limitations of linear programming.

- In all practical situations there are likely to be substantial problems involved in estimating the total quantities of scarce resources available. Furthermore, the final estimates used are likely to be subject to considerable uncertainty.

- There is an assumption of linearity. Each extra unit of a given product is supposed to change the contribution and the consumption of resources by the same amount. In practice, this assumption may be invalid except over small ranges. For example, in a profit maximisation problem, it may well be found that there are substantial changes in unit variable costs arising from increasing or decreasing returns to scale.

- The linear programming model is essentially static and is therefore not really suitable for analysing in detail the effects of changes over time.

- In some circumstances, a solution derived from a linear programming model may be of limited use if, for example, the variables may only take on integer values. A solution can be found by a combination of rounding up or down and trial and error, but this sort of approach is not really suitable for large-scale practical problems.

- The later part of this chapter has described how to solve a linear programming problem using the Simplex method. The method can be used with any number of decision variables, whereas the graphical method can only be applied to problems involving two decision variables.

- Make sure that you can formulate the linear programming problem and then set up an initial tableau. The method for setting up this tableau is as follows.

  Turn each constraint (ignoring non-negativity constraints) into an equation by introducing slack variables (which represent the amount of constraining resource or item that is unused).

  Express the objective function as an equation with the right-hand side equal to zero. Insert the slack variables into the equation, giving them zero coefficients.

  The initial feasible solution tested is that all the decision variables have a zero value but all the slack variables have a non-negative value.

  There should be a column for each variable and also a solution column.

  There is a row for each equation in the problem (which correspond with the coefficients of the variables in each of the revised constraints), and a solution row which holds the coefficients of the revised objective function.

- The final solution is reached when the shadow prices on the solution row are all positive. The shadow price indicates the amount by which contribution/profit would increase/decrease if more/less of the resource could be made available at its normal variable cost.

- Sensitivity analysis allows you to test the effect of having more or less of a scarce resource or of obtaining extra resources at a premium on cost.

Quick quiz

1   What is meant by an objective function?

2   What would the inequality $4x + 3y = 24$ look like when drawn on a graph?

3   What is the feasible region?

4   What is an iso-profit line?

5   How does the graphical solution of minimisation problems differ from that of maximisation problems?

6   Define the dual price of a resource.

7   What is a slack variable?

8   How is it possible to differentiate the final tableau from other tableaux?

9   What is a shadow price?

10   What is involved in doing sensitivity analysis with the Simplex method?

Answers to activities

1   If $5x + 1.5y = 400$, then if $x = 0$, $y = 267$ and if $y = 0$, $x = 80$.

    If $x + y = 150$, then if $x = 0$, $y = 150$ and if $y = 0$, $x = 150$.

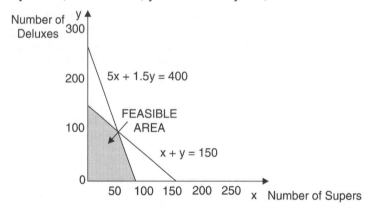

2   The new problem here is the inequality $y \geq 2x$. The equation $y = 2x$ is a straight line, and you need to plot two points to draw it, for example:

    (a)   when $x = 0$, $y = 0$
    (b)   when $x = 2$, $y = 4$

    Since $y \geq 2x$, feasible combinations of x and y lie above this line (if $x = 2$, y must be 4 or more).

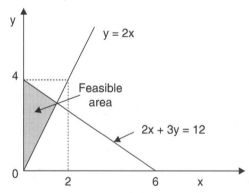

3   The decision variables are processing hours in each process. If we let the processing hours per week for process 1 be P_1 and the processing hours per week for process 2 be P_2 we can formulate an objective and constraints as follows.

    The objective is to maximise $70P_1 + 60P_2$, subject to the following constraints.

$$20P_1 + 30P_2 \le 2{,}700 \qquad \text{(material A supply)}$$
$$10P_1 + 20P_2 \le 2{,}000 \qquad \text{(material B supply)}$$
$$P_2 \le 80 \qquad \text{(maximum time for } P_2 \text{)}$$
$$P_1 + P_2 \le 120 \qquad \text{(total maximum time)}$$
$$P_1, P_2 \ge 0$$

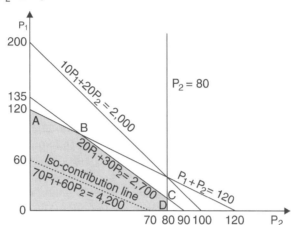

The feasible area is ABCDO.

The optimal solution, found by moving the iso-contribution line outwards, is at point A, where $P_1 = 120$ and $P_2 = 0$.

Total contribution would be $120 \times 70 = £8{,}400$ a week.

4   Feasible solutions are at the intersection of the constraints:

(1) and (2)	(1) and (3)	(1) and (4)	(2) and (3)	(2) and (4)	(3) and (4)
X = 2, Y = 4	X = 0, Y = 5	X = 10, Y = 0		X = 0, Y = 0	
Profit = 22	Profit = 20	Profit = 30		Profit = 0	

Profit is maximised when 10 units of product X and no units of product Y are produced.

5   The gradient of $2x + 3y = 450$ is $-2/3$. We therefore need:

£5/unit profit from Y < 2/3
Unit profit from Y > £7.50
Unit selling price of Y > £18.50

6   The optimum is at the following point.

$$3x + 6y = 12{,}000 \qquad (1)$$
$$5x + 2y = 10{,}000 \qquad (2)$$
$$15x + 6y = 30{,}000 \qquad (3) \quad ((2) \times 3)$$
$$12x = 18{,}000 \qquad (3) - (1)$$
$$x = 1{,}500$$
$$\therefore y = 1{,}250$$

Profit $= (1{,}500 \times 4) + (1{,}250 \times 2) = £8{,}500$.

225

With one extra machine hour, the optimum would be as follows.

$$
\begin{array}{rll}
3x + 6y &= 12,000 & (1) \\
5x + 2y &= 10,001 & (2) \\
15x + 6y &= 30,003 & (3) \quad ((2) \times 3) \\
12x &= 18,003 & (3) - (1) \\
x &= 1,500.25 & \\
y &= 1,249.875 &
\end{array}
$$

Profit = $(1,500.25 \times 4) + (1,249.875 \times 2) = £8,500.75$.

The dual price per machine hour is $£(8,500.75 - 8,500.00) = £0.75$

7　(a)　*Define variables*

Let x_1 be the number of Alphas produced/sold per period
Let x_2 be the number of Betas produced/sold per period
Let x_3 be the number of Gammas produced/sold per period

Establish constraints

$$
\begin{array}{rll}
2x_1 + 3x_2 + 2.5x_3 &\leq 1,920 & \text{(Process 1)} \\
3x_1 + 2x_2 + 2x_3 &\leq 2,200 & \text{(Process 2)} \\
0 \leq x_1 &\leq 200 & \text{(Sales)} \\
x_2, x_3 &\geq 0 & \text{(Non-negativity)}
\end{array}
$$

Establish objective functions

Maximise $C = 400x_1 + 200x_2 + 100x_3$ (Contribution)

To prepare the initial tableau we need to introduce slack variables.

Let x_4 = quantity of unused process 1 hours
Let x_5 = quantity of unused process 2 hours
Let x_6 = quantity of unused units of Alpha

The revised constraints are as follows.

$$
\begin{array}{rl}
2x_1 + 3x_2 + 2.5x_3 + x_4 &= 1,920 \\
3x_1 + 2x_2 + 2x_3 + x_5 &= 2,200 \\
x_1 + x_6 &= 200
\end{array}
$$

The objective function can be redefined as

$$C - 400x_1 - 200x_2 - 100x_3 + 0x_4 + 0x_5 + 0x_6 = 0$$

(b)　The initial Simplex tabulation is as follows.

Variable in solution	x_1	x_2	x_3	x_4	x_5	x_6	Solution
x_4	2	3	2.5	1	0	0	1,920
x_5	3	2	2	0	1	0	2,200
x_6	1	0	0	0	0	1	200
Solution	−400	−200	−100	0	0	0	0

8　Overall contribution = £181,333.30.

Since this is the optimal solution, contribution will fall by £66.67 per unit of Gamma produced. (If it were to rise, the solution would not be optimal.)

If the number of Process 1 hours were reduced/increased by one, contribution would fall/rise by £66.67.

If the upper limit on sales of Alpha were reduced/increased by one, contribution would fall/rise by £266.7.

9

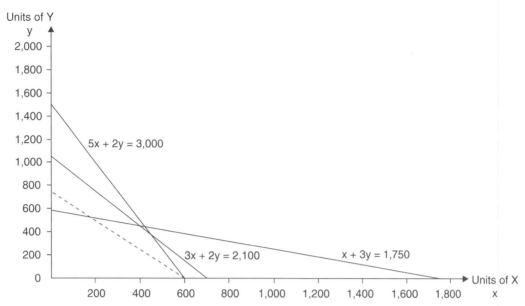

As the number of labour hours available increases, the line on the graph representing the constraint will move up the axes parallel to the original constraint. It will remain part of the boundary of the feasible area and a critical constraint until the point when it passes through the point (0, 1,050). At this point the labour hours available are (1 × 0) + (3 × 1,050) = 3,150. The shadow price of £1.1428 per hour is therefore valid for about 1,400 *extra* labour hours.

10 (a) The objective function is to:

Maximise   2a + 3b + 4c (contribution)

Subject to the constraints 5a + 2b + 4c ≤ 12,000 (process X hours)
           4a + 5b + 6c ≤ 24,000 (process Y hours)
           3a + 5b + 4c ≤ 18,000 (process Z hours)
              a, b, c ≥ 0

(b) Initial tableau

Variables in the solution	a	b	c	x	y	z	Solution
x	5	2	4	1	0	0	12,000
y	4	5	6	0	1	0	24,000
z	3	5	4	0	0	1	18,000
Solution	−2	−3	−4	0	0	0	0

(c) (i) The maximum contribution available is £14,000

Contribution would fall by £2.33 for every tank produced.

If the number of hours in Process X were reduced/increased by one, contribution would fall/rise by £0.667.

If the number of hours in Process Z were reduced/increased by one, contribution would fall/rise by £0.333.

Process Z hours would be fully utilised in the optimal solution.

(ii) If an order were to be received for 300 tanks and they were produced, contribution would fall by $300 \times £2.33 = £700$.

Assignment 8 (45 minutes)

A chemical company refines crude oil into petrol. The refining process uses two types of crude oil, heavy and light. A mixture of these oils is blended into either super or regular petrol.

In the refining process one gallon (g) of super is made from $^{7}/_{10}$ g of heavy crude and ½ g of light crude. One gallon of regular is made from ½ g of heavy crude and $^{7}/_{10}$g of light crude oil. (There is a refining loss of $^{1}/_{5}$g in each case.)

At present, 5,000g heavy crude and 6,000g of light crude oil are available for refining each day. Market conditions suggest that at least two thirds of the petrol should be super. The company sells super for £1.80 a gallon and regular for £1.65 a gallon, the profit being £0.25 and £0.10 a gallon respectively, and wishes to maximise total profit.

Required

(a) State the objective function and three constraints, one for heavy crude, one for light crude and one for market conditions.

(b) Graph the constraints and shade the feasible region.

(c) Deduce the optimal policy and the profit generated, and comment briefly on your answer.

(d) A qualified management accountant has seen your calculations and provided you with a long list of other matters that need to be taken into account, such as competitors' actions, the large number of other by-products from the refining process, the unpredictable actions of suppliers, distribution factors, and so on.

How can these matters be incorporated into the decision?

Chapter 9:
NETWORK ANALYSIS

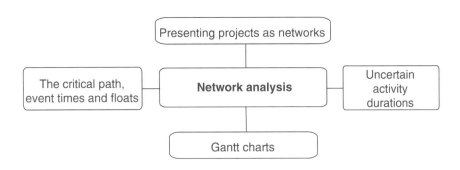

Introduction

A large project, such as building a bridge, will comprise many activities, which must be done in the right order. Network analysis is a way of mapping out the activities in a project, and showing their interrelationships: we will see how to draw a type of network diagram called an activity on arrow diagram.

Timing is often crucial in large projects. We will see how to find the critical path, which is a sequence of those activities which, were any of them to run late, would mean that the whole project was delayed. We will also see how to find the earliest time each activity might be able to start (an earliest event time) and the latest time by which it must be finished (a latest event time). We can then work out by how much an activity might be allowed to overrun (its float). Activities may take more or less time than anticipated, and so we will look at PERT, a method of dealing with such uncertainties. Finally we will look at Gantt charts, which can be used to estimate the amount of resources required for a project.

Your objectives

After completing this chapter, you should:

    (a)   be able to draw network diagrams using the activity on arrow presentation;

    (b)   understand the concept of dummy activities;

    (c)   be able to identify the critical path;

    (d)   be able to determine earliest event times and latest event times;

    (e)   be able to calculate an activity's float;

    (f)   be able to use PERT;

    (g)   be able to construct and use Gantt charts.

1 PRESENTING PROJECTS AS NETWORKS

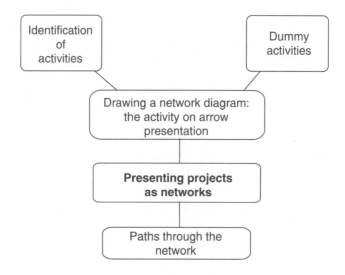

1.1 Network analysis is a technique for planning and controlling large projects, such as construction work, research and development projects or the computerisation of business systems. Network analysis helps managers to plan when to start various tasks, to allocate resources so that the tasks can be carried out within schedule, to monitor actual progress and to find out when control action is needed to prevent a delay in completion of the project. The events and activities making up the whole project are represented in the form of a diagram or chart. Network analysis is sometimes called critical path analysis (CPA) or critical path method (CPM).

Definition

Network analysis is basically concerned with the deployment of available resources for the completion of a complex task.

Drawing a network diagram: the activity on arrow presentation

1.2 Here is an example of a network for building the Channel Tunnel, with the whole project simplified to just three activities.

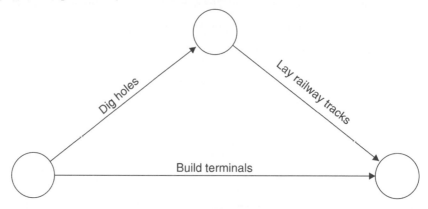

Figure 9.1 Channel Tunnel network diagram

The holes must be dug before the tracks can be laid, which is why laying the tracks follows on from digging the holes in the diagram. However, building the terminals in France and England can be done at the same time as the other two activities, which is why building the terminals runs across the page alongside those other activities in the diagram.

This form of network diagram is an activity on arrow diagram, which means that each activity within a project is represented on the diagram by an arrowed line. An alternative form of diagram is activity on node, but we shall use the activity on arrow presentation because it is easier to follow.

1.3 A project is analysed into its separate activities and the sequence of activities is presented in a network diagram. The flow of activities in the diagram is from left to right.

1.4 An *activity* within a network is represented by an arrowed line, running between one event and another event. An event is simply the start and/or completion of an activity, which is represented on the network diagram by a circle (called a *node*).

1.5 Let us suppose that in a certain project there are two activities A and B, and activity B cannot be started until activity A is completed. Activity A might be building the walls of a house, and activity B might be putting the roof on. This would be represented as follows.

Figure 9.2 Construction of network diagrams (1)

The rule is that an activity cannot start until all activities leading into the event at its start have been completed.

1.6 Events are usually numbered, just to identify them. In this example, event 1 is the start of Activity A, event 3 is the completion of Activity B, and event 2 is both the completion of A and the start of B.

1.7 Let us now suppose that another project includes three activities, C, D and E. Neither activity D nor E can start until C is completed, but D and E could be done simultaneously if required. This would be represented as follows.

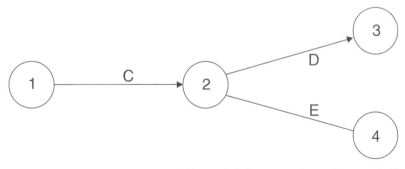

Figure 9.3 Construction of network diagrams (2)

In this diagram, event 2 represents the point when C is completed and also the point when D and E can start, so the diagram clearly shows that D and E must follow C.

1.8 A third possibility is that an activity cannot start until two or more activities have been completed. If H cannot start until F and G are both complete, then we would represent the situation like this.

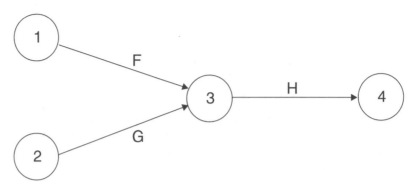

Figure 9.4 Construction of network diagrams (3)

EXAMPLE: NETWORK DIAGRAMS

Draw the network for the following project to build a factory.

Activity		Preceding activity
A:	lay foundations	–
B:	build walls	A
C:	lay drains	A
D:	install electricity cables	A
E:	fit window frames	B
F:	fit door frames	B
G:	fit windows	E
H:	fit doors	F
I:	plaster inside walls	G,H
J:	lay floor	C
K:	fit power outlets	D
L:	install machines	I, J, K

SOLUTION

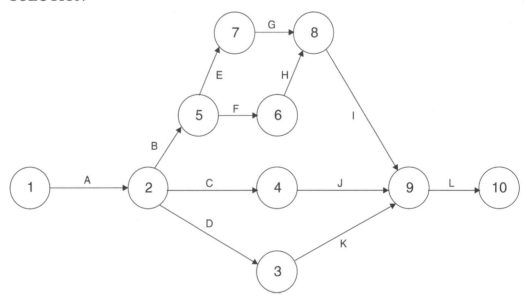

Activity 1

In the above network, could activities E and H be carried on simultaneously?

The identification of activities

1.9 Activities may be identified as either:

(a) activities A, B, C, D and so on; or
(b) activities 1–2, 2–5, 2–4, 2–3 and so on.

Dummy activities

1.10 It is a convention in network analysis that two activities are not drawn between the same events. The convention makes diagrams clearer.

To avoid having two activities running between the same events, we use a dummy activity. A dummy activity takes no time and no resources to complete.

Definition

A *dummy activity* is used in network analysis when two activities could start at the same time and finish at the same time too. It is represented by a broken arrowed line.

1.11 For example, suppose that the sequence of activities in a project to install a computer system is as follows.

Activity	*Preceding Activity*
A: install computer	–
B: write programs	A
C: hire trained staff	A
D: test system	B, C

In theory, we could draw the network as follows.

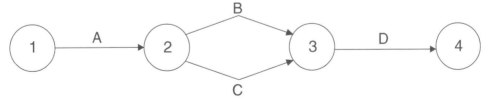

Figure 9.5 Theoretical network diagram of computer installation

By convention, this would be incorrect. Two separate activities must not start and end with the same events. The correct representation is shown below.

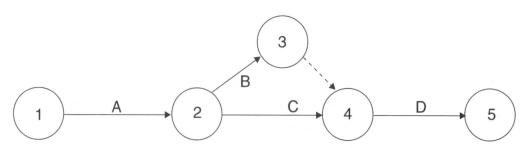

Figure 9.6 Actual network diagram of computer installation

1.12 Sometimes it is necessary to use a dummy activity not just to comply with the convention, but to preserve the basic logic of the network.

1.13 Consider the following example of a project to install a new office telephone system.

Activity	Preceding Activity
A: buy equipment	–
B: allocate extension numbers	–
C: install switchboard	A
D: install wiring	B, C
E: print office directory	B

The project is finished when both D and E are complete.

The problem arises because D can only start when both B and C have been finished, whereas E is only required to follow B. The only way to draw the network is to use a dummy activity.

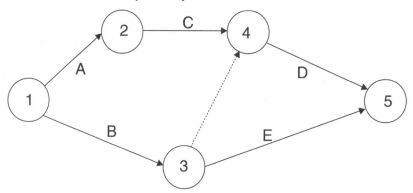

Figure 9.7 Network diagram with dummy activity

Paths through the network

1.14 Any network can be analysed into a number of different paths or routes. A path is simply a sequence of activities from the start to the end of the network. In the example above, there are just three paths.

(a) A C D;
(b) B Dummy D;
(c) B E.

Activity 2

List the paths through the network in the earlier example to build a factory with activities A – L.

2   THE CRITICAL PATH, EVENT TIMES AND FLOATS

Definition

The *critical path* is the path through the network with the greatest total duration

2.1   The time needed to complete each individual activity in a project must be estimated. This time is shown on the network above or below the line representing the activity. The duration of the whole project will be fixed by the time taken to complete the path through the network with the greatest total duration. This path is called the *critical path* and activities on it are known as *critical activities*. A network can have more than one critical path, if several paths tie for the greatest duration.

2.2   Activities on the critical path must be started and completed on time, otherwise the total project time will be extended. The method of finding the critical path is illustrated in the example below.

EXAMPLE: THE CRITICAL PATH

The following activities comprise a project to renovate a block of flats.

Activity	Preceding Activity	Duration (weeks)
A: replace windows in lounges	–	5
B: rewire	–	4
C: replaster walls of lounges	A	2
D: fit lights in lounges	B	1
E: decorate bedrooms	B	5
F: install plumbing	B	5
G: decorate lounges	C,D	4
H: decorate kitchens	F	3
I: decorate bathrooms	F	2

(a)   What are the paths through the network?
(b)   What is the critical path and what is its duration?

SOLUTION

The first step in the solution is to draw the network diagram, with the time for each activity shown.

A network should have just one start node and one completion node, and in the diagram below, this is achieved by introducing a dummy activity after activity I. Dummy activities always have zero duration.

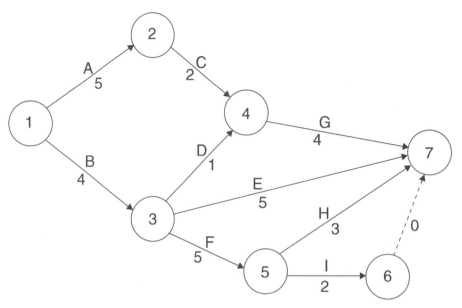

We could list the paths through the network and their durations as follows.

Path	Duration (weeks)	
A C G	(5 + 2 + 4)	11
B D G	(4 + 1 + 4)	9
B E	(4 + 5)	9
B F H	(4 + 5 + 3)	12
B F I Dummy	(4 + 5 + 2 + 0)	11

The critical path is the longest path, BFH, with a duration of 12 weeks. This is the minimum time needed to complete the project. Note that a network may have more than one critical path, if two or more paths have equal highest durations.

Activity 3

The following activities comprise a project to agree a price for some land to be bought for development.

Activity		Preceded by	Duration Days
P:	get survey done	–	4
Q:	draw up plans	–	7
R:	estimate cost of building work	Q	2
S:	get tenders for site preparation work	P	9
T:	negotiate price	R, S	3

Within how many days could the whole project be completed?

2.3   Listing paths through the network in this way is easy for small networks, but it becomes tedious for bigger and more complex networks.

Earliest event times and latest event times

2.4   Another way to find the critical path is to include earliest times and latest times for each event, showing them on the network diagram.

(a)   The earliest event time is the earliest time that any subsequent activities can start.

(b)   The latest event time is the latest time by which all preceding activities must be completed if the project as a whole is to be completed in the minimum time.

One way of showing earliest and latest event times is to divide each event node into three sections. These will record:

(a)   the event number;
(b)   the earliest event time. For the starting node in the network, this is time 0;
(c)   the latest event time.

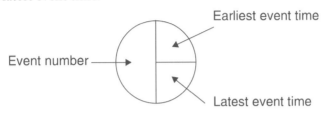

Figure 9.8 Earliest and latest event times

Earliest event times

2.5   The next step is to calculate the earliest event times. Always start at event 1 with its earliest starting time of 0. We will continue the previous example to show how times are calculated.

Work from left to right through the diagram calculating the earliest time that the next activity following the event can start. For example, the earliest event time at event 2 is the earliest time activity C can start. This is week $0 + 5 = 5$. Similarly, the earliest event time at event 3 is the earliest time D, E and F can start, which is week $0 + 4 = 4$, and the earliest time at event 5 is the earliest time activities H and I can start, which is $4 + 5 = $ week 9.

A slight problem occurs where more than one activity ends at the same node. For example, event 4 is the completion node for activities C and D. Activity G cannot start until both C and D are complete, therefore the earliest event time at event 4 is the higher of:

(a)   earliest event time, event 2 + duration of C = $5 + 2 = 7$ weeks;
(b)   earliest event time, event 3 + duration of D = $4 + 1 = 5$ weeks.

The earliest event time at event 4 is 7 weeks.

Similarly, the earliest event time at event 7 is the highest of:

Earliest event time, event 3 + duration of E $= 4 + 5 = 9$
Earliest event time, event 4 + duration of G $= 7 + 4 = 11$
Earliest event time, event 5 + duration of H $= 9 + 3 = 12$
Earliest event time, event 6 + duration of dummy activity $= 11 + 0 = 11$

The highest value is 12 weeks. This also means that the minimum completion time for the entire project is 12 weeks.

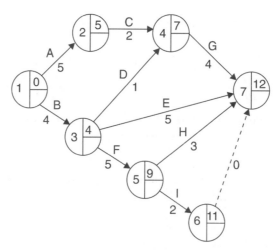

Figure 9.9 Calculating earliest event times

Activity 4

If activity C had taken four weeks, which earliest event times would have been affected, and what would they have changed to?

Latest event times

2.6 The next step is to calculate the latest event times. These are the latest times at which each event can occur if the project as a whole is to be completed in the shortest possible time, 12 weeks. The latest event time at the final event must be the same as the earliest event time, which in this example is 12 weeks.

Work from right to left through the diagram calculating the latest time at which each activity can start, if it is to be completed by the latest event time of the event at its end. The latest event time for:

(a) event 4 is 12 – 4 = week 8;
(b) event 6 is 12 – 0 = week 12;
(c) event 2 is 8 – 2 = week 6.

Event 5 might cause difficulties as two activities, H and I lead back to it.

(a) Activity H must be completed by week 12, and so must start at week 9.
(b) Activity I must also be completed by week 12, and so must start at week 10.

The latest event time at node 5 is the earlier of week 9 or week 10, that is, week 9. All activities leading up to node 5, which in this case is just F, must be completed by week 9 so that both H and I can be completed by week 12.

The latest event time at event 3 is calculated in the same way. It is the earliest time which enables all subsequent activities to be completed within the required time. Thus, at event 3, we have the following.

Subsequent event	Latest time of that event (a)	Intermediate activity	Duration of the activity (b)	Required event time at event 3 (a) – (b)
4	8	D	1	7
5	9	F	5	4
7	12	E	5	7

All activities before event 3 must be completed by week 4, to enable all subsequent activities to be completed within the required time.

Similarly, the latest event time at event 1 is the lower of:

Latest event time, event 2 minus duration of A = 6 − 5 = 1
Latest event time, event 3 minus duration of B = 4 − 4 = 0

The latest event time at event 1 is therefore 0. It must always be 0. If your calculations give any other value, you have made an error.

The final network diagram is now as follows. The critical path has been indicated by a double line.

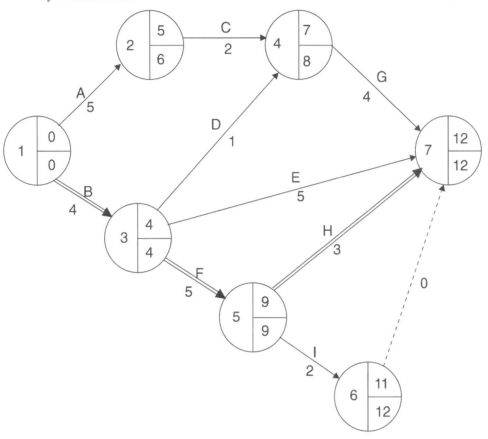

Figure 9.10 Final network diagram

Finding the critical path

2.7   Critical activities are those activities which must be started on time, otherwise the total project time will be increased. It follows that each event on the critical path must have the same earliest and latest times. The critical path for the above network is therefore B F H (events 1,3,5,7). An event with the same earliest and latest times is called a *critical event*.

BPP
PUBLISHING

Activity 5

The following activities comprise a project to make a film.

Activity		Preceded by	Duration Weeks
J:	negotiate distribution	–	6
K:	arrange publicity	J	5
L:	write screenplay	–	3
M:	hire cast and crew	L	5
N:	shoot and edit	M, Q	4
P:	design sets	L	2
Q:	build sets	P	1

What are the earliest and latest event times of the event at the end of activity P?

2.8 You may find that an activity connects two events each of which has the same earliest and latest event times, but that the activity itself is not critical.

For example, in the following extract from the example following paragraph 2.2, events 3 and 7 are on the critical path.

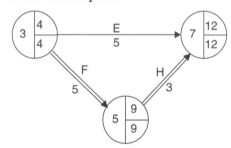

Figure 9.11 The critical path

Activity E, however, is not critical: the critical path goes through event 5. If you are in doubt as to whether an activity is on the critical path you should check to see whether it has any float (see below). All critical activities have zero float.

Float

2.9 Activities which are not on the critical path are non–critical, and they can, within limits:

(a) start late; and/or
(b) take longer than the time specified,

without holding up the completion of the project as a whole.

The float for any activity is the amount of time by which its duration could be extended up to the point where it would become critical. This is the same as the amount of time by which its duration could be extended without affecting the total project time.

The effect on the time available for preceding and subsequent activities is ignored. The total float for an activity is therefore equal to its latest finishing time minus its earliest starting time minus its duration.

For example, look at activity C in the above example to renovate a block of flats. This must be completed by week 8 if the total project time is not to be extended. It cannot be started until week 5 at the earliest, but as it only takes two weeks there is one spare week available. The float for activity C is $(8 - 5 - 2) = 1$ week.

> **Activity 6**
>
> What are the floats for activities D and G in the above example?

3 UNCERTAIN ACTIVITY DURATIONS

3.1 Network problems may be complicated by uncertainty in the durations of individual activities. For example, building works can easily be delayed by bad weather.

Definition

> *PERT (project evaluation and review technique)* is a form of network analysis which takes account of uncertainty.

3.2 Using PERT, optimistic, most likely and pessimistic estimates of durations are made for each activity in the project. These estimates are converted into a mean duration and a variance, using the following formulae.

(a) Mean $\mu = \dfrac{a + 4m + b}{6}$

where a = optimistic estimate of activity duration
m = most likely estimate of activity duration
b = pessimistic estimate of activity duration

(b) Variance $\sigma^2 = \dfrac{1}{36}(b-a)^2$

The standard deviation, σ, is $\dfrac{1}{6}(b-a)$.

Once the mean duration and the standard deviation of durations have been calculated for each activity, we can find the critical path using the mean activity durations.

EXAMPLE: PERT

A project consists of four activities.

Activity	Preceding activity	Optimistic (a) Days	Time to complete Most likely (m) Days	Pessimistic (b) Days
A	–	5	10	15
B	A	16	18	26
C	–	15	20	31
D	–	8	18	28

Analyse the project using PERT.

SOLUTION

The mean duration for each activity is calculated by the formula $\dfrac{a + 4m + b}{6}$

Activity	a + 4m + b	Divided by 6 Days
A	5 + 40 + 15 = 60	10
B	16 + 72 + 26 = 114	19
C	15 + 80 + 31 = 126	21
D	8 + 72 + 28 = 108	18

The standard deviation of durations for each activity is calculated by the formula $\dfrac{b - a}{6}$

Activity	b – a	Divided by 6 Days
A	15 – 5 = 10	1.67
B	26 – 16 = 10	1.67
C	31 – 15 = 16	2.67
D	28 – 8 = 20	3.33

The network can be drawn using the mean durations.

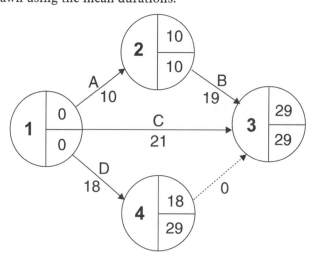

We add the *variances* of the uncertain activities in a path. We can do this provided the activity durations are independent.

Variance of activity A's time = 1.67^2	2.78
Variance of activity B's time = 1.67^2	2.78
Combined variance of path AB	5.56

The standard deviation of the durations of path AB is $\sqrt{5.56} = 2.36$ days.

4 GANTT CHARTS

Definition

> *Gantt charts* are line diagrams, with lines representing both time and activities. They can be used to estimate the amount of resources required for a project. Where activities are in a continuous 'chain', with one activity able to follow immediately after the other, these can be drawn as a continuous line on the chart.

EXAMPLE: GANTT CHARTS

Flotto Limited is about to undertake a project about which the following data is available.

Activity	Must be preceded by activity	Duration Days	Men required for the job
A	–	3	6
B	–	5	3
C	B	2	4
D	A	1	4
E	A	6	5
F	D	3	6
G	C,E	3	3

There is a labour force of nine men available, and each man is paid a fixed wage regardless of whether or not he is actively working on any day. Every man is capable of working on any of the seven activities. If extra labour is required during any day, men can be hired on a daily basis at the rate of £120 per day. If the project is to finish in the minimum time what extra payments must be made for hired labour?

SOLUTION

Draw the network to establish the duration of the project and the critical path. Then draw a Gantt chart, using the critical path as a basis, assuming that jobs start at the earliest possible time. Float times on chains of activities should be shown by a dotted line.

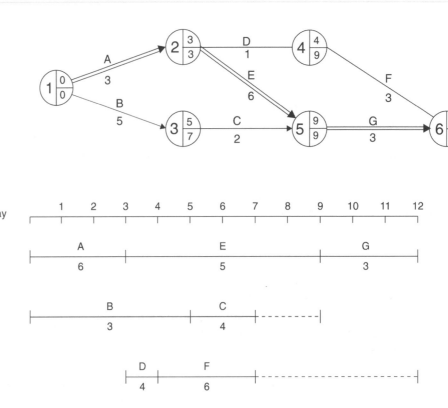

It can be seen that if all activities start at their earliest times, as many as 15 men will be required on any one day (days 6–7) whereas on other days there would be idle capacity (days 7–12). The problem can be reduced, or removed, by using up float time on non–critical activities. Suppose we deferred the start of activities D and F until the latest possible day. This would be the end of day 8/start of day 9 – leaving four days to complete the activities by the end of day 12.

The Gantt chart would be redrawn as follows.

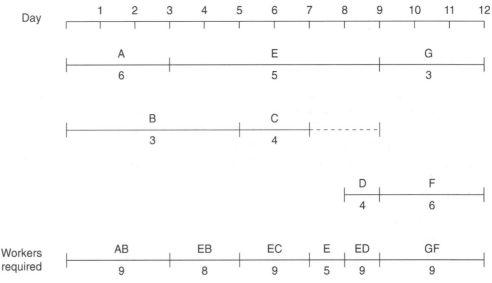

The project can be completed in the minimum time without hiring any additional labour.

Gantt charts used for control

4.1 Gantt charts can also be used very conveniently to show the progress of a project. Consider the following chart which shows progress on a project at day 10.

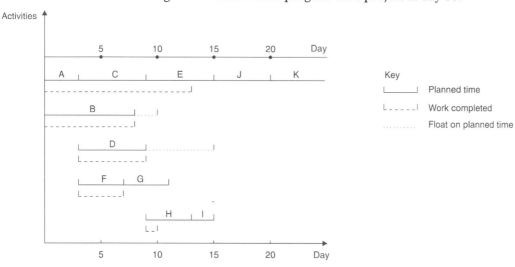

Figure 9.12 A Gantt chart

This chart shows that activities A, B, C and D have been completed; that work on the critical path is slightly ahead of schedule (equivalent to the end of the 13th day); that work on activity H is absolutely on schedule, but that work on F and G is well behind.

Activity 7

Thurnon plc are to initiate a project to study the feasibility of a new product. The end result of the feasibility project will be a report recommending the action to be taken for the new product. The activities to be carried out to complete the feasibility project are given below.

Activity	Description	Immediate predecessors	Expected time Weeks	Number of staff required
A:	preliminary design	–	5	3
B:	market research	–	3	2
C:	obtain engineering quotes	A	2	2
D:	construct prototype	A	5	5
E:	prepare marketing material	A	3	3
F:	costing	C	2	2
G:	product testing	D	4	5
H:	pilot survey	B, E	6	4
I:	pricing estimates	H	2	1
J:	final report	F, G, I	6	2

(a) Draw a network for the scheme of activities set out above. Determine the critical path and the shortest duration of the project.

(b) Assuming the project starts at time zero and that each activity commences at the earliest start date, construct a chart showing the number of staff required at any one time for this project.

NOTES

The investment in stock is a very important one for most organisations, both in terms of monetary value and relationships with customers. It is therefore vital that management establish and maintain an effective stock control system. The final chapter in this Course Book is entitled 'Inventory Control' and is concerned with the ways in which stock (inventory) can be controlled by management.

Chapter roundup

- A network represents a project by breaking it down into activities and showing their interdependence.

- Activities are represented by arrows, which are drawn between nodes which represent events. Dummy activities may be needed. Any sequence of activities from the start to the end of a network is a path through the network.

- The path with the greatest duration is the critical path. Any delay on this path will delay the project as a whole.

- The earliest event time for an event is the earliest time that activities starting at that event can start. The latest event time is the latest time by which all activities leading into that event must be completed if the whole project is to be completed in the minimum time.

- For events on the critical path, the earliest and latest event times are the same. Activities on the critical path have zero float: an activity's float is the latest event time of the event at its end minus the earliest event time of the event at its start minus its duration.

- If activity durations are uncertain, the PERT formulae can be used to estimate mean durations and variances of durations. The variances of the durations of activities on the critical path can then be added, and the probability that the duration of the critical path will exceed any given value can be computed.

- Gantt charts can be used to estimate the amount of resources required for a project.

Quick quiz

1   When is a dummy activity necessary in a network?

2   What is the critical path?

3   What is an activity's float?

4   What are the formulae used in PERT to estimate the mean and the standard deviation of an activity's duration?

5   Where we have a chain of activities with uncertain durations, can we add the standard deviations of their durations?

Answers to activities

1   Yes, E and H could be carried on simultaneously. Indeed, that might be the most sensible thing to do. If E took five days and F only took one day, H could be started while E was still in progress.

2   There are four paths, as follows.

    A B E G I L
    A B F H I L
    A C J L
    A D K L

PUBLISHING

3

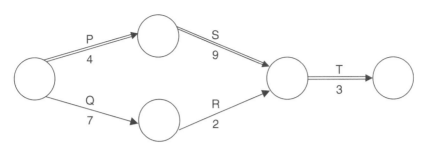

The paths are PST (4 + 9 + 3 = 16 days) and QRT (7 + 2 + 3 = 12 days). The minimum overall duration is 16 days. The critical path is PST.

4   The only earliest event times affected would be those for event 4 (revised to week 9) and for event 7 (revised to week 13).

5

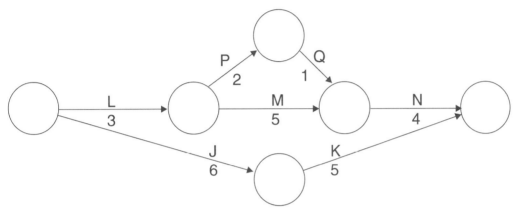

The critical path is LMN, with a duration of 12 weeks. The earliest event time for the event at the end of activity P is 3 + 2 = 5 weeks. The latest event time is 12 − 4 − 1 = 7 weeks.

6   Float for activity D = 8 − 4 − 1 = 3 weeks.

Float for activity G = 12 − 7 − 4 = 1 week.

7   (a)

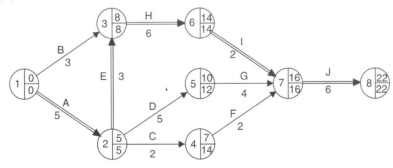

The critical path is AEHIJ, and the minimum total duration is 22 weeks.

(b) To construct a Gantt chart we need to list all possible paths through the network.

A E H I J
A D G J
A C F J
B H I J

Then using the critical path as the basis, we can construct the Gantt chart as follows.

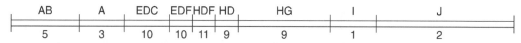

Assignment 9   **(45 minutes)**

The network for a project consisting of eight activities is shown below, together with the time (in days) required to complete each stage.

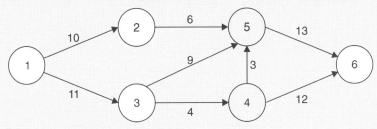

Required

(a) State the four possible paths through the network and the total time required to complete each one.

(b) Deduce the critical path, and state its duration and importance.

(c) Complete the five blank columns in the table below.

(d) Explain briefly the information conveyed by the total float.

Activity	Time	Earliest start	Earliest finish	Latest start	Latest finish	Total float
1-2	10					
1-3	11					
2-5	6					
3-5	9					
3-4	4					
4-5	3					
4-6	12					
5-6	13					

Chapter 10 :
INVENTORY CONTROL

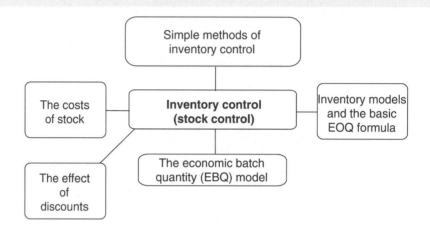

Introduction

Inventory (stock) is traditionally one of the key concerns of a business. This chapter considers a variety of methods by which it may be 'controlled'. In effect this means minimising the cost but not running out.

Your objectives

After completing this chapter you should:

(a)   know what the different costs associated with stock are;

(b)   understand the simple methods of stock control;

(c)   be able to calculate the reorder level and reorder quantity;

(d)   have an understanding of the basic economic quantity order (EOQ) model;

(e)   have an understanding of the economic batch quantity (EBQ) model;

(f)   understand the effect of discounts on the total cost of an order.

1 STOCK CONTROL LEVELS

Why hold stock?

1.1 The costs of purchasing stock are usually one of the largest costs faced by an organisation and, once obtained, stock has to be carefully controlled and checked.

1.2 The main reasons for holding stocks can be summarised as follows.

- To ensure sufficient goods are available to meet expected demand
- To provide a buffer between processes
- To meet any future shortages
- To take advantage of bulk purchasing discounts
- To absorb seasonal fluctuations and any variations in usage and demand
- To allow production processes to flow smoothly and efficiently
- As a necessary part of the production process (such as when maturing cheese)
- As a deliberate investment policy, especially in times of inflation or possible shortages

Holding costs

1.3 If stocks are too high, *holding costs* will be incurred unnecessarily. Such costs occur for a number of reasons.

(a) *Costs of storage and stores operations*. Larger stocks require more storage space and possibly extra staff and equipment to control and handle them.

(b) *Interest charges*. Holding stocks involves the tying up of capital (cash) on which interest must be paid.

(c) *Insurance costs*. The larger the value of stocks held, the greater insurance premiums are likely to be.

(d) *Risk of obsolescence*. The longer a stock item is held, the greater is the risk of obsolescence.

(e) *Deterioration*. When materials in store deteriorate to the extent that they are unusable, they must be thrown away with the likelihood that disposal costs would be incurred.

Costs of obtaining stock

1.4 On the other hand, if stocks are kept low, small quantities of stock will have to be ordered more frequently, thereby increasing the following *ordering* or *procurement costs*.

(a) *Clerical and administrative costs* associated with purchasing, accounting for and receiving goods

(b) *Transport costs*

(c) *Production run costs*, for stock which is manufactured internally rather than purchased from external sources

Stockout costs

1.5 An additional type of cost which may arise if stocks are kept too low is the type associated with running out of stock. There are a number of causes of *stockout costs*.

- Lost contribution from lost sales
- Loss of future sales due to disgruntled customers
- Loss of customer goodwill
- Cost of production stoppages
- Labour frustration over stoppages
- Extra costs of urgent, small quantity, replenishment orders

Objective of stock control

1.6 The overall objective of stock control is, therefore, to maintain stock levels so that the total of the following costs is minimised.

- Holding costs
- Ordering costs
- Stockout costs

Stock control levels

1.7 Based on an analysis of past stock usage and delivery times, a series of control levels can be calculated and used to maintain stocks at their optimum level (in other words, a level which minimises costs). These levels will determine 'when to order' and 'how many to order'.

(a) *Reorder level*. When stocks reach this level, an order should be placed to replenish stocks. The reorder level is determined by consideration of the following.

- The maximum rate of consumption
- The maximum lead time

The maximum lead time is the time between placing an order with a supplier, and the stock becoming available for use

Reorder level = maximum usage × maximum lead time

(b) *Minimum level*. This is a warning level to draw management attention to the fact that stocks are approaching a dangerously low level and that stockouts are possible.

Minimum level = reorder level – (average usage × average lead time)

(c) *Maximum level*. This also acts as a warning level to signal to management that stocks are reaching a potentially wasteful level.

Maximum level = reorder level + reorder quantity – (minimum usage × minimum lead time)

(d) *Reorder quantity*. This is the quantity of stock which is to be ordered when stock reaches the reorder level. If it is set so as to minimise the total costs associated with holding and ordering stock, then it is known as the economic order quantity.

(e) *Average stock*. The formula for the average stock level assumes that stock levels fluctuate evenly between the minimum (or safety) stock level and the highest possible stock level (the amount of stock immediately after an order is received, ie safety stock + reorder quantity).

Average stock = safety stock + ½ reorder quantity

1.8 We will look at some of these stock levels again in the next section of this chapter when we look at methods of inventory control.

Definitions

- The *lead time* is the time which elapses between the beginning and end of something, in this case between the placing of an order for stock and its eventual delivery. Thus, a supply lead time of two months means that it will take two months from the time an order is placed until the time it is delivered.

- *Stock-outs* arise when there is a requirement for an item of stock, but the stores or warehouse is temporarily out of stock.

- *Buffer stocks* are safety stocks held in case of unexpectedly high demand. Buffer stocks should only be required from time to time during the lead time between ordering fresh quantities of an item and their delivery. If there is excessive demand, or a delay in delivery, the buffer stocks might be used.

- The *order quantity* is the number of units of an item in one order. A fixed size is usually estimated for the order quantity.

- The *reorder level* is the balance of units remaining in stock, at which an order for more units will be placed.

Activity 1

A manufacturing firm holds an average of 40,000 items of stock. This is typically one month's supply. Stock items are bought for an average of £2.50 each. Further possibly relevant information from last year's financial and management accounts is as follows.

	£
Warehouse rent	8,000
Delivery charges (goods in)	24,000
Purchase department wages	45,400
Stores department wages	75,600
Purchase department overheads	31,400
Stores department overheads	34,800
Warehouse contents insurance	4,800

(a) What is the average cost of acquiring and holding a single item of stock?

(b) Would any other information be relevant?

2   SIMPLE METHODS OF INVENTORY CONTROL METHODS

2.1   A business needs to ensure that stock levels are high enough to avoid production stoppages. At the same time, it is undesirable that stock levels should be kept higher than necessary because management will wish to keep storage costs to a minimum. There are also administration and handling costs associated with ordering materials and accepting delivery from suppliers. An inventory control system can be instituted to minimise the combined costs of holding and ordering stocks, while maintaining high enough stock levels to avoid customer dissatisfaction.

2.2   Simple methods of inventory control are as follows.

- Demand reorder timing
- Perpetual inventory
- Periodic review

Demand reorder timing

2.3   Control of stock levels is often achieved by collecting, for each stores item, details of the amounts used in an *average period*, an *exceptionally busy period* and an *exceptionally slack period*. We will call these usage levels the *average level, maximum level* and *minimum level* respectively. *Suppliers' delivery period* or *lead time* would be analysed in the same way and a *maximum, average* and *minimum delivery time* ascertained.

2.4   With this information it is possible to calculate a level of stock (a *re-order level*) which will trigger a fresh purchase. If stock-outs are to be avoided, a prudent re-order level could be calculated as follows.

Re-order level = maximum delivery period × maximum usage

It is unnecessary to keep detailed records of stock levels at every moment. It is enough to perform occasional checks to ensure that stock has not fallen to the *re-order level*. This makes the method a suitable one to use for stock items of comparatively low value, where up-to-the-minute information on stock levels is an unnecessary luxury.

2.5   Another problem is to decide a re-order quantity, that is the quantity of the stock item which should be ordered when stocks have fallen to the re-order level. As we shall see, mathematical models can be used to calculate an optimum re-order quantity (one which minimises the combined costs of holding stocks and ordering stocks). For small value items such models are unnecessarily elaborate and management might choose a level which they estimate will minimise the administrative inconvenience of frequent re-ordering, without leading to excessively high levels of stock being held.

EXAMPLE: RE-ORDER LEVEL AND RE-ORDER QUANTITY

Component 697 is one of thousands of items kept in the store of a manufacturer. Usage of the component is expected to be at the rate of about 30,000 per year. Management believes that the maximum weekly usage is about 750 and the minimum weekly usage about 400. Experience has shown that suppliers deliver on average three weeks after an order is placed, but it can be as much as four weeks or as little as two weeks.

Suggest a re-order level and a re-order quantity for component 697.

SOLUTION

(a) Average weekly usage is approximately 600 per week. The average usage between the time an order is placed and the time delivery is received is equal to $600 \times 3 = 1,800$. The maximum usage during the supplier's lead time is $750 \times 4 = 3,000$. Management would be likely to fix a re-order level nearer to the maximum usage than to the average usage. A stock of 3,000 might be regarded as an acceptable re-order level.

(b) Assuming that component 697 is not a particularly valuable stock item, management will take a simple approach to fixing a re-order quantity. Perhaps six orders a year would be considered a suitable number, so that each order would be for two months stock. The re-order quantity would then be $30,000/6 = 5,000$.

Perpetual inventory

Definitions

A *perpetual inventory* method involves knowing stock levels of all items at all times. A record is kept of all items showing receipts, issues and balances of stock. Since in practice physical stocks may not agree with recorded stocks, (because of clerical errors, storekeepers' errors, pilferage etc) it is necessary to check the inventory by *continuous stocktaking*. Here a number of items are counted and checked daily or at frequent intervals and compared with the bin cards. Each item is checked at least once a year and any discrepancies are investigated and corrected immediately.

2.6 Perpetual inventory systems usually involve the upkeep of two sets of records.

(a) *Bin cards*. These show the physical balance of units in stock at any time.

(b) *Stores ledger records*. These show both the physical balance of units in stock at any time and also their valuation.

The physical balances on the bin cards and the stores ledger record should agree at all times, unless there has been a clerical error on one of the records.

2.7 A perpetual inventory system uses the same system of re-order levels to trigger a fresh purchase of stock as with the demand and supply system.

Periodic review

2.8 Periodic stocktaking is a process that involves physically counting and valuing all stock times at one set point in time, usually at the end of an accounting period.

2.9 Periodic stocktaking has a number of disadvantages when compared with continuous stocktaking.

2.10 The advantages of continuous stocktaking compared to periodic stocktaking are as follows.

NOTES

(a) The annual stocktaking is unnecessary and the disruption it causes is avoided.

(b) Regular skilled stocktakers can be employed, reducing likely errors.

(c) More time is available, reducing errors and allowing investigation.

(d) Deficiencies and losses are revealed sooner than they would be if stocktaking were limited to an annual check.

(e) Production hold-ups are eliminated because the stores staff are at no time so busy as to be unable to deal with material issues to production departments.

(f) Staff morale is improved and standards raised.

(g) Control over stock levels is improved, and there is less likelihood of overstocking or running out of stock.

Activity 2

A firm needs regular supplies of a material that has to be imported from South America. Lead time for delivery is typically 9 weeks but it can be between 5 and 13 weeks. The firm uses a minimum of about 2,000 kg per week and never more than 4,000 kg. It does not expect any increase or decrease in production levels in the foreseeable future. There is not room to store more than 60,000 kg at any one time. What re-order level and re-order quantity would you suggest?

---

3 INVENTORY MODELS AND THE BASIC EOQ FORMULA

3.1 The purpose of an inventory model is to help management to decide how to *plan* and *control* stocks efficiently, so as to minimise costs. Models may therefore estimate the following.

(a) The optimal size of an order for a particular item
(b) Whether the offer of a bulk purchase discount for large orders should be accepted
(c) The optimal re-order level for an item of stock
(d) How frequently orders should be placed

The basic EOQ formula

Definition

The *economic order quantity (EOQ)* or *economic batch quantity (EBQ)* is the order quantity for an item of stock which will minimise costs.

3.2 The assumptions used in the model are as follows.

(a) Demand is certain, constant and continuous over time.

BPP
PUBLISHING

(b) Supply lead time is constant and certain, or else there is instantaneous re-supply.

(c) Customers' orders cannot be held while fresh stocks are awaited.

(d) No stock-outs are permitted.

(e) All prices are constant and certain and there are no bulk purchase discounts.

(f) The cost of holding stock is proportional to the quantity of stock held.

3.3 At this stage, some symbols must be introduced.

Let   D = the usage in units for one time period (demand)

Co = the cost of making one order (relevant costs only)

Ch = the holding cost per unit of stock for one time period (relevant costs only)

Q = the re-order quantity

Average stock

3.4 If the lead time is zero or is known with certainty, then fresh stocks can be obtained when stocks fall to zero. When fresh stocks arrive, stocks will be at their maximum level which is Q. As demand is constant, the average stock will be Q/2. This is illustrated in the diagram below. As Ch is the holding cost per unit of stock, the cost of holding the average stock for one time period is (Q/2)Ch.

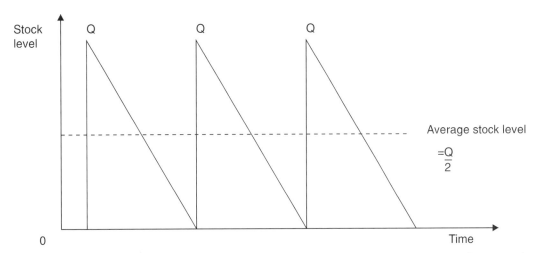

3.5 The number of orders for stock made in a time period depends upon the annual usage (D) and the re-order quantity (Q). The number of orders made in a time period will, equal D/Q. If the cost of making one order is Co then total ordering costs for the time period will equal CoD/Q.

3.6 The total cost per time period, T, equals

$$\frac{QCh}{2} + \frac{CoD}{Q}$$

The objective is to minimise T.

Since there are no stock-out costs, no buffer stocks and no bulk purchase discounts, these are the only items of cost which vary with the size of the order.

The formula for the *economic order quantity*, Q, can be derived from the above using elementary calculus. For now you should simply accept that

$$Q = \sqrt{\frac{2CoD}{Ch}}$$

EXAMPLE: THE EOQ FORMULA

The demand for a commodity is 40,000 units a year, at a steady rate. It costs £20 to place an order, and 40p to hold a unit for a year. Find the order size to minimise stock costs, the number of orders placed each year, and the length of the stock cycle.

SOLUTION

$$Q = \sqrt{\frac{2 \times 20 \times 40,000}{0.4}}$$

= 2,000 units

This means that there will be

$\dfrac{40,000}{2,000}$ = 20 orders placed each year, so that the stock cycle is

---

Activity 3

Placing an order for an item of stock costs £170. The stock costs £30 a unit, and annual storage costs are 15% of purchase price. Annual demand is 600,000 units. What is the economic order quantity?

$\dfrac{52 \text{ weeks}}{20 \text{ orders}}$ = 2.6 weeks.

A graphical approach

3.7   The variation of costs with order size can be represented by the following graph.

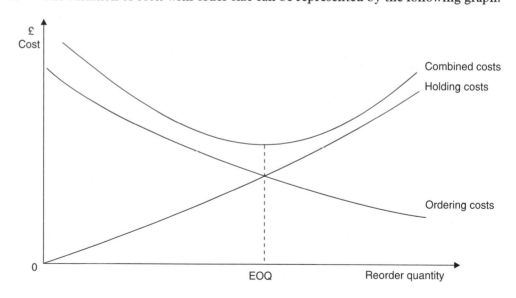

At the EOQ level of order size, ordering costs per period will equal stock holding costs:

$$\frac{QCh}{2} = \frac{CoD}{Q}$$

3.8 In the example on the previous page, where the EOQ was 2,000 units, costs were as follows.

	£
Annual ordering costs £20 × 20	400
Annual stock holding costs 2,000/2 × £0.40	400
Total annual costs of having stock	800

4 THE ECONOMIC BATCH QUANTITY (EBQ) MODEL

4.1 You may come across a problem in which the basic EOQ formula requires modification because re-supply is *gradual*, instead of instantaneous. Typically, a manufacturing company might hold stocks of a finished item, which is produced in batches. Once the order for a new batch has been placed, and the production run has started, finished output might be used before the batch run has been completed.

4.2 For example suppose that the daily demand for an item of stock is ten units, and the storekeeper orders 100 units in a batch. The rate of production is 50 units a day.

On the first day of the batch production run, the stores will run out of its previous stocks, and re-supply will begin. 50 units will be produced during the day, and ten units will be consumed. The closing stock at the end of day 1 will be $50 - 10 = 40$ units.

On day 2, the final 50 units will be produced and a further ten units will be consumed. Closing stock at the end of day 2 will be $(40 + 50 - 10) = 80$ units.

In eight more days, stocks will fall to zero.

4.3 The *minimum stock* in this example is zero, and the *maximum stock* is 80 units. The maximum stock is the quantity ordered (Q = 100) minus demand during the period of the batch production run which is $Q \times D/R$, where

D is the rate of demand
R is the rate of production
Q is the quantity ordered.

In our example, the *maximum stock* is $(100 - \frac{10}{50} \times 100) = 100 - 20 = 80$ units.

The *maximum stock* level, given gradual re-supply, is thus $Q - \frac{QD}{R} = Q(1 - D/R)$.

4.4 The position can be represented graphically as follows.

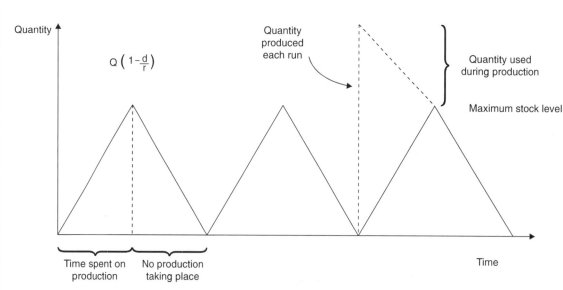

4.5 An amended EOQ formula is required because average stocks are not Q/2 but Q(1 – D/R)/2.

The amended formula is known as the *Economic Batch Quantity* or the EBQ formula, and is written as:

$$Q = \sqrt{\frac{2CoD}{Ch(1 - D/R)}}$$

where
- Q = the amount produced in each batch
- D = the usage per time period
- Co = the set up cost per batch
- Ch = the holding cost per unit of stock per time period
- R = the production rate per time period (see below)

4.6 When carrying out EBQ calculations (or EOQ calculations) make sure that the figures you use are compatible. For example do not mix in a usage figure per *month* with a production rate per *day*.

4.7 The 'production' rate may actually be a 'supply' rate: for example if X Ltd were only able to obtain 100 units of raw materials per day and one unit were needed per widget they could only *make* 100 widgets per day.

Activity 4

A company is able to manufacture its own components for stock at the rate of 4,000 units a week. Demand for the component is at the rate of 2,000 units a week. Set up costs for each production run are £50. The cost of holding one unit of stock is £0.001 a week. Calculate the economic production run.

> **Activity 5**
>
> If   Q = 6,000
>
>   D = 120,000
>
>   R = 160,000
>
>   Ch = £1.50
>
>   Co = £50
>
> what are the annual stock costs, excluding the cost of materials?

5   THE EFFECT OF DISCOUNTS

5.1   The solution obtained from using the simple EOQ formula may need to be modified if *bulk discounts* (also called *quantity discounts*) are available. The graph below shows the effect that discounts granted for orders of certain sizes may have on total costs.

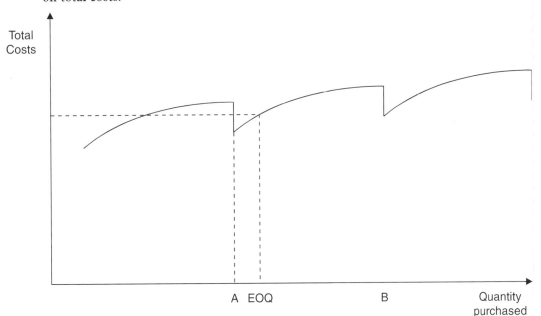

It can be seen from the graph that *differing bulk discounts* are given when the order quantity exceeds A, B and C. Furthermore the *minimum total cost*, in this case, is when quantity B is ordered rather than when the EOQ is ordered.

5.2   To decide mathematically whether it would be worthwhile taking a discount and ordering larger quantities, it is necessary to minimise the total of the following.

    (a)   Total material costs

    (b)   Ordering costs

    (c)   Stock holding costs

5.3   The total cost will be minimised:

    (a)   at the pre-discount EOQ level, so that a discount is not worthwhile; or

    (b)   at the minimum order size necessary to earn the discount.

EXAMPLE: BULK DISCOUNTS

The annual demand for an item of stock is 45 units. The item costs £200 a unit to purchase, the holding cost for one unit for one year is 15% of the unit cost and ordering costs are £300 an order.

The supplier offers a 3% discount for orders of 60 units or more, and a discount of 5% for orders of 90 units or more. What is the cost-minimising order size?

SOLUTION

(a)   The EOQ ignoring discounts is

$$\sqrt{\frac{2 \times 300 \times 45}{15\% \text{ of } 200}}$$

	£
Purchases (no discount) 45 × £200	9,000
Holding costs 15 units × £30	450
Ordering costs 1.5 orders × £300	450
Total annual costs	9,900

(b) With a discount of 3% and an order quantity of 60 units, costs are as follows.

	£
Purchases £9,000 × 97%	8,730
Holding costs 30 units × 15% of 97% of £200	873
Ordering costs 0.75 orders × £300	225
Total annual costs	9,828

(c) With a discount of 5% and an order quantity of 90 units, costs are as follows.

	£
Purchases £9,000 × 95%	8,550.0
Holding costs 45 units × 15% of 95% of £200	1,282.5
Ordering costs 0.5 orders × £300	150.0
Total annual costs	9,982.5

The cheapest option is to order 60 units at a time.

(d)   Note that the value of Ch varied according to the size of the discount, because Ch was a percentage of the purchase cost. This means that total holding costs are reduced because of a discount. This could easily happen if, for example, most of Ch was the cost of insurance, based on the cost of stock held.

Activity 6

A company uses an item of stock as follows.

Purchase price:	£96 per unit
Annual demand:	4,000 units
Ordering cost:	£300
Annual holding cost:	10% of purchase price
Economic order quantity:	500 units

Should the company order 1,000 units at a time in order to secure an 8% discount?

Sensitivity analysis

5.4 If there are doubts about the accuracy of the estimated ordering costs and holding costs, or there is uncertainty about the volume of demand, sensitivity analysis may be used to measure the effect on annual costs of selecting an EOQ based on inaccurate figures. We simply compare the actual costs with the costs which would have been incurred, had the correct EOQ been used.

EXAMPLE: SENSITIVITY ANALYSIS

Montelimar Ltd estimated that it would use 100 tons of Catcomine during the last financial year. The annual holding costs of Catcomine are £5 a ton. The cost of placing one order should be £10. Using the basic EOQ formula, Montelimar Ltd calculated that the economic order size was 20 tons and established a policy of ordering this quantity every time stocks were exhausted. At the end of the year the company found it had actually used 120 tons of Catcomine and that the actual cost of placing each order was £14. The managing director wishes to know the net financial effect of the bad forecasting.

SOLUTION

The actual costs incurred were as follows.

					£
Holding costs	$\dfrac{ChQ}{2}$	=	$\dfrac{5 \times 20}{2}$	=	50
Ordering costs	$\dfrac{CoD}{Q}$	=	$\dfrac{14 \times 120}{20}$	=	84
					$\overline{134}$

The economic order quantity should have been

$$\sqrt{\frac{2 \times 14 \times 120}{5}} \quad = \quad 25.92 \text{ tons}$$

The total costs would then have been as follows.

			£
Holding costs =	$\dfrac{5 \times 25.92}{2}$	=	64.80
Ordering costs =	$\dfrac{14 \times 120}{25.92}$	=	64.81
			$\overline{129.61}$

The company therefore incurred costs £4.39 higher than necessary. Thus the total costs are insensitive to modest forecasting errors.

Chapter roundup

- *Inventory control* aims to minimise the costs of holding stocks whilst also ensuring that stocks are available when required.

- *Simple methods of inventory control* include demand re-order timing, perpetual inventory and periodic review

- The *EOQ model* sets out the relationship between demand, ordering costs and holding costs. The *EOQ formula* is

$$Q = \sqrt{\frac{2C_oD}{C_h}}$$

- The EOQ model has to be modified for batch production to take account of the production rate. The *EBQ formula* is

$$Q = \sqrt{\frac{2C_oD}{C_h(1-D/R)}}$$

- Where *discounts* are available it is necessary to compare the annual costs of buying the EOQ without discounts and the annual costs of buying quantities that earn discounts.

Quick quiz

1   State the objective of stock control.

2   Explain the demand reorder timing method of inventory control.

3   What is perpetual inventory?

4   What are the assumptions of the EOQ model?

5   Why is an amended EOQ formula (sometimes called the EBQ formula) necessary?

6   At what order quantity might costs be minimised when bulk discounts are available?

7   When is sensitivity analysis useful?

Answers to activities

1   (a)

	£
Rent £(8,000/40,000) (W1)	0.20
Delivery £(24,000/480,000) (W2)	0.05
Purchasing £((45,400 + 31,400)/480,000)	0.16
Stores £((75,600 + 34,800)/480,000)	0.23
Insurance £(4,800/40,000)	0.12
	0.76

Workings

1   Only enough space for 40,000 items needs to be rented, and only 40,000 items need to be insured.

2   Delivery and other charges are for a whole year's stock. 12 × 40,000 = 480,000.

(b)   Many of the costs listed in Paragraphs 1.3 and 1.4 may also be relevant, particularly the cost of tying up £(2.50 + 0.76) × 40,000 = £130,400 of capital per month in stocks (interest paid or not earned, other more profitable uses of the money and so on), and the cost of any wastage of stock in storage. You should not have included production costs like materials handling, or wastage in the course of manufacturing.

Note that a more detailed analysis of all the figures given would also be useful. Part of these costs may not be connected with stock acquisition and holding.

2 Re-order level $\quad$ = 13 weeks $\times$ 4,000 kg

$\qquad\qquad\qquad\qquad$ = 52,000 kg

$\quad$ Re-order quantity $\quad$ = 60,000 – (52,000 – 10,000) (W)

$\qquad\qquad\qquad\qquad$ = 18,000 kg

Working

The firm will place an order when stocks reach 52,000 kg. It will use at least 5 weeks $\times$ 2,000 kg before the new delivery arrives and will therefore have up to (52,000 –10,000) kg left at this time. It can only hold 60,000 kg so the order must not take stock levels above this. In brief:

Re-order quantity = maximum stock – (re-order level – minimum usage in delivery period)

3 $C_o=$ $\qquad$ £170
$\quad$ $D =$ $\qquad$ 600,000
$\quad$ $C_h=$ $\qquad$ £30 $\times$ 15% = £4.50

$\quad$ EOQ $\qquad = \qquad \sqrt{\dfrac{2\times170\times600,000}{4.5}} = 6,733$ units

4 $Q = \qquad \sqrt{\dfrac{2\times50\times2,000}{0.001(1-2,000/4,000)}}$

$\qquad = \qquad$ 20,000 units (giving a stock cycle of 10 weeks)

5 The number of orders placed will be D/Q = 20

At £50 per order, ordering costs will be £1,000

Holding costs are based on average stocks which are Q(1 – D/R)/2 (see paragraph 4.5)

6,000 $\times$ ((1 – 120/160) $\div$ 2) = 750 units

750 $\times$ £1.50 = £1,125

Annual stock costs are therefore £2,125 plus the cost of materials

6 The total annual cost at the economic order quantity of 500 units is as follows.

	£
Purchases 4,000 $\times$ £96	384,000
Ordering costs £300 $\times$ (4,000/500)	2,400
Holding costs £96 $\times$ 10% $\times$ (500/2)	2,400
	388,800

The total annual cost at an order quantity of 1,000 units would be as follows.

	£
Purchases £384,000 × 92%	353,280
Ordering costs £300 × (4,000/1,000)	1,200
Holding costs £96 × 92% × 10% × (1,000/2)	4,416
	358,896

The company should order the item 1,000 units at a time, saving £(388,800 - 358,896) = £29,904 a year.

Assignment 10   **(45 minutes)**

(a)   A company purchases 25,000 litres of a material each year from a single supplier. At the moment, the company obtains the material in batch sizes of 800 litres. The material costs £16 a litre. The cost of ordering a new batch from the supplier is £32 and the cost of holding one litre in stock is £4 a year plus an interest cost equal to 15% of the purchase price of the material.

Required

(i)   Calculate the economic order quantity and the annual savings which would be obtained if this order quantity replaced the current order size.

(ii)   The supplier has agreed to offer a discount on orders above a certain size. He has offered the following price structure.

Order size	Unit cost
Litres	£
0 –500	16.00
501 - 999	15.20
1,000 or more	14.80

What is the cost-minimising order size?

(b)   A company has estimated the annual demand for an item of stock to be 48,000 units. The purchase price is £2 a unit, with a 2% discount for orders of 12,000 units or more.

The annual cost of holding one unit of stock is 15 pence. The cost of an order averages £100.

Required

(i)   Determine the economic order quantity ignoring the discount. How oten should orders be placed and what will be annual cost of holding stock?

(ii)   Delermine whether the discount should be obtained by ordering 12,000 units at a time.

ANSWERS TO ASSIGNMENTS

ANSWER TO ASSIGNMENT 1

Tutorial note. This question tests your understanding of non–linear cost behaviour and involves the manipulation of equations. Because there are three unknowns in the general form of a quadratic equation (a, b, c), you will need to use three simultaneous equations. Don't forget to label the axes and provide a title to the graph in (a)(ii).

Profit is the difference between revenue and costs and hence, in part (b)(iii), profit = revenue – cost.

(a) (i) The general form of a quadratic equation is $ax^2 + bx + c = 0$

We are given the following information.

Let x = size of batch.

When	x = 10,	cost = £700	(1)
	x = 20,	cost = £400	(2)
	x = 40,	cost = £1,600	(3)

We can substitute these values into $ax^2 + bx + c = cost$ to determine the values of a, b and c.

Using (1)	$100a + 10b + c$	=	700	(i)
Using (2)	$400a + 20b + c$	=	400	(ii)
Using (3)	$1,600a + 40b + c$	=	1,600	(iii)
	$400a + 40b + 4c$	=	2,800	(iv)(4 × (i))
	$20b + 3c$	=	2,400	(v)((iv) – (ii))
	$1,600\ a + 160b + 16c$	=	11,200	(vi)(4 × (iv))
	$120b + 15c$	=	9,600	(vii)((vi) – (iii))
	$120b + 18c$	=	14,400	(viii)(6 × (v))
	$3c$	=	4,800	(viii) – (vii)
	c	=	1,600	
	$120b$	=	14,400 – 28,800	Sub into (viii)
	b	=	–120	
	$100a – 1,200 + 1,600$	=	700	Sub into (i)
	$100a$	=	300	
	a	=	3	

The relationship is cost = $3x^2 – 120x + 1,600$

(ii) Substitute different values for x (batch size) into the equation above to determine the cost for different batch sizes.

Batch size	Cost
x	£
0	1,600
10	700
15	475
20	400
25	475
30	700
40	1,600
50	3,100

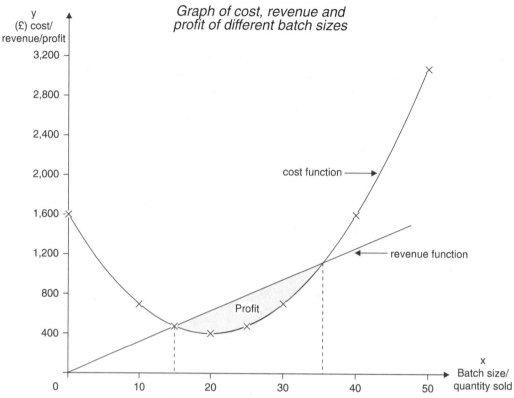

Graph of cost, revenue and profit of different batch sizes

(iii) From the graph, the batch size which minimises total cost is 20 (the x coordinate of the lowest point on the cost function curve).

(b) (i) Let x = quantity sold and y = revenue

If x = 0, y = 0
If x = 10, y = 10 × 30 = £300
If x = 50, y = 50 × 30 = £1,500

We can plot the revenue function on the graph using these values.

(ii) The product makes a profit when total revenue is greater than total cost. Revenue is greater than cost in the shaded region on the graph. The product therefore makes a profit if the batch size is between approximately 15 and 35.

(iii) Profit = revenue – cost

Revenue function is y = 30x because for every increase in x (quantity sold), revenue increases by £30.

$$\therefore \text{Profit} = 30x - (3x^2 - 120x + 1,600)$$
$$= 30x - 3x^2 + 120x - 1,600$$
$$= -3x^2 + 150x - 1,600$$

ANSWER TO ASSIGNMENT 2

Tutorial note. There is a danger with discursive questions such as this one of spending too much time on the question and writing too much, while not adequately addressing specific points raised in the question. The way to approach such questions is to draft out your answer in rough, making brief notes of the points you wish to make before starting to write out the answer properly. Five or ten minutes thought and note making beforehand will result in a much better answer.

(a)   *Define the target population*

Since the aim of the survey is to investigate means of increasing sales, the target population is those who do not currently buy the paper. Hence the newspaper itself cannot be used to collect the data.

Data collection method choices

The method of data collection selected by the company will have to take account of cost on the one hand and reliability of results on the other.

(i)   A postal survey would be the cheapest option but response rates are notoriously low, even where incentives such as entry into a prize draw are given, and it is impossible to ascertain the opinions of non-respondents. The results of such surveys are therefore very unreliable.

(ii)   All other methods involve the employment of staff to conduct interviews and these staff will need some training to ensure that they do not introduce interviewer bias. They are consequently more expensive.

       (1)   A telephone survey would avoid the costs of travel and would enable more interviews to be completed per day than face to face interviews. A slight problem is that some people do not have telephones but this is unlikely to be the case with the new readership in which the newspaper is interested. A more important problem is refusal to be interviewed, which is much greater in telephone surveys than face to face. All surveys are intrusive and it is easier to say 'no' to someone over the telephone. Additionally respondents may well be reluctant to disclose personal information such as age or income when no identification can be shown by the interviewer.

       (2)   From the standpoint of reliability of results, face to face interviews are the best data collection method. In this instance the area to be covered is small, so neither travel time nor cost need be a big problem. The company should be advised to use this method even if, for reasons of costs, it necessitates a somewhat smaller sample than a telephone survey.

(b)   The electoral register will provide an acceptable sampling frame and the sampling scheme should begin by stratifying the population according to area. Assuming that potential new readers have the same characteristics as existing readers, 10% of respondents should be selected randomly from rural areas, 30% from suburban and 60% from town. At the same time respondents can be stratified by gender since the electoral register shows forenames and half of those selected in each case should be female and half male.

It is not possible to stratify either by age or by income using the electoral register. This need not be a problem since non-readers may not be similar to readers in that respect. If the company strongly wishes to mirror its existing readership in these respects, the questionnaire should contain quota control questions which would enable the correct proportions of people in the various age and income groups to be interviewed.

If the company does not wish to survey any existing readers, such interviews could be aborted but they would actually be well advised to include existing readers. The proposed changes might perhaps alienate existing readers and the company would benefit from this information.

The electoral register would not give access to people below the age of 18 but this seems to be a minimal problem since the existing readership contains only a small proportion in this group and the proposed changes do not seem to be aimed at a young readership.

ANSWER TO ASSIGNMENT 3

(a) Cumulative monthly sales are the total of the sales so far, including the sales in the month in question.

The first figure in the moving annual total is calculated by taking the total sales for 20X1, adding those for January 20X2 and subtracting those for January 20X1. A similar approach is used for the rest of the year (adding on the new 20X2 month and deducting the corresponding 20X1 month).

	(i) Cumulative monthly sales	(ii) Moving annual total
Jan	54	490
Feb	109	515
Mar	164	540
April	219	561
May	269	574
June	315	581
July	358	584
Aug	399	585
Sept	439	585
Oct	479	580
Nov	521	573
Dec	565	565

(b) The Z chart shows monthly sales during 19X2, cumulative monthly sales and the moving annual total.

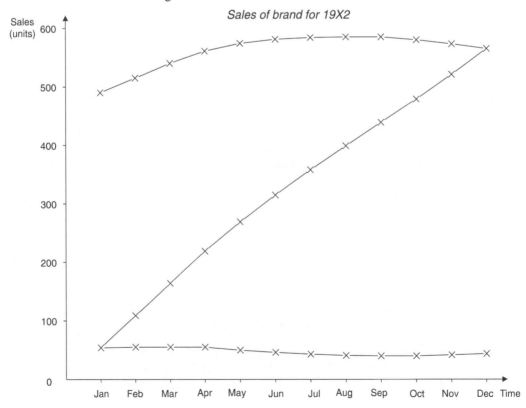

Sales of brand for 19X2

(c)   The monthly sales are fairly constant, reaching a peak of 55 units in April and a trough of 40 units in September and October.

The peak in April may be due to the advertising campaign in March. Sales are growing towards the end of the year, which could be a result of the advertising campaign in September. The trough between April and the end of the year may well be due to the competition.

The cumulative monthly sales grow fairly steadily during the year.

The moving annual total (a form of trend) shows that, although sales were increasing until August, there was a slight decline towards the end of the year.

ANSWER TO ASSIGNMENT 4

Tutorial note. The main requirement of this question is to use the Retail Prices Index (RPI) to find real earnings. We have given the general formula for this at the beginning. In such a question you cannot be expected to show all your workings but should include examples of your workings so that the examiner can see your method.

(a)   Deflated value at constant 1988 prices

$$= \text{value given} \times \frac{\text{RPI for 1988}}{\text{RPI for the time being considered}}$$

For example, February 1989, deflated value $= 104.9 \times \dfrac{107}{111.5} = 100.7$

Production industries index at constant 1988 prices (to one decimal place)

1989	
Feb	100.7
May	100.6
Aug	100.9
Nov	101.9
1990	
Feb	101.7
May	100.2
Aug	100.0
Nov	101.8
1991	
Feb	102.3
May	103.6
Aug	103.9
Nov	104.0

Average earnings in production industries have risen by 31.8% from 1988 to the end of 1991 but when adjusted for inflation the real increase is seen to be only 4%. The increase did not occur gradually over the whole period. By August 1990 earnings were identical to their 1988 value in real terms and the real 4% increase occurred between then and November 1991.

(b)   We need to do two sets of calculations: update the £5,000 using the Average Earnings Index for service industries with May 1989 as the base period and convert the £5,000 into real terms using the RPI.

Time	Value of pension (pa)	Chain index £	Value in real terms	Chain index £
May 1989	5,000.00	100	5,000.00	100
Nov 1989	$5,000 \times \dfrac{112.7}{107.2} = 5,256.53$	105	5,152.17*	103**
Nov 1990	$5,000 \times \dfrac{123.0}{107.2} = 5,736.94$	109	5,652.17	110
Nov 1991	$5,000 \times \dfrac{129.7}{107.2} = 6,049.44$	105	5,895.65	104

* Example of workings: $5,000 \times \dfrac{118.5}{115} = 5,152.17$

** $\left[1 + \left(\dfrac{5,152.17 - 5,000}{5,000}\right)\right] \times 100 = 103$

The value of the pension has increased in real terms: in the middle year its value was more or less in line with the RPI but in the other periods its value increased above the rate of the RPI.

ANSWER TO ASSIGNMENT 5

(a)   Our calculations must relate to the current year.

Our values for x relate to the midpoints of the age groups. The age groups cover five years and hence the midpoints are two and a half years from the lower limit.

Age group (years)	Midpoint x	Frequency f	fx	x^2	fx^2
25 < 30	27.5	5	137.5	756.25	3,781.25
30 < 35	32.5	10	325.0	1,056.25	10,562.50
35 < 40	37.5	13	487.5	1,406.25	18,281.25
40 < 45	42.5	28	1,190.0	1,806.25	50,575.00
45 < 50	47.5	21	997.5	2,256.25	47,381.25
50 < 55	52.5	12	630.0	2,756.25	33,075.00
55 < 60	57.5	8	460.0	3,306.25	26,450.00
60 < 65	62.5	3	187.5	3,906.25	11,718.75
		100	4,415.0		201,825.00

$$\text{Mean} = \frac{\Sigma fx}{\Sigma f} = \frac{4,415}{100} = 44.15 \text{ years}$$

$$\text{Standard deviation} = \sqrt{\frac{\Sigma fx^2}{\Sigma f} - \bar{x}^2}$$

$$= \sqrt{\frac{201,825}{100} - 44.15^2} = 8.31 \text{ years}$$

(b)

	Now	Five years ago	Absolute change	% change
Mean (years)	44.15	49.05	–4.90	–10%
Standard deviation (years)	8.31	8.45	–0.14	–2%

The mean age has dropped by 10%, principally because most of the workforce have shifted from being in the 50+ age groups to being in the 25 to 50 age groups. This shift downwards in the age of the workforce has had very little effect on the standard deviation, however.

(c) A multiple or compound bar chart will best illustrate changes in the age structure of the workforce over the five–year period.

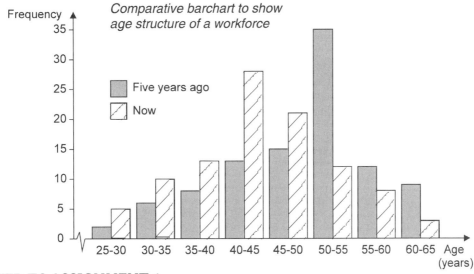

ANSWER TO ASSIGNMENT 6

Tutorial note. The only problem you may have had with this question was failing to spot that the units for maintenance were £10s, not £s.

(a) $b = \dfrac{n\Sigma xy - \Sigma x \Sigma y}{n\Sigma x^2 - (\Sigma x)^2}$, $a = \dfrac{\Sigma y}{n} - \dfrac{b\Sigma x}{n}$

x	y	xy	x^2
2	60	120	4
8	132	1,056	64
6	100	600	36
8	120	960	64
10	150	1,500	100
4	84	336	16
4	90	360	16
2	68	136	4
6	104	624	36
10	140	1,400	100
60	1,048	7,092	440

$b = \dfrac{10 \times 7,092 - 60 \times 1,048}{10 \times 440 - 60^2} = \dfrac{8,040}{800} = 10.05$

$a = \dfrac{1,048}{10} - 10.05 \times \dfrac{60}{10} = 44.5$

Hence maintenance cost £(10) = 44.5 + 10.05 × age

(b)

Age	1	2	3	4	5	6	7	8	9	10
Cost (£)	545.5	646	746.5	847	947.5	1,048	1,148.5	1,249	1,349.5	1,450

The cost is given by substituting the age into the above equation and multiplying the result by 10.

(c) Estimated cost for 12-year-old vehicle is 10 × (44.5 + 10.05 × 12) = £1,651

The validity of making such an estimate depends on whether or not the cost behaviour is linear. It is unlikely that maintenance cost varies in direct proportion to the age of a vehicle since a vehicle tends to cost increasingly more to maintain the older it gets. An exponential growth model may therefore be more appropriate.

Twelve years is outside the range of the data, albeit not far outside, which reduces the reliability of the estimate. Other factors such as mileage, type of journey and driver and so on may also affect the maintenance cost. The estimate is therefore nothing more than a rough approximation.

ANSWER TO ASSIGNMENT 7

(a)

Year	Quarter	Sales (thousands of units)	Moving annual total (thousands of units)	Moving average of annual total (thousands of units)	Centred moving average (trend) (thousands of units)	Seasonal variation (thousands of units)
20X1	Q4	14				
20X2	Q1	16				
	Q2	30	100	25	25.5	4.5
	Q3	40	104	26	26.0	14.0
	Q4	18	104	26	26.5	−8.5
20X3	Q1	16	108	27	27.5	−11.5
	Q2	34	112	28	27.5	6.5
	Q3	44	108	27	27.0	17.0
	Q4	14	108	27	27.5	−13.5
20X4	Q1	16	112	28	29.0	−13.0
	Q2	38	120	30		
	Q3	52				

(b)

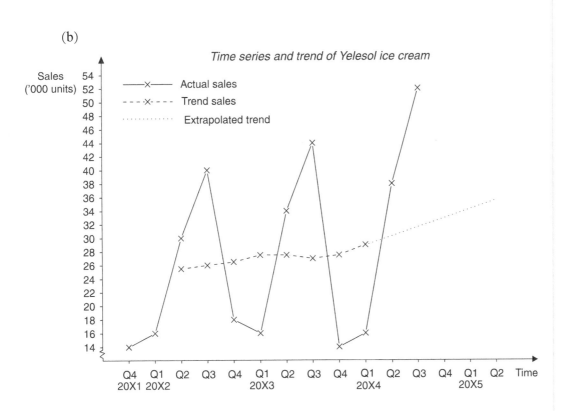

Time series and trend of Yelesol ice cream

(c)

	Q_1	Q_2	Q_3	Q_4
20X2		4.50	14.00	−8.50
20X3	−11.50	6.50	17.00	−13.50
20X4	−13.00			
Total	−24.50	11.00	31.00	−22.00
Average	−12.25	5.50	15.50	−11.00

(d) The extrapolated trend line would seem to indicate the following forecast trend values.

20X4	Q_4	33.0
20X5	Q_1	34.5

Adjusting by the seasonal variations gives the following forecast.

20X4	Q_4	33 − 11	= 22	ie 22,000 units
20X5	Q_1	34.5 − 12.25	= 22.25	ie 22,250 units

ANSWER TO ASSIGNMENT 8

Tutorial note. This was a straightforward maximisation problem, but you may have found the formulation of the market conditions constraint a little tricky. Note how it appears on the graph.

(a) Let the quantities produced in gallons be x of super and y of regular.

The objective is to maximise profit given by 0.25x + 0.10y, subject to the following constraints.

Heavy crude: $\frac{7}{10}x + \frac{1}{2}y \leq 5,000$, or $7x + 5y \leq 50,000$ (1)

Light crude: $\dfrac{1}{2}x + \dfrac{7}{10}y \le 6{,}000$, or $5x + 7y \le 60{,}000$ (2)

Market conditions: $x \ge 2y$ (3)

Tutorial note. At least 2/3 of the petrol should be super. The total petrol is $x + y$ and the quantity of super is x hence $x \ge (x + y) \times 2/3$, or $3x \ge 2x + 2y$, or $x \ge 2y$.

(b)   Non negativity constraints $x \ge 0$, $y \ge 0$ are also assumed.

For line (1), intercepts on the axes are as follows.

     If $x = 0$, $y = 50{,}000/5 = 10{,}000$
     If $y = 0$, $x = 50{,}000/7 = 7{,}143$

For line (2), intercepts are as follows.

     If $x = 0$, $y = 60{,}000/7 = 8{,}571$
     If $y = 0$, $x = 60{,}000/5 = 12{,}000$

For line (3), convenient points to plot are as follows.

     If $x = 0$, then $y = 0$
     If $x = 10{,}000$, $y = 5{,}000$

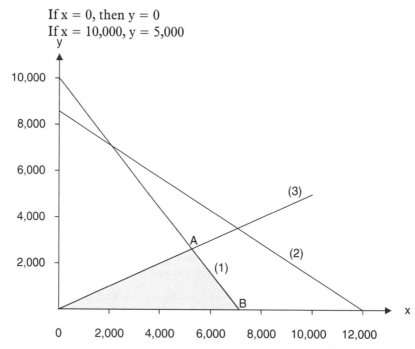

(c)

Vertex	x	y	Profit = $0.25x + 0.1y$
			£
A	5,263	2,632	1,579
B	7,143	0	1,786

The optimal policy is to produce no regular petrol and 7,143 gallons of super petrol. The profit generated will be £1,786.

This policy will use all supplies of heavy crude but will leave a surplus of light crude. If this policy were followed throughout the industry it seems likely that the cost of light crude would fall, which would disproportionately reduce the cost of regular petrol. Assuming also that there is a market for regular petrol, this policy would make a higher price for it possible. Both would tend to increase the unit contribution of regular petrol. The above policy would therefore be likely to need modifying in the light of market changes, and should be seen by the company as a fairly short-term policy.

(d)   The graphical method of solving resource allocation problems cannot be used when there are more than two decision variables. There are a number of mathematical techniques that can be used in these circumstances, for example the *Simplex method* which involves introducing slack variables into the equations to represent unused resources, shortfall in demand and so on and step–by–step trial calculations until the optimum solution is found.

In practice, faced with these sorts of difficulty the business will construct a mathematical model of the scenarios on a computer and use software tools specially designed to solve such problems.

ANSWER TO ASSIGNMENT 9

(a)
Path	Time required	
1, 2, 5, 6	10 + 6 + 13	= 29 days
1, 3, 5, 6	11 + 9 + 13	= 33 days
1, 3, 4, 6	11 + 4 + 12	= 27 days
1, 3, 4, 5, 6	11 + 4 + 3 + 13	= 31 days

(b)   The critical path is therefore 1, 3, 5, 6. Its duration of 33 days is the minimum duration of the entire project. The importance of this critical path derives from the fact that, if the project is to be completed in the minimum time, the three activities on the critical path must each start on time and may not have their durations extended.

(c)   *Tutorial note.* The question did not ask for a network to be drawn showing earliest and latest event times but it is easier to complete the table with the aid of such a diagram.

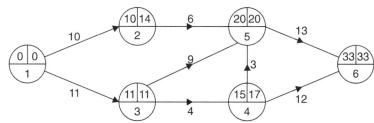

Activity	Time	Earliest Start	Earliest finish	Latest start	Latest finish	Total float
1 - 2	10	0	10	4	14	4
1 - 3	11	0	11	0	11	0
2 - 5	6	10	16	14	20	4
3 - 5	9	11	20	11	20	0
3 - 4	4	11	15	13	17	2
4 - 5	3	15	18	17	20	2
4 - 6	12	15	27	21	33	6
5 - 6	13	20	33	20	33	0

(d)   The total float tells us the absolute maximum number of days by which an activity's duration may be extended without increasing the duration of the entire project.

It is important to note that the total float does not tell us whether use of the float on one activity will reduce the float available on other activities. For example, activities 3 - 4 and 4 - 5 both have total floats of two days but if 3 - 4 is extended by two days then 4 - 5 will become critical and will have zero total float.

ANSWER TO ASSIGNMENT 10

(a) (i) $EOQ = \sqrt{\dfrac{2CoD}{Ch}} = \sqrt{\dfrac{2 \times 32 \times 25,000}{4 + (15\% \times 16)}} = \sqrt{250,000} = 500$ litres

	800 litres per order		500 litres per order	
		£		£
Holding costs	$\left(\dfrac{800}{2} \times £6.40\right)$	2,560	$\left(\dfrac{500}{2} \times £6.40\right)$	1,600
Ordering costs	$\left(\dfrac{25,000}{800} \times £32\right)$	1,000	$\left(\dfrac{25,000}{500} \times £32\right)$	1,600
		3,560		3,200

The annual saving would be £(3,560 − 3,200) = £360.

(ii)   The EOQ does not fall into one of the discount bands, therefore we do no need to recalculate it.

We need to compare the annual costs of the following order sizes:

(1)   EOQ of 500, as calculated above
(2)   501 (the lower boundary of the first discount band)
(3)   1000 (the lower boundary of the second discount band)

	Order 500 units £	Order 501 units £	Order 1,000 units £
Cost of purchases:			
(1) at £16.00 (× 25,000)	400,000		
(2) at £15.20 (× 25,000)		380,000	
(3) at £14.80 (× 25,000)			370,000
Holding costs:			
(1) at £6.40 (× 250)	1,600		
(2) at £4 + (15% of £15.20)		1,576	
(3) at £4 + (15% of £14.80)			3,110
Ordering costs at £32			
(1) 50 orders	1,600		
(2) $\dfrac{25,000}{501}$ orders (say 50 orders)		1,600	
(3) 25 orders			800
	403,200	383,176	373,910

The economic order quantity is now 1,000 units, to take advantage of the bulk purchase discounts. This is £(403,200 − 373,910) = £29,290 a year cheaper than ordering 500 litres at a time.

(b) (i) Total annual demand = 48,000 units.

$$Q = \sqrt{\frac{2(100 \times 48,000)}{0.15}} = \sqrt{64,000,000}$$

Orders must be placed every $\dfrac{8,000}{48,000} \times 12$ months = 2 months

The annual stockholding cost will be $\dfrac{QCh}{2} = \dfrac{8,000}{2} \times £0.15 = £600$

(ii) At an order size of 8,000 units, total costs are as follows.

	£
Stockholding cost	600
Ordering cost $6 \times £100$	600
Purchases $48,000 \times £2$	96,000
	97,200

At an order size of 12,000 units, total costs are as follows.

	£
Stockholding cost $(12,000/2) \times £0.15$	900
Ordering cost $(48,000/12,000) \times £100$	400
Purchases $48,000 \times £2 \times 0.98$	94,080
	95,380

The discount should be obtained, saving £(97,200 − 95,380) = £1,820 a year.

GLOSSARY

Additive model A model for time series analysis which assumes that the components of the series are independent of each other, an increasing trend not affecting the seasonal variations, for example.

Arithmetic mean Calculated from the sum of values of items divided by the number of items. The arithmetic mean of a variable x is shown as $\bar{x}$ ('x bar').

Attribute Something an object has either got or not got.

Bar chart A method of presenting data in which quantities are shown in the form of bars on a chart, the length of the bars being proportional to the quantities.

Base weighted index See Laspeyre indices.

Breakeven point The point at which neither profit nor loss occurs.

Buffer stock Safety stocks held in case of unexpectedly high demand. Buffer stocks should only be required from time to time during the lead time between ordering fresh quantities of an item and their delivery. If there is excessive demand, or a delay in delivery, the buffer stocks might be used.

Census A survey in which all of the population is examined.

Coefficient of correlation Measures the degree of correlation between two variables.

Coefficient of determination The square of the correlation coefficient, r^2. This measures the proportion of the total variation in the value of one variable that can be explained by variations in the value of the other variable.

Combination A set of items, selected from a larger collection of items, regardless of the order in which they are selected.

Continuous stocktaking A number of items are counted and checked daily or at frequent intervals and compared with the bin cards. Each item is checked at least once a year and any discrepancies are investigated and corrected immediately.

Contribution The difference between sales value and the marginal cost of sales.

Correlation Variables are said to be correlated when the value of one variable is related to the value of another.

Critical path In network analysis, the longest sequence of consecutive activities through the network.

Cube root The value which, when multiplied by itself twice, equals the original number.

Cumulative frequency distribution Can be used to show the total number of times that a value above or below a certain amount occurs.

Data A scientific term for facts, figures, information and measurements.

Deseasonalisation The process of removing seasonal variations from data to leave figures indicating the trend.

Decimals A way of showing parts of a whole.

Dual price The amount by which the value of total contribution will go up (or down) if one unit more (or less) of a scarce resource is made available.

Dummy activity Used in network analysis when two activities could start at the same time and finish at the same time too. It is represented by a broken arrowed line.

Economic order quantity (EOQ) The order quantity for an item of stock which will minimise costs.

Equation An expression of the relationship between variables.

Expected value A weighted average value, based on probabilities.

Feasible area The area on a graph of a linear programming problem within which all the inequalities are satisfied.

Fractions A way of showing parts of a whole.

Frequency The number of times each value occurs.

Frequency distribution (or **frequency table**) Records the number of times each value occurs.

Gantt charts A line diagram, with lines representing both time and activities. It can be used to estimate the amount of resources required for a project. Where activities are in a continuous 'chain' of one able to follow immediately after the other, these can be drawn as a continuous line on the chart.

Geometric progression A sequence of numbers in which there is a common or constant ratio between adjacent terms.

Histogram A data presentation method for (usually) grouped data of a continuous variable. Visually similar to a bar chart but frequencies are represented by areas covered by the bar rather than by their height.

Historigram A graph of a time series.

Identity matrix (I) A square matrix which behaves like the number 1 in multiplication.

Index A measure, over time, of the average changes in the values (prices or quantities) of a group of items. An index comprises a series of index numbers.

Index relative (or **relative**) The name given to an index number which measures the change in a single distinct commodity.

Integer A whole number, either positive or negative.

Intercept The point at which a straight line crosses the y axis.

Inter-quartile range The difference between the values of the upper and lower quartiles, hence showing the range of values of the middle half of the population.

Laspeyre indices Indices that use weights from the base period and are therefore sometimes called base weighted indices.

Lead time The time which elapses between the beginning and end of something, in this case between the placing of an order for stock and its eventual delivery. Thus, a supply lead time of two months means that it will take two months from the time an order is placed until the time it is delivered.

Linear equation An equation of the form y = a + bx.

Linear programming A technique for solving problems of profit maximisation (or cost minimisation) and resource allocation. The word 'programming' is simply used to denote a series of events. The various aspects of the problem are expressed as linear equations.

Linear regression analysis (**least squares method**) A technique for estimating the equation of a line of best fit.

Logarithm The power to which 10 must be raised to equal a given number.

Matrix (plural **matrices**) An array or table of numbers or variables.

Mean deviation A measure of the average amount by which the values in a distribution differ from the arithmetic mean.

Median The value of the middle member of a distribution once all of the items have been arranged in order of magnitude.

Mode An average which indicates the most frequently occurring value.

Moving averages Consecutive averages of the results of a fixed number of periods.

Multiplicative model A model for time series analysis which expresses each actual figure as a proportion of the trend.

Negative correlation Low values of one variable are associated with high values of the other, and high values of one variable with low values of the other.

Network analysis A technique basically concerned with the deployment of available resources for the completion of a complex task.

Non-linear equations Equations in which one variable varies with the nth power of another, where n > 1.

Null matrix A matrix in which every element is 0.

Objective function The mathematical expression of the aim of a linear programming exercise.

Ogive Used to show the cumulative number of items with a value less than or equal to, or alternatively greater than or equal to, a certain amount.

Order quantity The number of units of an item in one order. A fixed size is usually estimated for the order quantity.

Paasche indices Use current time period weights; in other words the weights are changed every time period.

Pearsonian correlation coefficient See coefficient of correlation.

Percentage Indicates the relative size or proportion of an item.

Permutation A set of items, selected from a larger group of items, in which the order of selection or arrangement is significant.

Perpetual inventory This method of stock control involves knowing stock levels of all items at all times. A record is kept of all items showing receipts, issues and balances of stock.

Pie chart Shows pictorially the relative sizes of the component elements of a total.

Positive correlation Low values of one variable are associated with low values of the other, and high values of one variable are associated with high values of the other.

Price index Measures the change in the money value of a group of items over time.

Primary data Data collected especially for the purpose of whatever survey is being conducted.

Product moment correlation coefficient See coefficient of correlation.

Project evaluation and review technique (PERT) A form of network analysis that takes account of uncertainty.

Proportional model See multiplicative model.

Quadratic equations A type of non-linear equation in which one variable varies with the square (or second power) of the other variable.

Quantiles A collective term for quartiles, deciles and percentiles, and any other similar dividing points for analysing a frequency distribution.

Quantity index (also called a **volume index**) Measures the change in the non-monetary values of a group of items over time.

Random sample A sample selected in such a way that every item in the population has an equal chance of being included.

Range The difference between the highest observation and the lowest observation.

Raw data Primary data which have not been processed at all, but are still just (for example) a list of numbers.

Reciprocal The reciprocal of a number is 1 divided by that number.

Reorder level The balance of units remaining in stock, at which an order for more units will be placed.

Residual The difference between the actual results and the results which would have been predicted (for a past period for which we already have data) by the trend line adjusted for the average seasonal variation.

Sampling Involves selecting a sample of items from a population.

Sampling frame A numbered list of all the items in the population.

Scattergraph method Involves plotting pairs of data for two related variables on a graph to produce a scattergraph, and then to use judgement to draw what seems to be a line of best fit through the data.

Seasonal variations Short-term fluctuations in recorded values, due to different circumstances which affect results at different times of the year, on different days of the week and so on.

Secondary data Data which have already been collected elsewhere, for some other purpose, but which can be used or adapted for the survey being conducted.

Semi-logarithmic graph This has a normal horizontal axis against which time is plotted but, on the vertical axis, equal intervals represent equal proportional changes in the variable. For example, the distance on the axis between y = 10 and y = 30 is the same as the distance between y = 30 and y = 90 (both represent a three-fold increase).

Sensitivity analysis Involves changing significant variables in order to determine the effect of these changes on the planned outcome.

Shadow price See dual price.

Simplex technique A linear programming technique which tests a number of feasible solutions to a problem until the optimal solution is found. The technique is a repetitive step-by-step process and therefore an ideal computer application. If the manual process is used, however, this is done in the form of a tableau (or 'table' or 'matrix') of figures.

Simultaneous equations Two or more equations which are satisfied by the same variable values.

Skewness The asymmetry of a frequency distribution curve.

Slack variable The amount of a constraining resource or item that is unused.

Spearman's rank correlation coefficient Measures the correlation between the order or rank of two variables.

Square root A value which, when multiplied by itself, equals the original number.

Standard deviation Square root of the variance.

Stock-outs These arise when there is a requirement for an item of stock, but the stores or warehouse is temporarily out of stock.

Table A matrix of data in rows and columns, with the rows and columns having titles.

Time series A series of figures or values recorded over time.

Trend The underlying long-term movement over time in the values of the data recorded.

Unit matrix See identity matrix.

Variable Something which can be measured. Variables may be classified as discrete (can only take a finite or countable number of values within a given range) or continuous (may take on any value).

Variance Average of the squared mean deviation for each value in a distribution.

Vector A table of numbers or variables which has just one row or column.

Z chart A form of time series chart.

INDEX

ORDER FORM

Any books from our HNC/HND range can be ordered in one of the following ways:

- Telephone us on **020 8740 2211**
- Send this page to our **Freepost** address
- Fax this page on **020 8740 1184**
- Email us at **publishing@bpp.com**
- Go to our website: **www.bpp.com**

We aim to deliver to all UK addresses inside 5 working days. Orders to all EU addresses should be delivered within 6 working days. All other orders to overseas addresses should be delivered within 8 working days.

BPP Publishing Ltd
Aldine House
Aldine Place
London W12 8AW
Tel: 020 8740 2211
Fax: 020 8740 1184
Email: publishing@bpp.com

Full name: _____

Day-time delivery address: _____

_____

_____ Postcode _____

Day-time telephone (for queries only): _____

Please send me the following quantities of books:

Core

		No. of copies	Price	Total
Unit 1	Marketing (8/00)		£7.95	
Unit 2	Managing Financial Resources (8/00)		£7.95	
Unit 3	Organisations and Behaviour (8/00)		£7.95	
Unit 4	Organisations, Competition and Environment (8/00)		£7.5	
Unit 5	Quantitative Techniques for Business (8/00)		£7.95	
Unit 6	Legal and Regulatory Framework (8/00)		£7.95	
Unit 7	Management Information Systems (8/00)		£7.95	
Unit 8	Business Strategy (8/00)		£7.95	

Option

Units 9-12	Business & Finance (1/2001)		£10.95	
Units 13-16	Business & Management (1/2001)		£10.95	
Units 17-20	Business & Marketing (1/2001)		£10.95	
Unit 21-24	Business & Personnel (1/2001)		£10.95	

Other Material

	Workbook (3/00)		£9.95	

Sub Total	£

Postage & Packaging

UK : Course book £3.00 for first plus £2.00 for each extra, Workbook £2.00 for first plus £1.00 for each	£
Europe : (inc. ROI) Course book £5.00 for first plus £4.00 for each extra, Workbook £2.50 for first plus £1.00 for each	£
Rest of the world : Course book £20.00 for first plus £10.00 for each extra, Workbook £2.50 for first plus £1.00 for each	£

Grand Total	£

I enclose a cheque for £_____ (cheque to BPP Publishing Ltd) or charge to Access/VISA/Switch

Card number: ⬜⬜⬜⬜⬜⬜⬜⬜⬜⬜⬜⬜⬜⬜⬜⬜⬜⬜⬜

Issues number (Switch only): _____

Start date: _____ Expiry date: _____

Signature _____

REVIEW FORM & FREE PRIZE DRAW

We are constantly reviewing, updating and improving our Course Books. We would be grateful for any comments or thoughts you have on this Course Book. Cut out and send this page to our Freepost address and you will be automatically entered in a £50 prize draw.

Jed Cope
HNC/HND Range Manager
BPP Publishing Ltd, FREEPOST, London W12 8BR

Full name: _____

Address: _____

_____

_____ Postcode _____

Where are you studying?

Where did you find out about BPP range books?

Why did you decide to buy this Course Book?

Have you used our texts for the other units in your HNC/HND studies?

What thoughts do you have on our:

• Introductory pages

• Topic coverage

• Summary diagrams, icons, chapter roundups and quick quizzes

• Activities and assignments

The other side of this form is left blank for any further comments you wish to make.

Please give any further comments and suggestions (with page number if necessary) below.

FREE PRIZE DRAW RULES

1   Closing date for 31 January 2001 draw is 31 December 2000. Closing date for 31 July 2001 draw is 30 June 2001.

2   Restricted to entries with UK and Eire addresses only. BPP employees, their families and business associates are excluded.

3   No purchase necessary. Entry forms are available upon request from BPP Publishing. No more than one entry per title, per person. Draw restricted to persons aged 16 and over.

4   Winners will be notified by post and receive their cheques not later than 6 weeks after the relevant draw date.

5   The decision of the promoter in all matters is final and binding. No correspondence will be entered into.